Instructor's Manual

for

A Concise Introduction to Logic

Ninth Edition

Instructor's Manual

for

A Concise Introduction to Logic
Ninth Edition

Patrick J. Hurley
University of San Diego

THOMSON
WADSWORTH

Australia • Canada • Mexico • Singapore • Spain • United Kingdom • United States

Printed in the United States of America
1 2 3 4 5 6 7 09 08 07 06 05

Printer: Thomson West

ISBN 0-495-00025-6

For more information about our products, contact us at:
Thomson Learning Academic Resource Center
1-800-423-0563

For permission to use material from this text or product, submit a request online at
http://www.thomsonrights.com.
Any additional questions about permissions can be submitted by email to **thomsonrights@thomson.com.**

Thomson Higher Education
10 Davis Drive
Belmont, CA 94002-3098
USA

Asia (including India)
Thomson Learning
5 Shenton Way
#01-01 UIC Building
Singapore 068808

Australia/New Zealand
Thomson Learning Australia
102 Dodds Street
Southbank, Victoria 3006
Australia

Canada
Thomson Nelson
1120 Birchmount Road
Toronto, Ontario M1K 5G4
Canada

UK/Europe/Middle East/Africa
Thomson Learning
High Holborn House
50–51 Bedford Row
London WC1R 4LR
United Kingdom

Latin America
Thomson Learning
Seneca, 53
Colonia Polanco
11560 Mexico
D.F. Mexico

Spain (including Portugal)
Thomson Paraninfo
Calle Magallanes, 25
28015 Madrid, Spain

CONTENTS

Preface

Prior editions of this Manual have contained sample tests for instructors. Beginning with this ninth edition the sample tests have been moved to a separate publication, "Test Bank for *A Concise Introduction to Logic* by Patrick J. Hurley," ISBN 0-495-00849-4. To receive a copy, please contact your Wadsworth Sales Rep. Contact information is available at www.philosophy.wadsworth.com. The Test Bank contains three new tests for each of the first six chapters of the book and one test for each of the last three chapters.

Another change to be found in this Manual concerns the natural deduction exercises in Chapters 7 and 8. Beginning with the last edition of the textbook, I adopted the practice of confining each line in a proof to the application of a single rule of inference. A pressing publication date did not allow carrying this change into the Instructor's Manual. However, with this ninth edition, the practice of one rule per line applies to the Manual as well.

I always welcome comments from instructors regarding their use of the textbook, the CD, and this Manual. Such comments have provided the basis for many of the improvements that have been incorporated in successive editions. I can be reached at phurley@sandiego.edu.

Instructor's Manual

for

A Concise Introduction to Logic

Ninth Edition

Exercise Answers

Exercise 1.1
Part I

1. P: Titanium combines readily with oxygen, nitrogen, and hydrogen, all of which have an adverse effect on its mechanical properties.
    C: Titanium must be processed in their absence.

2. P: The good, according to Plato, is that which furthers a person's real interests.
    C: In any given case when the good is known, men will seek it.

3. P: The denial or perversion of justice by the sentences of courts, as well as in any other manner, is with reason classed among the just causes of war.
    C: The federal judiciary ought to have cognizance of all causes in which the citizens of other countries are concerned.

4. P: When individuals voluntarily abandon property, they forfeit any expectation of privacy in it that they might have had.
    C: A warrantless search and seizure of abandoned property is not unreasonable under the Fourth Amendment.

5. P_1: Artists and poets look at the world and seek relationships and order.
    P_2: But they translate their ideas to canvas, or to marble, or into poetic images.
    P_3 Scientists try to find relationships between different objects and events.
    P_4: To express the order they find, they create hypotheses and theories.
    C: The great scientific theories are easily compared to great art and great literature.

6. P_1: The animal species in Australia are very different from those on the mainland.
    P_2: Asian placental mammals and Australian marsupial mammals have not been in contact in the last several million years.
    C: There was never a land bridge between Australia and the mainland

7. P_1: After October 1963, when Hurricane Flora devastated the island and killed more than a thousand people, the Cuban government overhauled its civil defense system.
    P_2: It was so successful that when six powerful hurricanes thumped Cuba between 1996 and 2002 only 16 people died.
    P_3: And when Hurricane Ivan struck Cuba in 2004 there was not a single casualty, but the same storm killed at least 70 people in other Caribbean countries.
    C: Cuba's record on disaster prevention is impressive.

8. P_1: The classroom teacher is crucial to the development and academic success of the average student.
    P_2: Administrators simply are ancillary to this effort.
    C: Classroom teachers ought to be paid at least the equivalent of administrators at all levels, including the superintendent.

Exercise 1.1

9. P₁: An agreement cannot bind unless both parties to the agreement know what they are doing and freely choose to do it.
   C: The seller who intends to enter a contract with a customer has a duty to disclose exactly what the customer is buying and what the terms of the sale are.

10. P₁: Punishment, when speedy and specific, may suppress undesirable behavior.
    P₂: Punishment cannot teach or encourage desirable alternatives.
    C: It is crucial to use positive techniques to model and reinforce appropriate behavior that the person can use in place of the unacceptable response that has to be suppressed.

11. P₁: High profits are the signal that consumers want more of the output of the industry.
    P₂: High profits provide the incentive for firms to to expand output and for more firms to enter the industry in the long run.
    P₃: For a firm of above average efficiency, profits represent the reward for greater efficiency.
    C: Profit serves a very crucial function in a free enterprise economy, such as our own.

12. P₁: My cat regularly used to close and lock the door to my neighbor's doghouse, trapping their sleeping Doberman inside.
    P₂: Try telling a cat what to do, or putting a leash on him--he'll glare at you and say, "I don't think so. You should have gotten a dog."
    C: Cats can think circles around dogs.

13. P₁: Private property helps people define themselves.
    P₂: Private property frees people from mundane cares of daily subsistence.
    P₃: Private property is finite.
    C: No individual should accumulate so much property that others are prevented from accumulating the necessities of life.

14. P₁: To every existing thing God wills some good.
    P₂: To love any thing is nothing else than to will good to that thing.
    C: It is manifest that God loves everything that exists.

15. P₁: The average working man can support no more than two children.
    P₂: The average working woman can take care of no more than two children in decent fashion.
    C: Women of the working class, especially wage workers, should not have more than two children at most.

16. P₁: The nations of planet earth have acquired nuclear weapons with an explosive power equal to more than a million Hiroshima bombs.
    P₂: Studies suggest that explosion of only half these weapons would produce enough soot, smoke, and dust to blanket the Earth, block out the sun, and bring on a nuclear winter that would threaten the survival of the human race.
    C: Radioactive fallout isn't the only concern in the aftermath of nuclear explosions.

17. P_1: An ant releases a chemical when it dies, and its fellows carry it away to the compost heap.
    P_2: A healthy ant painted with the death chemical will be dragged to the funeral heap again and again.
    C: Apparently the communication is highly effective.

18. P: Every art and every inquiry, and similarly every action and pursuit, is thought to aim at some good.
    C: The good has been rightly declared to be that at which all things aim.

19. P_1: Antipoverty programs provide jobs for middle-class professionals in social work, penology and public health.
    P_2: Such workers' future advancement is tied to the continued growth of bureaucracies dependent on the existence of poverty.
    C: Poverty offers numerous benefits to the non-poor.

20. P_1: Corn is an annual crop.
    P_2: Butchers meat is a crop which requires four or five years to grow.
    P_3: An acre of land will produce a much smaller quantity of the one species of food (meat) than the other.
    C: The inferiority of the quantity (of meat) must be compensated by the superiority of the price.

21. P_1: Loan oft loses both itself and friend.
    P_2: Borrowing dulls the edge of husbandry.
    C: Neither a borrower nor lender be.

22. P_1: Take the nurse who alleges that physicians enrich themselves in her hospital through unnecessary surgery.
    P_2: Take the engineer who discloses safety defects in the braking systems of a fleet of new rapid-transit vehicles.
    P_3: Take the Defense Department official who alerts Congress to military graft and overspending.
    P_4: All know that they pose a threat to those whom they denounce and that their own careers may be at risk.
    C: The stakes in whistleblowing are high.

23. P_1: If a piece of information is not "job relevant," then the employer is not entitled qua employer to know it.
    P_2: Sexual practices, political beliefs, associational activities, etc., are not part of the description of most jobs
    P_3: They do not directly affect one's job performance.
    C: They are not legitimate information for an employer to know in the determination of the hiring of a job applicant.

24. P_1: One of the most noticeable effects of a dark tan is premature aging of the skin.
    P_2: The sun also contributes to certain types of cataracts, and, what is most worrisome, it plays a role in skin cancer.
    C: Too much sun can lead to health problems.

Exercise 1.1

25. P_1: It is generally accepted that by constantly swimming with its mouth open, the shark is simply avoiding suffocation.
    P_2: This assures a continuous flow of oxygen-laden water into their mouths, over their gills, and out through the gill slits.
    C: Contrary to the tales of some scuba divers, the toothsome, gaping grin on the mouth of an approaching shark is not necessarily anticipatory.

26. P: If you place a piece of Polaroid (for example, one lens of a pair of Polaroid sunglasses) in front of your eye and rotate it as you look at the sky on a clear day, you will notice a change in light intensity with the orientation of the Polaroid.
    C: Light coming from the sky is partially polarized.

27. P_1: The secondary light [from the moon] does not inherently belong to the moon, and is not received from any star or from the sun.
    P_2: In the whole universe there is no other body left but the earth.
    C: The lunar body (or any other dark and sunless orb) is illuminated by the earth.

28. P_1: Anyone familiar with our prison system knows that there are some inmates who behave little better than brute beasts.
    P_2: If the death penalty had been truly effective as a deterrent, such prisoners would long ago have vanished.
    C: The very fact that these prisoners exist is a telling argument against the efficacy of capital punishment as a deterrent.

29. P_1: REM (rapid eye movement) sleep studies conducted on adults indicate that REM pressure increases with deprivation.
    P_2: This would not occur if REM sleep and dreaming were unimportant.
    C: REM sleep and dreaming are necessary in the adult.

30. P_1: World government means one central authority, a permanent standing world police force, and clearly defined conditions under which this force will go into action.
    P_2: A balance of power system has many sovereign authorities, each controlling its own army, combining only when they feel like it to control aggression.
    C: World government and the balance of power are in many ways opposites.

Part II.

1. College sports are as much driven by money as professional sports.

2. The creation of a multilingual society is contrary to the best interests of all of us.

3. The competitive aspect of team sports is having a negative impact on the health and fitness of our children.

4. Business majors are robbing themselves of the true purpose of collegiate academics, a sacrifice that outweighs the future salary checks.

5. The sale and purchase of recreational drugs should be legalized.

6. Congress should not cut the National Institutes of Health budget.

7. The religious intolerance of television preachers must not be tolerated.

8. Patients should not be offered elective Cesarean section.

9. Parents who truly love their children allow them to fail once in a while.

10. Protecting the environment requires that we limit population growth.

Part III

1. Logic: The organized body of knowledge, or science, that evaluates arguments.

2. Argument: A group of statements one or more of which (the premises) are claimed to provide support for, or reasons to believe, one of the others (the conclusion).

3. Statement: A sentence that is either true or false.

4. Premise: A statement in an argument that sets forth evidence or reasons.

5. Conclusion: The statement in an argument that the premises are claimed to support or imply.

6. Conclusion indicator: A word that provides a clue in identifying the conclusion.

7. Premise indicator: A word that provides a clue in identifying the premises.

8. Inference: The reasoning process used to produce an argument.

9. Proposition: The information content of a statement.

10. Truth value: The attribute by which a statement is either true or false.

Part IV

1.	True	6.	False
2.	False	7.	True
3.	False	8.	True
4.	False	9.	True
5.	True	10.	True

Exercise 1.2

Exercise 1.2
Part I

1. Nonargument (explanation)

2. Nonargument; conditional statement

3. Argument (conclusion: Freedom of the press is the most important of our constitutionally guaranteed freedoms.)

4. Nonargument (illustration)

5. Nonargument (piece of advice)

6. Argument (conclusion: Mosquito bites are not always the harmless little irritations most of us take them to be.)

7. Argument (conclusion: If stem-cell research is restricted, then people will die prematurely.)

8. Argument (conclusion: Fiction provides us with the opportunity to ponder how people react in uncommon situations, and to deduce moral lessons, psychological principles, and philosophical insights from their behavior.)

9. Nonargument (statement of belief)

10. Nonargument (report)

11. Argument (conclusion: Any interest of the state in protecting the woman from an inherently hazardous procedure, except when it would be equally dangerous for her to forgo it, has largely disappeared.)

12. Nonargument (expository passage)

13. Nonargument (opinion)

14. Nonargument (report of an argument)

15. Argument (conclusion: Economics is of practical value in business.)

16. Nonargument (piece of advice)

17. Nonargument (loosely associated statements)

18. This passage could be interpreted as either an argument or an explanation (or both). If it is interpreted as an argument, the conclusion is: Most business organizations include a credit department which must reach a decision on the credit worthiness of each prospective customer.

19. Argument (conclusion: For organisms at the sea surface, sinking into deep water usually means death.)

20. Nonargument (temporal meaning of "since"; "hence" indicates an explanation.)

21. Argument (conclusion: Dachshunds are ideal dogs for small children.)

22. Argument (conclusion: Atoms can combine to form molecules, whose properties are generally very different from those of the constituent atoms.)

23. Argument (conclusion: The coarsest type of humor is the practical joke.)

24. Nonargument (conditional statement)

25. Nonargument (explanation)

26. Argument (conclusion: Words are slippery customers.)

27. Nonargument (report)

28. Argument (conclusion: A person never becomes truly self-reliant.)

29. Nonargument (opinion)

30. Nonargument (illustration)

31. This passage could be both an argument and an explanation (conclusion: In areas where rats are a problem, it is very difficult to exterminate them with bait poison.)

32. Both an argument and an explanation (conclusion: Men are less likely to develop osteoporosis until later in life than women and seldom suffer as severely.)

33. Argument (conclusion: Newspapers, radio, and television are essential for a democracy.)

34. Nonargument (loosely associated statements)

35. Argument (conclusion: The plane mirror remains an important element in the modern arsenal of sophisticated optical devices.)

Part II

1. Nonargument

2. Argument (conclusion: The emphasis on computers in elementary schools is harmful.)

Exercise 1.2

3. This passage is probably best considered a nonargument, but it could be rephrased to form an argument. (Possible conclusion: Something is wrong with our approach to education.)

4. Nonargument

5. Argument (conclusion: In opposing obligatory prayer in the public schools I am actually serving my God.)

6. Argument (conclusion: Religious fundamentalists are preventing our children from learning science. *Or* We must eliminate the influence of religious fundamentalism in our public schools.)

7. Argument (conclusion: The poor quality of parenting and the lack in continuity of adult care provided to many U.S. children contribute to a passivity and a sense of helplessness that hobbles individuals for the remainder of their lives.)

8. Argument (conclusion: Global capitalism is attended by serious inequities.)

9. Argument (main conclusion: The suggestion by socio-biologists that stepparent child abuse has evolutionary advantages is superficial. Intermediate conclusion: there are plenty of loving and generous stepparents around.)

10. Nonargument

Part IV

1. Argument from example: An argument that purports to prove something by giving one or more examples of it.

2. Conditional statement: An "if ... then ..." statement

3. Antecedent: The component of a conditional statement that immediately follows the word "if."

4. Consequent: The component of a conditional statement that immediately follows the word "then"; the component of a conditional statement that is not the antecedent

5. Sufficient condition: The condition represented by the antecedent of a conditional statement

6. Necessary condition: The condition represented by the consequent of a conditional statement

7. Explanation: A statement or group of statements intended to shed light on some event

8. Explanandum: The component of an explanation that indicates the event or phenomenon to be explained

9. Explanans: The component of an explanation that ex plains the event indicated by the explanandum

10. Illustration: A kind of nonargument composed of statements intended to show what something means or how something is done.

11. Expository passage: A kind of Nonargument consisting of a topic sentence and one or more other sentences that expand or elaborate on the topic sentence.

Part V

1. True	6. True
2. False	7. True
3. False	8. True
4. True	9. True
5. True	10. True

Part VI

1. Sufficient: If something is a tiger, then it is an animal.

2. Necessary: If something is not an animal, then it is not a tiger. *Or*: If something is a tiger, then it is an animal.

3. Sufficient: If a person drinks water, then he will quench his thirst.

4. Necessary: If a person has no racquet, then he/she cannot play tennis. *Or*: If a person plays tennis, then he/she has a racquet.

5. Necessary: If a person does not pull the cork, then he/she cannot drink a bottle of expensive wine. *Or*: If a person drinks a bottle of expensive wine, then he/she has pulled the cork.

6. Sufficient: If someone steps on a cat's tail, then the cat will yowl.

7. Sufficient: If leaves burn, then smoke is produced.

8. Necessary: If a person does not pay attention, then he/she will not understand a lecture. *Or*: If a person understands a lecture, then he/she pays attention.

9. Sufficient: If a person takes a swim in the North Sea, then he/she will cool off.

10. Necessary: If a person does not open the door, then he/she cannot cross the threshold. *Or*: If a person crosses the threshold, then he/she has opened the door.

Exercise 1.3

Exercise 1.3
Part I

1. Deductive (argument based on mathematics; also, the conclusion follows necessarily from the premises.)

2. Inductive (argument based on signs)

3. Inductive (prediction; also, there is an inductive indicator word and the conclusion follows only probably from the premise.)

4. Deductive (categorical syllogism; also, the conclusion follows necessarily from the premises.)

5. Inductive (generalization)

6. Deductive (the conclusion follows necessarily from the premise)

7. Inductive (causal inference; also, the conclusion follows only probably from the premise.)

8. Deductive (the conclusion follows necessarily from the premises.)

9. Inductive (causal inference)

10. Inductive (argument from analogy; also, the conclusion follows only probably from the premises.)

11. Deductive (argument from definition)

12. Deductive (disjunctive syllogism; also, the conclusion follows necessarily from the premises.)

13. Inductive (argument from authority; also, the conclusion follows only probably from the premise.)

14. Deductive (hypothetical syllogism; also, the conclusion follows necessarily from the premises.)

15. Inductive (causal inference; also, there are inductive indicator words.)

16. Deductive (the conclusion follows necessarily from the premise.)

17. Deductive (the conclusion follows necessarily from the premises.)

18. Inductive (prediction)

19. Inductive (causal inference)

20. Deductive (the conclusion follows necessarily from the premise.)

21. The use of the indicator "manifestly deduced" and the quasi-geometrical approach suggest that this argument is deductive. Nevertheless the argument could be interpreted as an inductive causal inference: Reasoning from the appearances to the reality behind the appearances.

22. Deductive (the conclusion follows necessarily from the premise; this example might also be interpreted as an argument from definition--the definition of "refraction.")

23. Inductive (prediction; also, the conclusion follows only probably from the premises.)

24. Deductive (the conclusion follows necessarily from the premises.)

25. Inductive (causal inference: the dog's familiarity with the visitor caused the dog to be silent.)

26. Deductive (the conclusion follows necessarily from the premises.)

27. Deductive (the conclusion follows necessarily from the premises.)

28. Inductive (causal inference; also, the word "may" suggests a probabilistic inference.)

29. Inductive (causal inference; also, the tentative flavor of "should indicate" suggests an inductive argument.)

30. Deductive (the conclusion follows necessarily from the premise.)

Part II

1. Deductive argument: An argument in which the arguer claims that it is impossible for the conclusion to be false given that the premises are true

2. Inductive argument: An argument in which the arguer claims that it is improbable that the conclusion be false given that the premises are true

3. Argument based on mathematics: A deductive argument in which the conclusion depends on some purely arithmetic or geometric computation or measurement

4. Argument from definition: A deductive argument in which the conclusion is claimed to depend merely upon the definition of some word or phrase used in the premise or conclusion

5. Categorical syllogism: A syllogism in which all three statements are categorical propositions; a syllogism in which all three statements begin with the words "all," "no" or "some"

Exercise 1.4

6. Hypothetical syllogism: A syllogism having a conditional statement for one or both of its premises

7. Disjunctive syllogism: A syllogism having a disjunctive statement for one of its premises

8. Argument from analogy: An inductive argument that depends on the existence of a similarity between two things or states of affairs

9. Generalization: An inductive argument that proceeds from the knowledge of a selected sample to some claim about the whole group

10. Prediction: An inductive argument that proceeds from our knowledge of the past to a claim about the future

11. Argument from authority: An inductive argument that concludes something is true because a presumed expert or witness has said that it is

12. Argument based on signs: An inductive argument that proceeds from the knowledge of a sign to a claim about the thing or situation that the sign symbolizes

13. Causal inference: An inductive argument that proceeds from knowledge of a cause to a claim about an effect, or from knowledge of an effect to a claim about a cause

14. Particular statement: A statement that makes a claim about one or more (but not all) members of a class

15. General statement: A statement that makes a claim about all the members of a class

Part III

1. True	6. False	11. True
2. True	7. True	12. False
3. True	8. False	13. True
4. True	9. False	14. False
5. False	10. False	15. False

Exercise 1.4
Part I

1. Valid, unsound; false premises, false conclusion.

2. Valid, sound; true premise, true conclusion.

3. Invalid, unsound; true premises, false conclusion.

4. Valid, sound; true premise, true conclusion.

5. Invalid, unsound; false premise, true conclusion.

6. Valid, unsound; one false premise, true conclusion.

7. Invalid, unsound; true premise, true conclusion.

8. Valid, unsound; one false premise, true conclusion.

9. Valid, sound; true premises, true conclusion.

10. Valid, unsound; one false premise, false conclusion.

11. Invalid, unsound; false premise, false conclusion.

12. Valid, sound; true premises, true conclusion.

13. Invalid, unsound; true premises, true conclusion.

14. Valid, unsound; one false premise, true conclusion.

15. Valid, sound; true premise, true conclusion.

Part II

1. Strong, cogent; true premise, probably true conclusion.

2. Weak, uncogent; true premise, probably false conclusion.

3. Strong, uncogent; false premise, probably false conclusion.

4. Weak, uncogent; true premise, probably false conclusion.

5. Strong, cogent; true premises, probably true conclusion.

6. Weak, uncogent; true premise, probably false conclusion.

7. Strong, uncogent; false premise, probably true conclusion.

8. Strong, cogent; true premises, probably true conclusion.

9. Weak, uncogent; true premise, undecided truth value of conclusion.

10. Strong, cogent; true premise, probably true conclusion.

11. Strong, uncogent; false premise, probably false conclusion.

12. Strong, uncogent; false premise, probably false conclusion.

Exercise 1.4

13. Weak, uncogent; true premises, probably false conclusion.

14. Strong, cogent; true premise, probably true conclusion.

15. Strong, uncogent; false premise, probably false conclusion.

Part III

1. Deductive, valid

2. Inductive, weak

3. Inductive, strong

4. Deductive, valid, unsound

5. Deductive, valid

6. Inductive, strong

7. Inductive, weak

8. Deductive, invalid

9. Inductive, strong

10. Deductive, invalid

11. Inductive, weak

12. Deductive, invalid

13. Inductive, weak

14. Deductive, valid, unsound

15. Inductive, strong

16. Deductive, invalid

17. Deductive, valid

18. Deductive, valid

19. Inductive, strong

20. Deductive, invalid

Part IV

1. Valid argument: An argument in which it is impossible for the conclusion to be false given that the premises are true

2. Invalid argument: A deductive argument in which it is possible for the conclusion to be false given that the premises are true

3. Sound argument: A deductive argument that is valid and has all true premises

4. Unsound argument: A deductive argument that is either invalid or has one or more false premises (or both)

5. Strong argument: An inductive argument in which it is improbable that the conclusion be false given that the premises are true

6. Weak argument: An inductive argument in which the conclusion does not follow probably from the premises

7. Cogent argument: An inductive argument that is strong and has all true premises

8. Uncogent argument: An inductive argument that is either weak or has one or more false premises (or both)

Part V

1. False	6. True	11. False
2. True	7. False	12. True
3. False	8. False	13. False
4. True	9. True	14. False
5. True	10. False	15. False

Exercise 1.5
Part I

1. All G are S.   All cats are animals.   (T)
   All Q are S.   All dogs are animals. (T)
   All G are Q.   All cats are dogs.   (F)

2. No C are E.   No cats are dogs.   (T)
   Some P are not C.   Some animals are not cats. (T)
   Some E are not P.   Some dogs are not animals. (F)

3. No P are M.   No cats are dogs.   (T)
   All P are R.   All cats are animals.   (T)
   No M are R.   No dogs are animals. (F)

4. No I are P.   No fish are mammals.   (T)
   Some I are not F.   Some fish are not cats.   (T)
   Some F are not P.   Some cats are not mammals.   (F)

5. Some P are W.   Some animals are dogs. (T)
   No W are T.   No dogs are fish.   (T)
   No P are T.   No animals are fish.   (F)

6. All S are T.   All dogs are mammals.   (T)
   All S are M.   All dogs are animals.   (T)
   All M are T.   All animals are mammals. (F)

7. No P are H.   No dogs are fish.   (T)
   No C are H.   No mammals are fish.   (T)
   No P are C.   No dogs are mammals. (F)

8. Some T are S   Some cats are animals. (T)
   Some S are U.   Some animals are dogs. (T)
   Some T are U.   Some cats are dogs.   (F)

15

9. All A are G.   All dogs are animals.   (T)
   Some A are I.   Some dogs are mammals.   (T)
   Some I are not G.   Some mammals are not animals. (F)

10. Some S are not O.   Some dogs are not fish.   (T)
    Some G are not O.   Some animals are not fish.   (T)
    Some S are not G.   Some dogs are not animals.   (F)

Part II

1. If A then E.   If George Washington was assassinated, then George Washington
                   is dead.
   Not A.   George Washington was not assassinated.
   Not E.   George Washington is not dead.

2. If C then P.   If George Washington was assassinated, then George Washington
                   is dead.
   P.   George Washington is dead.
   C.   George Washington was assassinated.

3. If H then C.   If Lassie is a dog, then Lassie is an animal.
   If E then C.   If Lassie is a cat, then Lassie is an animal.
   If H then E.   If Lassie is a dog, then Lassie is a cat.

4. If E, then
   either D or C. If Tom Cruise is a man, then he is either a mouse or a human.
   If D, then I.   If Tom Cruise is a mouse, then he has a tail.
   If E, then I.   If Tom Cruise is a man, then he has a tail.

5. All H who are P are D.   All humans who are female are women.
   All H are D.   All humans are women.

6. Some W are C.   Some fruits are purple.
   Some W are H.   Some fruits are lemons.
   Some W are CH.   Some fruits are purple lemons.

7. All C with L are either S or I.   All cats with fur are either mammals or dogs.
   All C are I.   All cats are dogs.

8. All M that are R
   are B that are I.   All animals that are cats are felines that are mammals.
   All M are I.   All animals are mammals.

9. All D are either I or G.   All dogs are either mammals or fish.
   Some D are I.   Some dogs are mammals.
   Some D are G.   Some dogs are fish.

10. All R that are F
    are either L or H.
    <u>All R are H.</u>
    All F are L.

All cats that are mammals are either dogs or animals.
<u>All cats are animals.</u>
All animals are dogs.

Exercise 1.6
Part I

1.
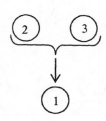

2.
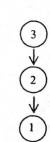

3.
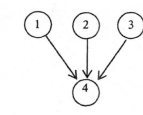

4.
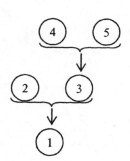

5.
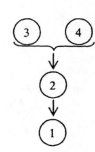

6.
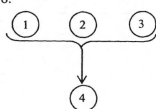

7.
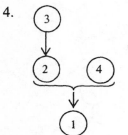

8.
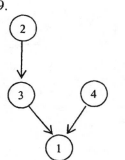

9.
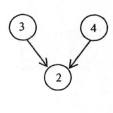

10.
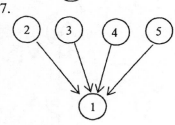

Exercise 1.6

Part II

1.
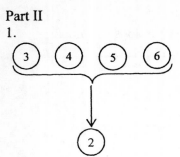

2.
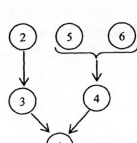 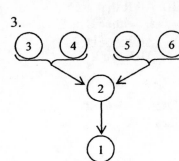

3.

4.
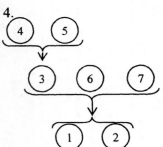 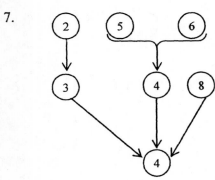

5.
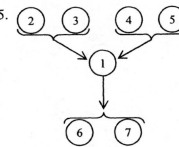

6.
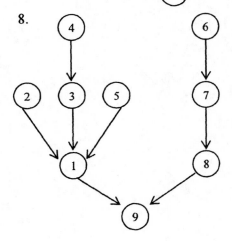 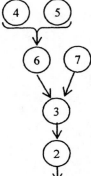

7.
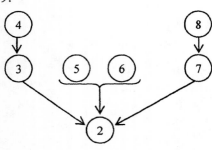

8.
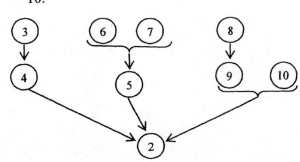

9.

10.

11.

12.

13.

14.

15.

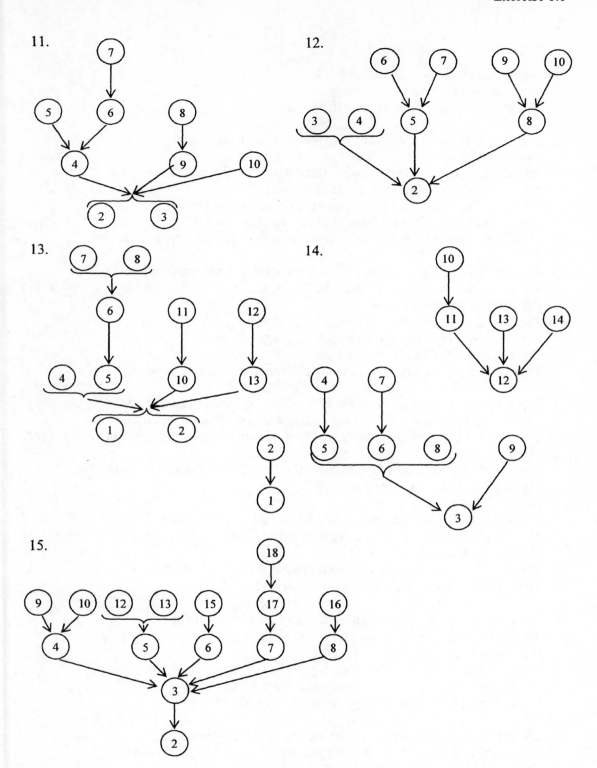

Exercise 2.1

Exercise 2.1
Part II

1. In dog sled races the dogs are tortured.
   Torturing animals is morally wrong.
   Therefore, dog sled races are morally wrong.

2. The children of Somalia are starving and covered with flies.
   Such a condition is extremely evil.
   A God that is loving would want to eliminate this evil if he is aware of it.
   A God that is ever-present is aware of this evil.
   A God that is omnipotent has the power to eliminate this evil.
   The evil in Somalia has not been eliminated by any God.
   Therefore, there is no God that is loving, ever-present, and omnipotent.

3. The beliefs of the creationists are mistaken, ignorant, and superstitious.
   No beliefs that are mistaken, ignorant, and superstitious should be taught in school.
   Evolution is a scientific truth.
   The beliefs of the creationists contradict evolution.
   Parents have a right to have their children taught the truth.
   The majority of parents favor the teaching of evolution.
   Therefore, the beliefs of the creationists should not be taught in school.

4. Free ownership of guns is as noble as belief in God and intestinal fortitude.
   Belief in God and intestinal fortitude made our country great and free.
   Continued belief in God and intestinal fortitude are necessary to keep our country the way it is.
   Free ownership of guns is no less important than God and intestinal fortitude.
   Therefore, gun control is wrong.

5. All killers should pay for their crimes by spending many years in jail.
   The insanity plea allows killers to spend as little as six months in a mental hospital and then be released.
   The insanity plea allows killers to avoid what is coming to them.
   Therefore, the insanity plea should be abolished.

6. Abortion and infanticide have produced a holocaust in our nation.
   These practices have resulted in the death of millions of innocent children.
   It is wrong to kill innocent children.
   All of us should oppose what is wrong.
   The Human Life Bill would outlaw abortion and infanticide.
   Therefore, all of us should support the Human Life Bill.

7. The celebration of cultural diversity causes social fragmentation.
   The celebration of cultural diversity is symptomatic of a split personality.
   The people who set this country up framed one nation, indivisible.
   The celebration of cultural diversity works against the intention of these people.
   The celebration of cultural diversity erodes national identity.
   Therefore, the celebration of cultural diversity is wrong.

8. A kind and loving God wants children to be happy, well-fed, cared for, and loved.
   The pro-choice attitude insures that the children who are born will be happy, well-fed, cared for, and loved.
   Therefore, God favors the pro-choice attitude.
   and
   The Catholic Church opposes pro-choice.
   Whatever opposes pro-choice fosters famine and disease in Third World nations.
   Anything that fosters famine and disease is wrong.
   The policies of the Catholic Church are outdated.
   Whatever is wrong and outdated should be changed.
   Therefore, the Catholic Church should change its policy in favor of pro-choice.

9. Over thousands of years, organized religion has solved no social problems.
   Organized religion has exacerbated social problems by promoting fear, superstition, and irrational mythologies.
   Organized religion recommends that we solve these problems through prayer.
   Prayer is a waste of time.
   Prayer lulls the supplicant into inactivity.
   Inactivity solves nothing.
   Therefore, organized religion takes the wrong approach to solving social problems, and the correct approach is reality based, empirical, and rational.

10. Liberalism has excessively enlarged the welfare system.
    Liberalism has made welfare recipients indolent and irresponsible.
    The liberals refuse to acknowledge or correct the defects in this system.
    Liberalism has made the criminal justice system too sensitive to the criminal and too insensitive to the victim of crime.
    Liberalism has given more rights to the criminal than to the ordinary citizen.
    Liberalism has promoted sex and violence in the school system.
    Liberals have opposed prayer in the schools.
    Therefore, liberalism is bad.

Part III

1. Probably verbal (ambiguity). Does "sound" designate a subjective perception or an objective disturbance of the air (or some other medium)?

2. Factual and verbal (vagueness). What do we mean by "art"? Also, Barbara appears committed to the idea that there is a true and eternal essence of art that excludes such things as graffiti, whereas Vickie would probably deny this.

3. Factual. Did Shaquille O'Neal score 37 points or 34 points?

4. Probably verbal (ambiguity). By "violence" do we mean intentional hostility exerted by one human against another, or the operation of blind physical forces? Possibly a combination of verbal and factual. Is human violence caused by the operation of physical forces just as other physical events are?

5. Probably a combination of verbal (ambiguity) and factual. Does "death" mean the point at which the soul takes leave of the body, or the point at which life terminates? Also, Kathy appears to claim that an afterlife exists, whereas Anne appears to deny this.

6. Verbal (ambiguity). Does "education" refer to formal schooling only, or to schooling plus informal study?

7. Factual. Did Paul go to Knoxville or Nashville?

8. Verbal (ambiguity). Does "euthanasia" refer to passive measures to end life or active measures?

9. A combination of verbal (vagueness) and factual. What does "music" mean? Also, Cheryl claims that Metallica makes good sounds, whereas Oliver claims it does not.

10. Factual. When was the Battle of Trafalgar fought, and when did Nelson die?

11. Verbal (ambiguity). Eric thinks "metaphysics" refers to the study of magic and ghosts, while Leah is using the word in its more proper sense as designating the branch of philosophy that deals with ultimate questions of existence.

12. Probably a combination of verbal (ambiguity) and factual. Does "intelligence refer to IQ or to practical abilities? Also, Harold claims that Steinbeck's classes are worth taking, whereas Joyce appears to deny this.

13. Probably a combination of verbal (ambiguity and vagueness) and factual. First, does "freedom" mean the absence of external constraint only, or the absence of both internal and external constraint? Second, given the former, is it appropriate to punish the perpetrator of evil acts even though those acts might be internally compelled?

14. Factual in two ways. First, is the sun's volume greater or less than the earth's, and second, is gravity proportional to a body's mass or its volume? Of course, both disputants are mistaken about the comparative mass of the sun and earth.

15. Verbal (vagueness or possibly ambiguity). What is the meaning of "sexual relations"?

16. Verbal (vagueness). How much must one earn to be overpaid?

17. Possibly a combination of verbal (vagueness and/or ambiguity) and factual. First, there may be a factual dispute about how RU-486 works (factual). Second, Brian may be claiming that human life begins with conception, and anything that prevents the continuation of such life is immoral; while Elaine appears to deny part or all of this claim (vagueness). Third, does "abortion" mean the removal of an implanted ovum only, or does it include the prevention of implantation (ambiguity)?

18. Verbal (vagueness) and possibly factual. What is required for something to be called a food? Also, Penny considers marijuana to be relevantly similar to alcohol and coffee, whereas Sam does not.

19. Verbal (vagueness). When is someone considered to be poor?

20. Verbal (ambiguity) and possibly factual. By "right" Joseph intends human right, and Stephen intends civil right. Also, Joseph may be arguing that there are no rights apart from legislative action.

Exercise 2.2
Part I

1.   extortion - term
     laborious - nonterm
     cunningly - nonterm
     practitioner - term
     seriousness - term
     forever - could be a term; e.g. "Forever is a long time."
     whoever studies - term
     interestingly impassive - nonterm
     scarlet - term
     reinvestment - term
     therefore - nonterm
     Thomas Jefferson - term
     Empire State Building - term
     annoy - nonterm
     render satisfactory - nonterm
     graceful dancer - term
     wake up - nonterm
     not only - nonterm
     tallest man on the
     squad - term
     mountaintop - term
     between - nonterm
     since - nonterm

2.   drum: round, loud
     politician: gregarious, double-talking, elected
     devil: crafty, evil, powerful
     wolf: carnivorous, four-legged, dangerous
     Mona Lisa: expensive, mysterious, hanging in the Louvre
     Statue of Liberty: made of copper, standing in New York harbor, given by France
     fanatic: narrow-minded, dogmatic, obsessed
     carrot: edible, crunchy, orange
     riot: destructive, irrational, uncontrollable
     piano: large, having eighty-eight keys, made of wood

Exercise 2.3

3. newspaper: St. Louis Post Dispatch, Chicago Tribune, Washington Post
scientist: Enrico Fermi, Paul Dirac, Werner Heisenberg
manufacturer: Boeing, General Dynamics, Intel
river: Rhine, Amazon, Volga
opera: Rigoletto, La Traviata, Aida
tallest mountain on earth: Everest
prime number less than ten: two, three, five, seven
Governor of New York: George Pataki
language of Canada: English, French
Scandinavian country: Sweden, Norway, Denmark, Finland, Iceland

4a. plant, tree, conifer, spruce, Sitka spruce
 b. vehicle, car, sports car, Italian sports car, Maserati
 c. person, professional person, Doctor of Medicine, surgeon, brain surgeon
 d. animal, mammal, marsupial, kangaroo, wallaby
 e. polygon, quadrilateral, parallelogram, rectangle, square

Part II

1. False   6. True
2. True   7. True
3. True   8. True
4. False   9. False
5. False   10. True

Exercise 2.3
Part I

	9. Stipulative	18. Stipulative
1. Precising	10. Theoretical	19. Lexical
2. Persuasive	11. Precising	20. Precising
3. Stipulative	12. Theoretical	21. Theoretical
4. Lexical	13. Stipulative	22. Precising
5. Theoretical	14. Persuasive	23. Persuasive
6. Lexical	15. Lexical	24. Lexical
7. Persuasive	16. Persuasive	25. Stipulative
8. Precising	17. Theoretical	

Part II

2. Capital: (1) The seat of government of a state or nation; (2) The head of a column.
Depression: (1) A period of low economic activity; (2) Dejection or sadness.

4. Energy: A physical unit equal to the mass multiplied by the speed of light squared.
Atom: A fundamental unit of matter consisting of a nucleus composed of protons and neutrons and an outer shell of electrons.

5. Conservative: A responsible person interested in preserving the values of the past.
   Conservative: A stodgy curmudgeon who is afraid of change.

   Socialism: An enlightened form of government that ensures that the basic human needs of all the people are met.
   Socialism: A depraved form of government that violates the God-given right to own property and dispose of it as one chooses.

Part III

1. False
2. True
3. True
4. False
5. True

6. True
7. False
8. False
9. True
10. True

Exercise 2.4
Part I

1. Subclass
2. Genus and difference
3. Operational
4 Enumerative
5. Etymological
6. Synonymous
7. Demonstrative
8. Enumerative
9. Subclass
10. Operational
11. Etymological
12. Enumerative
13. Genus and difference
14. Operational
15. Subclass

16. Etymological
17. Synonymous
18. Genus and difference
19. Enumerative
20. Demonstrative
21. Genus and difference
22. Synonymous
23. Operational
24. Enumerative
25. Subclass
26. Synonymous
27. Etymological
28. Genus and difference
29. Operational
30. Subclass

Part II

1a. "Skyscraper" means the Empire State Building, Chrysler Building, Sears Tower, etc.
   Nonsynonymous term: "Buildings"

b. Corporation: General Motors, Ford, Daimler-Chrysler (auto maker)

c. Island: Oahu, Maui, Kauai (Hawaiian island)

d. Composer: Bruckner, Mahler, Strauss (nineteenth century Austrian male)

Exercise 2.4

   e. Novel: Jane Eyre, Wuthering Heights, Oliver Twist (motion picture)

2a. Ocean: Atlantic, Pacific, Indian, Arctic

   b. Continent: North America, South America, Europe, Africa, Australia, Asia, Antarctica

3a. "Animal" means a horse, bear, lion, and so on.
Nonsynonymous term: "Mammal"

   b. Fish: skipjack, yellow fin, albacore (tuna)

   c. Vehicle: Pontiac, Cadillac, Oldsmobile (automobile)

   d. Gemstone: diamond, sapphire, ruby (very hard object)

   e. Polygon: triangle, square, hexagon (figure)

4a. Quadrilateral: irregular quadrilateral, trapezoid, parallelogram, rectangle, square

   b. Circulating American coin: penny, nickel, dime, quarter, half dollar, dollar

5a. "Intersection" means crossing.

   b. Fabric: cloth

   c. Nucleus: center

   d. Abode: dwelling

   e. Wedlock: marriage

   f. Cellar: basement

   g. Summit: top

   h. Apparel: clothing

6a. A person is a "genius" if and only if that person can earn a score of 140 on an IQ test.

   b. A metal is "ferromagnetic" if and only if a magnet sticks to it when placed in contact with it.

   c. A substance is "fluorescent" if and only if it glows when an ultraviolet light shines on it.

   d. A solution is "alkaline" if and only if litmus paper turns blue when dipped into it.

e. Light is "polarized" if and only if its intensity changes when viewed through a piece of rotating Polaroid.

7a. "Drake" means a male duck.

b. Biologist: A scientist who studies life

c. Felony: A very serious crime

d. Widow: A woman whose husband has died

e. Library: A room or building for housing books

8a. Morphology: Derived from the Greek *morphe* (form) and *logos* (reason, speech, account). The morphology of something (such as an animal or plant) gives an account or explanation of the form or structure of that thing.

b. Isomorphic: Derived from the Greek *isos* (equal, same) and *morphe* (form). Something is isomorphic to something else if it has the same form, shape, or structure.

c. Isotropic: Derived from the Greek *isos* (equal, same) and *tropos* (turn, way, manner). Something exhibits isotropic properties (such as the velocity of light) if it has the same value when measured in different directions. In other words, no matter which way you turn, the value is the same.

d. Phototropic: Derived from the Greek *phot-* from *phos* (light) and *tropos* (turn). Something (such as a plant) is phototropic if it turns toward the light.

e. Photography: Derived from the Greek *phot-* from *phos* (light) and *graphein* (to write). Photography is a process by which an image is produced by the action of light. In other words, the image is "written" by light.

f. Lithography: Derived from the Greek *lithos* (stone) and *graphein* (to write). Lithography is a printing process by which an image is transferred from an ink-embedded stone (or metal) plate to a piece of paper.

g. Lithology: Derived from the Greek *lithos* (stone) and *logos* (word, reason, speech, account). Lithology is the study of rocks. In other words, lithology gives an account or explanation of rocks.

h. Psychology: Derived from the Greek *psyche* (spirit, soul) and *logos* (word, reason, speech, account). Psychology is the study of the soul (mind) or of disorders that afflict the soul.

Exercise 2.5

Part III
1. False   6. False
2. True   7. False
3. False   8. True
4. False   9. True
5. True   10. True

Exercise 2.5

1. Too narrow: The definiens excludes images made of bronze, wood, plaster, etc.

2. Circular

3. No reference is made to the context.

4. Figurative

5. Improper grammar

6. Fails to state the essential meaning: No reference is made to the purpose of an iPod.

7. Negative

8. Circular: What is an IQ test? A test that measures intelligence? Also too narrow?

9. Too broad: The definiens also includes overtures, concertos, incidental music, etc.

10. Affective terminology

11. Obscure

12. Ambiguous: What includes definitions? Is it logic or arguments?

13. Improper grammar

14. Too narrow: Houses can also be made of brick, etc.

15. Figurative language (contains a metaphor.)

16. Circular

17. Fails to indicate the context

18. Vague, possibly ambiguous

19. Vague

20. Negative

21. Figurative language (contains a metaphor.)

22. Improper grammar; vague; too broad: "Sailboat" also includes ketches, sloops, and yawls.

23. Affective terminology; perhaps also figurative language

24. Ambiguous: One player defeats another before who can remove whose men from the board?

25. Too broad: The definiens also denotes violins, violas, and string bass.

26. Affective terminology

27. Figurative language

28. Fails to state the essential meaning: The definition says nothing about the purpose of a clock, which is to tell the time. Also too narrow: the definiens excludes 24 hour clocks, digital clocks, and other clocks without numerals on their face.

29. Obscure

30. Too broad: The definiens also denotes salmon, tuna, swordfish, etc.

31. Affective terminology

32. Improper grammar

33. Negative, fails to convey the essential meaning

34. Too broad: The definiens also includes pencils, crayons, etc. Also too narrow: Pens can be used on material other than paper.

35. Too broad (brandy is also made from grapes) and too narrow (some wines are made from fruits other than grapes).

Exercise 3.1

1. Formal fallacy

2. Informal fallacy

3. Formal fallacy

4. Informal fallacy

5. Informal fallacy

6. Formal fallacy

7. Informal fallacy

8. Informal fallacy

9. Formal fallacy

10. Formal fallacy

Exercise 3.2

Exercise 3.2
Part I

1. Appeal to pity

2. Argument against the person, circumstantial

3. Red herring

4. Accident

5. Appeal to the people, indirect variety

6. Argument against the person, abusive

7. Appeal to force

8. Straw man

9. Missing the point

10. *Tu quoque* (you too)

11. No fallacy

12. Appeal to the people, direct variety

13. Red herring

14. Appeal to pity

15. Accident

16. Argument against the person, circumstantial

17. Argument against the person, abusive

18. No fallacy

19. Straw man

20. Appeal to force

21. Red herring

22. Appeal to the people, indirect variety

23. No fallacy (MacDowell has presented no argument.)

24. *Tu quoque*

25. Missing the point

Part II

1.	False	6.	False
2.	True	7.	True
3.	False	8.	True
4.	True	9.	True
5.	False	10.	True

Part III

The fallacies are noted in brackets throughout the text:

"Thanks for saving us a seat," Jodie says to her friend Frank, as she and Liz sit down with coffee cups in hand in the crowded cafeteria.

"No problem," Frank says.

"We were late getting out of Professor Conklin's social problems class," Jodie says disgustedly. "He's such a jerk! He always keeps us late, and he's the most arrogant snob I've ever met." [No fallacy. No argument of Prof. Conklin is being attacked.]

"I've heard that," Frank says. "What's he covering in class now?"

"Sexual harassment in the workplace," Jodie replies. "But that *is* a real problem these days."

"How so?"

"Well, my friend Amelia is a dispatcher for a trucking company, and she's told me about dozens of times she's been a victim of sexual harassment. The truckers have *Playboy* centerfolds tacked up all over the place, they constantly leer at her, they're always asking her for dates. One of them even pats her rear when she leans over at the drinking fountain." [No fallacy]

Frank laughs. "Well, there is such a thing as the First Amendment, which supposedly guarantees freedom of expression. You wouldn't want to deny these guys their freedom of expression, would you?" [Accident]

"Freedom of expression my eye!" explodes Jodie, looking incredulously at Frank. "Patting someone's rear isn't freedom of expression, it's abusive physical contact. So it's not protected by the First Amendment. [No fallacy] Men! The trouble with you, Frank, is you're a typical man. If you were a woman, you'd see these things for what they are," she says, looking at Liz for support. [*Ad hominem* circumstantial]

Liz nods her head in strong agreement.

"Well, says Frank, "I think your friend is lucky to have a job, what with all the people out of work these days. I've got a friend who's spent half his retirement savings just putting food on the table for his family, after losing his job. He was in the construction business, which is dead right now. And in other parts of the country it's even worse. You should tell Amelia to quit complaining." [Red herring]

31

"Stop giving me the run-around," demands Jodie, offended. "The trouble with you men is, you always look at women as sex objects. That makes sexual harassment inevitable." [Red herring]

"What do you mean?" protests Frank. "It's you women who treat us men like sex objects. What about all your make-up and perfume? And the tight pants and all the see-through stuff you wear? You think men are just a pack of animals--nothing but instinct--and you think that will make us fall for you. Isn't that how you see us?" [*Tu quoque*]

"I won't dignify that with a reply," fumes Jodie. "Anyone who isn't blind can see that Amelia's being victimized by those truckers. [*Ad hominem* abusive] If you can't see it, maybe pouring this hot coffee over your thick head will wake you up!" she threatens. [Appeal to force]

"Calm down," says Frank with a startled look. "Everyone is beginning to stare at us. Okay, suppose I agree that Amelia is a victim. The question is, what do we do about it?"

"To begin with," says Jodie firmly, "the trucking company should transfer Amelia out of dispatch and give her a better job, like executive secretary in the regional office. Her husband ran out on her recently, leaving her with all five kids--and little Tommy needs braces. She could really use the extra money." [Appeal to pity]

"You're joking!" Frank laughs sarcastically. "Didn't you tell me once that Amelia never finished high school and is functionally illiterate? She could never handle a job like that." [No fallacy]

Thinking for a moment, Jodie then replies, "well, maybe you're right. But at least the company should adopt a policy forbidding all forms of sexual harassment. Maybe that would make the truckers see how abusive they are, and then they might stop acting that way. [No fallacy] Practically every company in the country has such a policy, but Amelia's bosses are dragging their feet." [Appeal to the people--indirect]

"Okay. But then how do you define sexual harassment?" Frank asks. "'Cause if you can't define it, any policy is useless."

"Well, I don't exactly know," Jodie hesitates. "I'll have to think about that."

"Aha! I knew it!" exclaims Frank, triumphantly. "You can't define it, which means you don't even know if it exists! [Missing the point] If you weren't such a radical feminist, you would see that all these claims of sexual harassment are hooey." [*Ad hominem* abusive]

"Me, radical?" Jodie explodes. "The truth is you're a radical sexist. [*Tu quoque*] What you're saying is, women are only chattel, like they were two hundred years ago, and men can use or abuse them any way they please. [Straw man] Liz, that's what he's saying, isn't it?"

"Absolutely," Liz affirms.

"What a crazy argument," says Frank scornfully. "What you're saying is, we should abolish all distinctions between men and women and create a unisex society in which everyone acts like a bunch of robots. [Straw man] Isn't that right, Liz?"

"No, not at all," insists Liz. "She's trying to--"

"You're completely insane, Frank" Jodie interrupts, rising determinedly from her chair, "and your arguments are wacko!" [*Ad hominem* abusive]--and then she throws the remains of her coffee at Frank. [No fallacy] The other students who have been listening to the heated argument rise up shouting, "Right on Jodie!" Some begin chanting, "End sex harassment! End sex harassment!" As more students join the demonstration, they surrounded Frank, gesturing crudely. [Appeal to the people--direct]

Angry and humiliated, he breaks away and dashes out the door.

Exercise 3.3
Part I

1. Hasty generalization (converse accident)

2. Weak analogy

3. Appeal to unqualified authority

4. Slippery slope

5. No fallacy

6. False cause

7. Appeal to ignorance

8. No fallacy

9. Hasty generalization (converse accident)

10. Appeal to unqualified authority. (The senator's statement is a case of politically motivated hysteria mongering.)

11. No fallacy

12. Slippery slope

13. Weak analogy

14. Appeal to ignorance

15. False cause

Part II

1.	False	6.	True
2.	True	7.	True
3.	False	8.	False
4.	False	9.	True
5.	True	10.	True

Part III

1. Hasty generalization

2. Missing the point

Exercise 3.3

3. No fallacy. (A promise is not an argument.)

4. Argument against the person, circumstantial

5. Accident

6. No fallacy. (Hawking is a qualified authority.)

7. False cause (gambler's fallacy)

8. Appeal to force

9. Appeal to the people, indirect variety

10. Straw man

11. Weak analogy

12. No fallacy

13. Red herring

14. Argument against the person, abusive

15. No fallacy

16. Missing the point

17. Appeal to unqualified authority. (Would the answer be the same if Bush's statement were a mere slip of the tongue?)

18. Missing the point

19. Weak analogy

20. Argument against the person, circumstantial

21. Appeal to pity

22. No fallacy

23. *Tu quoque*

24. Red herring

25. Appeal to ignorance

26. Accident

27. No fallacy? Weak analogy?

28. False cause

29. Appeal to unqualified authority

30. Slippery slope

Part IV
The fallacies are noted in brackets throughout the text:

"Hi! Glad you could make it," Ralph says to his friend Claudia, at a Friday night party. "Hey, you just missed a great discussion that Tom, Ruben, and I were having about abduction by extraterrestrials. Ruben just left, but he said he's been reading this book by Whitley Strieber--I think it's called *Transformation*--in which Strieber describes being kidnapped by creatures from outer space."

"Good grief! You don't actually believe that nonsense, do you?" Claudia asks increduloulsy. [Possible *ad hominem* abusive]

"Well, I don't think Strieber would lie. Also, Ruben told us an amazing personal story. He was out camping a year ago, and after he'd killed off a couple of six packs of Moosehead, he says he saw a UFO. So, I think we have to conclude there really are UFOs." [Appeal to unqualified authority]

"What a joke!" Claudia laughs scornfully. "Ruben was probably hallucinating. [No fallacy] By the way, didn't he fail most of his classes last semester? His parents are spending a fortune for his education, and all he does is party, sleep, and ignore his studies. I think that's immoral. [Red herring] As for Strieber, does he give any evidence?"

"As a matter of fact, he does," Ralph replies smugly. "Apparently, a few years ago, he was driving with his wife on some country road, when both of them experienced an unusual blackout. When they woke up, they were thirty-five miles further down the road, and they had no recollection of how they got there. Later, both began having dreams about extraterrestrials performing experiments on them while they were on board their spacecraft. Extraterrestrials must have abducted them, then hypnotized them so they wouldn't remember what had happened." [False cause]

"Oh yeah, now I remember who Strieber is," answers Claudia, caustically. He's that weirdo who dreams up all kinds of fantastic stories just so he can write books about them and make lots of money. [*ad hominem* abusive and circumstantial] If you give that sickie one minute of your time, then you're crazier than he is." [*Ad hominem* abusive]

"I think you're prejudiced," Ralph says. "Why, recent surveys show that sixty-four percent of the American public believe in UFOs, and the number is growing every day. That alone should convince you they're real." [Appeal to the people--indirect]

"You've got to be kidding," Claudia mutters, shaking her head in disbelief.

"Well then, consider this," insists Ralph. "There are hundreds of people out there who've had similar dreams and the same unaccounted for time lapses. They can't all be fantasizing." [No fallacy]

"I know that Strieber is a kook," Claudia persists, "so all the others must be too." [Hasty generalization]

"Now, now, aren't we jumping to conclusions?" her friend asks condescendingly. [No fallacy]

Exercise 3.3

"Not at all. First it was UFOs and little green men. Now those little creatures are abducting people and experimenting on them. Before long they'll be manipulating our genes and trying to infiltrate the human race. In the end, everyone will suspect everyone else of being an alien, mass terror will prevail, and civilization will collapse!" Claudia exclaims in mock horror. [Slippery slope]

"Don't be a fool!" Ralph barks, irritated. "The problem with you is, you're an agnostic. [*Ad hominem* circumstantial] Obviously, you're saying we should refuse to believe in anything we can't clearly see or touch. So, logically, God doesn't exist, and there is no immortal soul. [Straw man] Tom, that's what she's saying, isn't it?"

"More or less," Tom agrees halfheartedly.

"Again, not at all," Claudia responds. "What I'm saying is, people have to be just a little bit critical about what they believe. Apparently you believe any cockamamie story that comes your way. You're just so gullible. If you keep it up, everyone and their dog will take you for a ride." [Probably no fallacy]

"Oh yeah? If I were you, I'd take a close look at my own beliefs," Ralph gibes. "Didn't I see you reading the astrology column just the other day? [*Tu quoque*] Nobody in their right mind believes in astrology. [*Ad hominem* abusive] Maybe I should start screaming 'Claudia believes in astrology! Claudia believes in astrology!' Then everyone will gawk at you, and that sexy physics major you're dying to get a date with will think you're a nut." [Appeal to force]

"Oh, shut up!" says Claudia, blushing. "I may read the astrology column, but I certainly don't believe it. I just read it for fun. But, the fact is, during the past twenty-five years there have been thousands of alleged sightings of UFOs, and not a single one has led to any solid evidence of their existence. [No fallacy] What do you make of that?"

"I think we should look at this situation the other way around," Ralph says. Up until now, nobody has shown that UFOs don't exist, so I think we should give those people who claim they have seen them the benefit of the doubt. We should believe in UFOs and extraterrestrials until the sightings are proven false. [Appeal to ignorance]

"Well, okay, let's suppose, just for the sake of argument, that I admit the existence of UFOs and their little green drivers. How are we supposed to respond to them? What are we supposed to do?" Claudia asks.

"For starters, we should extend an open invitation to them," answers Ralph. "They may come from a dying planet where millions of their compatriots desperately struggle for survival. Their sun may be burning out, their water supply exhausted, and their soil poisoned with toxic chemicals. Surely they deserve a second chance on a new planet." [Appeal to pity]

"Maybe so," Claudia says in a patronizing tone. "And now that you mention it, we probably have a legal obligation to let them in. Our current immigration laws say that we have to admit at least ten thousand applicants annually, from every major nation. If those aliens would just sign the right papers, we'd have to give them permanent residency. [Accident] However, what worries me is, they may have the wrong intentions. After all, didn't they conduct experiments on those people they abducted?"

"Yes, but don't we experiment on animals? If the animals don't complain, why should we? [Weak analogy] Also, medical experimentation often leads to wonderful new cures. I'm certain we have nothing to worry about," says Ralph, proud of his logic. [Missing the point] "Humph! I hope you're right. Well, I've got to go now--and don't let any green men kidnap you," Claudia says with a barb.

"And you either," Ralph answers.

36

Exercise 3.4
Part I

1. False dichotomy

2. Composition

3. Equivocation (on "good")

4. Amphiboly

5. Complex question

6. Division

7. Begging the question

8. No fallacy

9. Suppressed evidence (the hidden conditions for getting a free trip prevent most people from ever actually receiving one.)

10. Equivocation (on "ring")

11. Complex question

12. Division

13. Composition

14. No fallacy

15. Amphiboly

16. Suppressed evidence (The arguer ignores the time value of money. In today's dollars, the $90,000 is worth several times that figure, and, given that the pay-back will be spread out over several years, the present value of the $200,000 is significantly less than that figure.)

17. False dichotomy

18. No fallacy

19. Division

20. Begging the question

21. Composition

Exercise 3.4

22. Complex question

23. Amphiboly

24. Equivocation

25. Begging the question

Part II

1.	True	6.	False	11.	True
2.	True	7.	True	12.	False
3.	True	8.	False	13.	True
4.	True	9.	False	14.	False
5.	False	10.	True	15.	True

Part III

1. Argument against the person, circumstantial

2. Amphiboly

3. Appeal to unqualified authority

4. Equivocation

5. Composition

6. Appeal to the people (indirect variety)

7. Begging the question

8. Hasty generalization (converse accident)

9. Appeal to ignorance

10. Division

11. Weak analogy

12. Composition

13. False cause (oversimplified cause)

14. Red herring

15. Complex question

16. Appeal to unqualified authority

17. Argument against the person, abusive and circumstantial

18. Appeal to pity

19. Composition

20. False dichotomy

21. Division

22. Weak analogy

23. Equivocation

24. No fallacy

25. Straw man

26. Amphiboly

27. Begging the question

28. Accident

29. Appeal to force

30. Suppressed evidence

31. Red herring

32. *Tu quoque*

33. Slippery slope

34. Amphiboly

35. Begging the question

36. Appeal to unqualified authority

37. False cause (gambler's fallacy)

38. Weak analogy

39. Equivocation

40. Begging the question

41. Division

42. No fallacy

43. Missing the point or suppressed evidence.

44. False dichotomy

45. Appeal to ignorance

46. Hasty generalization

47. Missing the point

48. False cause

49. Composition

50. Complex question

Part IV

"Thanks for giving me a lift home," Paul says to his friend Steve, as they head toward the freeway.

"No problem; it's on my way," says Steve.

"Uh oh," warns Paul suddenly, "watch out ahead. Looks like the police have pulled somebody over."

"Thanks," Steve says. "Hope they don't beat the guy up."

"Not a chance," says Paul. "Why would you say that?"

"You're an optimist," answers Steve. "Most cops are animals; they beat up on anybody they want to. You remember Rodney King, don't you? Those cops in LA put King in the hospital for no reason at all. That should prove I'm right." [Hasty generalization]

"I think you're overreacting," Paul says. "Daryl Gates, the LA Police Chief at the time, said the King incident was an aberration. Since he was chief, I think we should take him at his word." [Appeal to unqualified authority]

"But Gates was a lunatic who refused to acknowledge even our most basic rights," Steve persists. "Also, if you recall, he was forced to resign after the King incident. [No fallacy--Gates made no argument] I know we don't live in LA, but our police department is just as bad as theirs. So, you can bet that our friend back there is just as abusive as any of them." [Division]

"Wait a minute," Paul argues, "as far as I know, nobody has ever proved that our police force is the slightest bit violent. You've no right to draw such a conclusion." [Appeal to ignorance]

"Well, listen to this," Steve counters, as he changes lanes and turns onto the freeway. "About a week ago, I was with my friend Casey. When I left him, he was perfectly okay; but he was picked up for going through a stop sign on the way home. I saw him a couple of days later, and he had a big bruise under his right eye. The cop who stopped Casey must have hit him with his baton." [False Cause--*post hoc*]

"Hold on. Did you ask Casey what happened?"

"No. I didn't have to," says Steve, a bit righteously. "I asked Casey's wife what happened between Casey and the cop, and she said he hit him. Those were her exact words, so that was good enough for me. I bet the cop's a maniac." [Amphiboly--who hit whom?]

"Good grief," answers his friend. "How long will it take you to get over your warped view of things?" [Complex question]

"My way of looking at things isn't warped," Steve insists. "The problem is, you and I are both white. If you were black, you'd see things differently. [*ad hominem* circumstantial] Police brutality toward African-Americans is way out of hand."

"Well," counters Paul, "a study done recently by an independent agency might interest you. According to that study, for every African-American whom the police use force against, there's a white person they also use force against. That proves the police treat African-Americans no worse than they do whites." [Begging the question: "Doesn't this assume that the number of blacks in the population equals the number of whites?" or possibly, composition]

"I've never heard of that study, but it seems to me there must be something wrong with it," insists Steve.

"Well, the results of that study are born out in my experience," says Paul. "I've been pulled over three or four times in the past couple of years, and the officers have always been extremely courteous. I can only conclude that the vast majority of these allegations of police brutality are the product of fertile imaginations." [Suppressed evidence or hasty generalization]

"Again, your naiveté amazes me," Steve answers, dumbfounded. "First of all, you forget that you're white and you drive a new Mercedes. Don't you think that makes a difference? [No fallacy] In fact, that's the trouble with all these arguments that downplay police brutality. They're all concocted by white people." [*Ad hominem* circumstantial]

"Well, the fact remains that we have a major crime problem in this country," Paul argues. "Combating crime requires a few concessions, and you do want to combat crime, don't you?" [Begging the question]

"Sure," Steve replies grudgingly, "but at what expense? Do innocent people have to get their heads bashed in?" [No fallacy]

"Well, I think what it comes down to is this," says Paul. "Either you allow the police to use whatever force they find necessary, or the criminals will take over this country. Now you certainly don't want that to happen, do you?" [False dichotomy]

"No, but that's the crucial question," Steve says, exiting from the freeway. "When and how much force is necessary?" [No fallacy]

"Well, you remember when the police apprehended that serial killer a few weeks ago? When the police made the arrest, the killer attacked them. So, the police can use force when attacked." [No fallacy]

"I agree," responds Steve thoughtfully. "But what about the way the police treated those peaceful right-to-lifers who were demonstrating in front of the abortion clinic the other day? Many of them were elderly and posed no physical threat. But the cops used those contraptions--what do you call them, nimchucks, nomchucks, I don't know--to squeeze the old folks' wrists, causing great pain and injury, and they hit the old people on the head with their batons. Do you think that was necessary?!" [No fallacy]

"Of course it was," answers Paul, agitatedly. "Those people attacked the police--they hurled epithets at them." [Equivocation on "attack"--verbal attack, physical attack]

"Honestly, I don't know how we've managed to stay friends all these years," Steve says with some frustration. "By the way, do you know what it says on the back of all police cars? It says 'To Protect and Serve.' Now if you hired a servant to take care of you, you'd get rid of him if he disobeyed you. Right?"

"Probably."

"Well, isn't it true," Steve asks, "that whenever a police officer disobeys one of us taxpayers, that officer should be fired?" [Weak analogy]

"That may be stretching it a bit," Paul laughs.

"But seriously," continues Steve, "I think what we need is some screening device to keep violent types from ever becoming cops."

"Well, you'll be happy to know that exactly such a device has been used for the past twenty-one years," Paul states. "Before entering the police academy, every applicant goes through a battery of psychological tests that positively eliminates all the macho types and the ones prone to violence. This ensures the individual officers are nonviolent, so we know the entire police force is nonviolent." [Composition]

"Hmm. Maybe your so-called solution is really the problem," Steve suggests, as he pulls up in front of Paul's house. We've had psychological testing for twenty-one years, and all that time, police violence has been on the rise. Perhaps we should get rid of the testing program." [False cause--*non causa pro causa*]

"Well, I don't know about the logic of that," Paul muses, stepping out of the car. "But like you said, we've been friends for a long time, so I guess we can disagree. Thanks for the ride and the discussion. See you tomorrow!"

"Sure," Steve murmurs. "Tomorrow."

Exercise 3.5
Part I

1. Missing the point, begging the question, or suppressed evidence. (Is any activity justified by the mere fact that it amounts to good business? Also, the arguer ignores the moral question of exporting a product that kills its users.)

2. Appeal to pity

3. Begging the question. (Is it likely that every woman will enlist and that every one of those will be killed?) Also possible straw man.

4. Composition

5. Missing the point; red herring; also, begging the question?

6. *Tu quoque*

7. No fallacy? Weak analogy?

8. Appeal to pity

9. Begging the question. (Does money invested in the stock market actually produce jobs?). Composition? (The fact that some politicians are corrupt and self-serving does not mean that the whole government is). Hasty generalization? (The fact that some programs are wasteful and useless does not mean that all of them are.)

10. Appeal to unqualified authority. The statement "Only a fool . . . ." suggests argument against the person, abusive.

11. Complex question

12. No fallacy? Weak analogy?

13. False cause (oversimplified cause), suppressed evidence, begging the question. (There is little or no evidence of any causal connection between malpractice suits and the decision of some obstetricians to leave the field. An unmentioned factor is the inconvenience of being on call twenty-four hours per day waiting for patients to deliver. There is also little or no evidence of any genuine "lawsuit crisis.")

14. Argument against the person, abusive; argument against the person, circumstantial

15. Slippery slope

16. Begging the question. (The argument appears to run in a circle.)

17. False dichotomy

18. Two cases of weak analogy; also, argument against the person, circumstantial

19. Slippery slope

20. False dichotomy; also, begging the question and/or false cause. (Will a smoking ban in restaurants actually cause smokers to stay away?)

21. Appeal to pity

22. False cause? No fallacy?

23. Missing the point or red herring; also, begging the question?

24. Argument against the person, abusive

25. False cause (post hoc ergo propter hoc)

26. Begging the question. (Just because your emotional reaction was that of losing a baby, does that mean the fetus is really a baby?)

27. Missing the point. (Pledging allegiance to the flag is a symbolic statement of support for the Constitution, which guarantees freedom of expression--including flag burning). Also, weak analogy (between flag burning and libel)

28. Suppressed evidence? Composition? Begging the question? No fallacy? (The Commerce Clause of the U.S. Constitution and pertinent federal legislation prohibits unfair trade practices between states. No equivalent regulations exist for international trade.)

29. No fallacy? Weak analogy?

30. Suppressed evidence? (Men and women usually differ in physical strength.) Begging the question? (Is it likely that physical attraction will lead to injury or rape?) No fallacy?

31. Appeal to the people (direct variety). Also, appeal to pity? Begging the question? (Does the fact that former pets were once loved make any difference?)

32. *Tu quoque*. Also, red herring

33. False cause (*post hoc*). But the argument is almost certainly whimsical or facetious.

34. Appeal to the people (direct variety)?

35. Appeal to force

36. Hasty generalization and/or weak analogy

37. False dichotomy? No fallacy?

38. Equivocation. (The advertiser makes it appear that the buyer will save 60% of the entire cost of a vacation instead of merely 60% of the cost of a plane ticket.) Possibly composition

39. Begging the question. (Must we all die prematurely in a nuclear holocaust?) Also possibly red herring

40. Appeal to unqualified authority; also, slippery slope

41. Begging the question and/or weak analogy. (Is the forced extinction of animal and plant species caused by industrial growth just another form of evolution? Is this forced extinction justified?)

42. Weak analogy and/or red herring; also, begging the question (Is the fetus a child?).

43. Several cases of weak analogy; also, argument against the person, abusive?

44. *Tu quoque*; also, appeal to force?

45. Complex question

46. Begging the question (Is the fetus a child?); also, straw man

47. Hasty generalization

48. Slippery slope

49. Appeal to unqualified authority. Also, the last paragraph suggests a hasty generalization.

50. Missing the point. (Whether such roadblocks are reasonable or unreasonable is a question for the courts to decide--not the general public.) Also, possibly appeal to the people.

51. Argument against the person, abusive (against the ACLU). Also, missing the point or begging the question. (If the mere possibility of hidden contraband justifies a search, then won't all Fourth Amendment rights be destroyed?)

52. Hasty generalization. Also, argument against the person, abusive? Also, begging the question or red herring?

53. Argument against the person, circumstantial; also, begging the question (Are talk-show participants informed and unbiased spokespersons?)

54. Begging the question or suppressed evidence (Individual tax payers are never consulted as to how tax revenues should be allocated.)

55. Weak analogy

56. Argument against the person, abusive; *tu quoque*; also, begging the question (Does the possibility that the Japanese would have used the atomic bomb against us justify our use of it against them?)

57. Weak analogy (between being overweight, too tall, or too short--which require special uniforms--and being gay)

58. Weak analogy? No fallacy?

59. Suppressed evidence. (Even though assault rifles might be used in few crimes, when they are used, they often inflict tremendous damage.) Begging the question (Is it likely that we will ever be justified in using assault rifles against government troops?)

60. Weak analogy? No fallacy?

Exercise 4.2

Exercise 4.1

1. Quantifier: some; Subject term: airport screeners; Copula: are; Predicate term: officials who harass frail grandmothers

2. Quantifier: no; Subject term: persons who live near airports; Copula: are; Predicate term: persons who appreciate the noise of jets

3. Quantifier: all; Subject term: oil-based paints; Copula: are; Predicate term: products that contribute significantly to photochemical smog

4. Quantifier: some; Subject term: preachers who are intolerant of others' beliefs; Copula: are not; Predicate term: television evangelists

5. Quantifier: all; Subject term: trials in which a coerced confession is read to the jury; Copula: are; Predicate term: trials in which a guilty verdict can be reversed

6. Quantifier: some; Subject term: artificial hearts; Copula: are; Predicate term: mechanisms that are prone to failure

7. Quantifier: no; Subject term: sex education courses that are taught competently; Copula: are; Predicate term: programs that are currently eroding public morals

8. Quantifier: some; Subject term: universities that emphasize research; Copula: are not; Predicate term: institutions that neglect undergraduate education

Exercise 4.2
Part I

1. **E** proposition, universal, negative, subject and predicate terms are distributed.

2. **A** proposition, universal affirmative, subject distributed, predicate undistributed.

3. **I** proposition, particular affirmative, subject and predicate undistributed.

4. **O** proposition, particular negative, subject undistributed, predicate distributed.

5. **A** proposition, universal affirmative, subject distributed, predicate undistributed.

6. **E** proposition, universal negative, subject and predicate distributed.

7. **I** proposition, particular affirmative, subject and predicate undistributed.

8. **O** proposition, particular negative, subject undistributed, predicate distributed.

Part II

1. No drunk drivers are threats to others on the highway.

2. All wildlife refuges are locations suitable for condominium developments.

3. Some slumlords are not persons who eventually wind up in jail.

4. Some CIA operatives are champions of human rights.

Part III.

1. Some owners of pit bull terriers are persons who can expect expensive lawsuits.

2. Some tax proposals that favor the rich are not fair proposals.

3. All grade school administrators are persons who choke the educational process.

4. No residents of Manhattan are people who can afford to live there.

Part IV.

1. Some oil spills are not events catastrophic to the environment.

2. Some alcoholics are persons with a healthy diet.

3. No Mexican vacations are episodes that end with Montezuma's revenge.

4. All corporate lawyers are persons with a social conscience.

Exercise 4.3
Part I

Exercise 4.3

Part II

1.	Invalid	6.	Invalid	11.	Invalid
2.	Valid	7.	Invalid	12.	Invalid
3.	Invalid	8.	Valid	13.	Invalid
4.	Valid	9.	Invalid	14.	Valid
5.	Invalid	10.	Valid	15.	Invalid

Part III

1. No S are B.

   All S are B.
   Invalid

2. F: Some L are V.

   No L are V.
   Valid

3. All T are P.

   Some T are P.
   Invalid;
   Existential Fallacy

4. All M are C.

   F: Some M are not C.
   Valid

5. F: No J are N.

   Some J are not N.
   Invalid

48

6. Some C are A.

Some C are not A.
Invalid

7. No F are S.

F: All F are S
Invalid;
Existential Fallacy

8. F: No C are T.

Some C are T
Valid

9. F: Some S are not C.

F: Some S are C.
Invalid

10. No V are A.

F: Some V are A.
Valid

Exercise 4.3

11. No T are A.

Some T are not A.
Invalid;
Existential fallacy

12. Some C are O.

No C are O.
Invalid

13. F: Some S are not O.

Some S are O.
Invalid;
Existential fallacy

14. F: All W are L.

Some W are not L.
Valid

15. F: Some C are D.

F: All C are D.
Invalid;
Existential fallacy

Exercise 4.4
Part I

1.	No Non-B are A.	True
2.	Some non-B are non-A.	Und.
3.	No A are B.	False
4.	All non-B are A.	False
5.	Some B are not non-A.	Und.
6.	Some non-A are not B.	True
7.	Contraposition	Und.
8.	Obversion	True
9.	Conversion	Und.
10.	Obversion	False
11.	Contraposition	True
12.	Conversion	False

Part II

1a. All storms intensified by global warming are hurricanes. (Not logically equivalent)

b. No completely successful procedures are sex-change operations. (Logically equivalent)

c. Some works that celebrate the revolutionary spirit are murals by Diego Rivera. (Logically equivalent)

d. Some substances with a crystalline structure are not forms of carbon. (Not logically equivalent)

2a. No radically egalitarian societies are societies that preserve individual liberties. (Logically equivalent)

b. All cult leaders are people who brainwash their followers. (Logically equivalent)

c. Some college football coaches are not persons who slip money to their players. (Logically equivalent)

d. Some budgetary cutbacks are actions unfair to the poor. (Logically equivalent)

3a. All physicians eligible to practice are physicians with valid licenses. (Logically equivalent)

b. No migrants refused asylum are persecuted migrants. (Not logically equivalent)

c. Some politicians who want to increase taxes are politicians who defend Social Security. (Not logically equivalent)

Exercise 4.4

   d.   Some supporters of civil unions are not supporters of gay marriage. (Logically equivalent)

Part III

1. Invalid (illicit conversion)

2. Valid

3. Valid

4. Invalid (illicit contraposition)

5. Valid

6. Valid

7. Valid

8. Invalid (illicit conversion)

9. Invalid (illicit contraposition)

10. Valid

11. Valid

12. Invalid (illicit contraposition)

13. Invalid (illicit conversion)

14. Valid

15. Invalid (illicit conversion)

16. Invalid (illicit contraposition)

17. Valid

18. Invalid (illicit conversion)

19. Valid

20. Valid

Exercise 4.5
Part I

1. (a) false, (b) true, (c) false

2. (a) undetermined, (b) undetermined, (c) true

3. (a) false, (b) false, (c) true

4. (a) undetermined, (b) true, (c) undetermined

5. (a) undetermined, (b) false, (c) undetermined

6. (a) false, (b) true, (c) true

7. (a) false, (b) undetermined, (c) undetermined

8. (a) true, (b) false, (c) true

Part II

1. Valid

2. Invalid (illicit subalternation)

3. Valid

4. Invalid (existential fallacy)

5. Invalid (illicit subcontrary)

6. Valid

7. Invalid (illicit contrary)

8. Valid

9. Invalid (existential fallacy)

10. Invalid (illicit subcontrary)

11. Valid

12. Invalid (unnamed fallacy)

13. Invalid (existential fallacy)

14. Invalid (illicit contrary)

Exercise 4.5

15. Valid

Part III

1. All non-B are A. (True)

2. All A are non-B. (False)

3. All A are B. (True)

4. Some non-A are B. (Undetermined)

5. Some A are non-B. (True)

6. No non-B are non-A. (Undetermined)

7. No non-A are B. (False)

8. Some A are B. (False)

9. No non-B are A. (False)

10. Some non-A are not non-B. (True)

11. Contradictory (False)

12. Conversion (True)

13. Obversion (False)

14. Subalternation (Undetermined)

15. Conversion (Undetermined)

16. Contradictory (True)

17. Contraposition (True)

18. Subalternation (True)

19. Contrary (Undetermined)

20. Subcontrary (True)

Part IV

1. Valid

2. Valid

3. Invalid (illicit subcontrary)

4. Invalid (illicit contraposition)

5. Valid

6. Invalid (existential fallacy)

7. Valid

8. Valid

9. Invalid (illicit conversion)

10. Invalid (illicit contrary)

11. Valid

12. Invalid (illicit contraposition)

13. Invalid (illicit subcontrary)

14. Valid

15. Valid

Part V

1.   All I are C.
       Some I are C.   (Subalt.)
       Some C are I.   (Conv.)

2.   No non-G are E.
       Some non-G are not E.   (Subalt.)
       Some non-E are not G.   (Contrap.)

3.   F: Some F are non-T.
       F: Some F are not T.   (Obv.)
       All F are T.   (Contradic.)

Exercise 4.6

4. All E are A.
    F: No E are A.   (Contrary)
    F: No A are E.   (Conv.)
    F: All A are non-E.   (Obv.)

5. No non-P are F.
    No F are non-P.   (Conv.)
    All F are P.   (Obv.)
    F: Some F are not P.   (Contradic.)

6. F: Some G are non-B.
    F: Some G are not B.   (Obv.)
    Some G are B.   (Subcon.)
    Some B are G.   (Conv.)

7. Some P are not non-S.
    Some P are S.   (Obv.)
    Some S are P.   (Conv.)
    F: No S are P.   (Contradic.)

8. F: No non-H are F.
    F: No F are non-H.   (Conv.)
    F: All F are H.   (Obv.)
    Some F are not H.   (Contradic.)

9. F: Some non-L are not S.
    Some non-L are S.   (Subcon.)
    Some S are non-L.   (Conv.)
    Some S are not L.   (Obv.)

10. F: Some F are not A.
    F: No F are A.   (Subalt.)
    F: No A are F.   (Conv.)
    F: All A are non-F.   (Obv.)

Exercise 4.6
Part I

1. Some A are not B.

   No A are B.
   Invalid

56

2. F: Some A are B.

F: All A are B.
Invalid, Boolean;
Conditionally valid,
Aristotelian

3. F: No A are B.

Some A are B.
Valid, Boolean

4. All A are B.

F: No A are B.
Invalid, Boolean;
Conditionally valid,
Aristotelian

5. Some A are B.

F: Some A are not B.
Invalid

6. Some A are not B.

F: All A are B.
Valid, Boolean

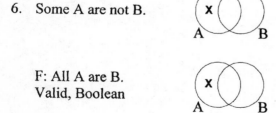

57

Exercise 4.6

7. F: Some A are B.

No A are B.
Valid, Boolean

8. F: All A are B.

Some A are B.
Invalid, Boolean;
Conditionally valid,
Aristotelian

9. F: All A are B.

No A are B.
Invalid

10. No A are B.

Some A are not B.
Invalid, Boolean;
Conditionally valid,
Aristotelian

Part II

1. No S are B.

F: Some S are B.
Valid, Boolean and
Aristotelian

2. F: Some P are not V.

Some P are V.
Invalid, Boolean;
Valid, Aristotelian;
Existential fallacy,
Boolean

3. No L are O.

Some L are not O.
Invalid;
Existential fallacy,
Boolean and Aristotelian

4. F: Some D are A.

Some D are not A.
Invalid, Boolean;
Valid, Aristotelian;
Existential fallacy,
Boolean

5. All R are I.

No R are I.
Invalid

6. F: All S are P.

Some S are not P.
Valid, Boolean and
Aristotelian

7. All P are F.

F: No P are F.
Invalid;
Existential fallacy,
Boolean and Aristotelian

8. F: Some G are not U.

F: No G are U.
Invalid, Boolean;
Valid, Aristotelian;
Existential fallacy,
Boolean

9. Some H are D.

F: No H are D.
Valid, Boolean and
Aristotelian

10. F: Some T are Q.

All T are Q.
Invalid

11. No F are C.

F: All F are C.
Invalid, Boolean;
Valid, Aristotelian;
Existential fallacy,
Boolean

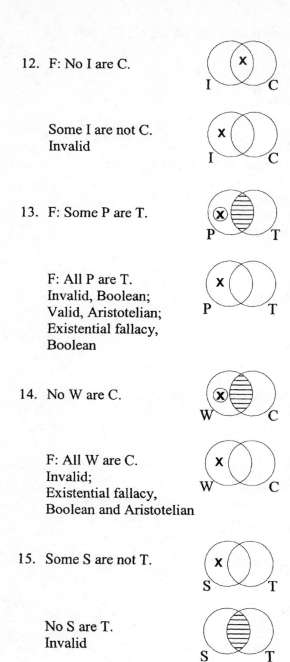

12. F: No I are C.

   Some I are not C.
   Invalid

13. F: Some P are T.

   F: All P are T.
   Invalid, Boolean;
   Valid, Aristotelian;
   Existential fallacy,
   Boolean

14. No W are C.

   F: All W are C.
   Invalid;
   Existential fallacy,
   Boolean and Aristotelian

15. Some S are not T.

   No S are T.
   Invalid

Exercise 4.7
Part I

1. All banks that make too many risky loans are banks that will fail.

2. No women military officers are persons eligible for combat duty.

3. All times security measures are lax are times terrorist attacks succeed.

Exercise 4.7

4. All substances identical to bromine are substances extractable from seawater.

5. Some guilt feelings are not psychological aberrations.

6. All jazz fans are admirers of Duke Ellington.

7. No halogens are chemically inert elements.

8. All television shows that depict violence are shows that incite violence.

9. No manipulators are persons who make good marriage partners.

10. All ships that fly the Jolly Roger are pirate ships.

11. All times she's depressed are times she gains weight.

12. All times she gains weight are times she's depressed.

13. All bachelors are unmarried men.

14. All times warmth is applied to pain are times warmth relieves pain.

15. All persons identical to Joseph J. Thomson are persons who discovered the electron.

16. Some organic silicones are things used as lubricants.

17. All vehicles suitable for deep space exploration are nuclear powered vehicles.

18. All heavenly bodies with tails are comets.

19. Some giant stars are things in the Tarantula Nebula.

20. All pregnant women who drink alcohol are women who risk giving birth to a deformed child.

21. All shellfish that make pearls are oysters.

22. All persons who believe Noah's ark lies beneath the snows of Ararat are persons given to flights of fancy.

23. All things identical to the electroscope are devices for detecting static electricity.

24. Some times are times there are concerts in Central Park.

25. All cities identical to Berlin are cities that were the setting for the 1936 Olympic Games. *or* All events identical to the 1936 Olympic Games are events that took place in Berlin.

26. No times in January are times the Kentucky Derby is run.

27. All ways of getting rid of a temptation are ways that consist in yielding to it.

28. All places there is smoke are places there is fire.

29. All times lunar eclipses occur are times the moon is full.

30. All times sunspot activity increases are times radio transmissions are disrupted.

31. All ores identical to pitchblende are radioactive ores.

32. No rats are animals that left the sinking ship, and all non-rats are animals that left the sinking ship.

33. All pesticides that contain DDT are dangerous pesticides.

34. All novels written by John Grisham are novels about lawyers.

35. All persons who hesitate are persons who are lost.

36. All modern corporations are entities run in the interest of their managers.

37. All times a rainbow occurs are times the sun is shining.

38. All persons who suffer allergic reactions are persons with a weakened immune system.

39. No pineapples are fruits that ripen after they are picked, and all non-pineapples are fruits that ripen after they are picked.

40. Some corporate raiders are persons known for their integrity, and some corporate raiders are not persons known for their integrity.

41. Some monkeys are animals found in the jungles of Guatemala.

42. All monkeys are mammals.

43. All persons identical to me are persons who like strawberries. *or* All things identical to strawberries are things I like.

44. No passengers are persons allowed to smoke on board the aircraft.

45. Some flowers are not fragrant things.

46. All places Cynthia wants to travel are places Cynthia travels.

47. All true flying mammals are bats.

48. Some rivers are not things that run to the sea.

Exercise 4.7

49. No physicists are persons who understand the operation of superconductors.

50. Some apartment dwellers are persons victimized by crime.

51. Some forced labor camps are things in China.

52. All measures that increase efficiency are measures that improve profitability.

53. Some dolphins are animals swimming between the breakers.

54. No feathers are heavy things.

55. Some picnics are events entirely free of ants, and some picnics are not events entirely free of ants.

56. All civil rights that are human rights are unalienable rights.

57. All things she pleases to say are things she says.

58. All Net surfers are computer buffs.

59. All felines are cats.

60. All things Renee is told to do are things Renee does.

Part II.

1. Some third generation computers are machines that take dictation.

2. All cars that young lawyers drive are BMWs.

3. No cartilaginous fishes are vertebrates with a bony skeleton, and all vertebrates that are not cartilaginous fishes are vertebrates with a bony skeleton.

4. No downhill skiers who suffer from altitude sickness are effective competitors.

5. All substances identical to cobalt are ferromagnetic metals.

6. No nuclear pacifists are persons who believe a just war is possible.

7. No matadors are persons who succumb easily to fear.

8. All companies identical to Google are companies looking forward to a bright future.

9. All toxic dumps that are ecological catastrophes are toxic dumps that leak.

10. All hungry crocodiles are dangerous animals.

Exercise 5.1
Part I

1. Major term: things that produce intense gravity.
   Minor term: extremely dense objects.
   Middle term: neutron stars.
   Mood, figure: **AAA**-3; invalid

2. Major term: insects that should be killed.
   Minor term: dragonflies.
   Middle term: insects that eat mosquitoes.
   Mood, figure: **EAE**-1; valid, Boolean and Aristotelian

3. Major term: environmentally produced diseases.
   Minor term: psychological disorders.
   Middle term: inherited afflictions.
   Mood, figure: **EOI**-2; invalid

4. Major term: good witnesses.
   Minor term: hypnotized persons.
   Middle term: persons who mix fact with fantasy.
   Mood, figure: **EIO**-1; valid, Boolean and Aristotelian

5. Major term: good absorbers of ultraviolet rays.
   Minor term: things destroyed by chlorine.
   Middle term: ozone molecules.
   Mood, figure: **AAI**-3; invalid, Boolean; valid, Aristotelian

Part II

1. All B are D.
   No R are D.
   No R are B.
   AEE-2
   Valid, Boolean and Aristotelian

2. No K are Y.
   Some Y are L.
   Some L are not K.
   EIO-4
   Valid, Boolean and Aristotelian

3. All W are M.
   No R are W.
   Some R are M.
   AEI-1
   Invalid

Exercise 5.1

4. No M are F.
   All M are I.
   Some I are not F.
   EAO-3
   Invalid, Boolean; valid, Aristotelian

5. Some M are I.
   No I are P.
   Some P are M.
   IEI-4
   Invalid

6. All C are U.
   Some A are not U.
   Some A are not C.
   AOO-2
   Valid, Boolean and Aristotelian

7 All P are E.
   All L are P.
   Some L are E.
   AAI-1
   Invalid

8. Some H are not P.
   No H are R.
   Some R are not P.
   OEO-3
   Invalid

9. No P are T.
   All A are T.
   No A are P.
   EAE-2
   Valid, Boolean and Aristotelian

10. Some O are not C.
    All S are O.
    Some S are C.
    OAI-1
    Invalid

Part III

1. Some M are not P.
   All M are S.
   No S are P.

2. No P are M.
   Some M are S.
   All S are P.

3. All M are P.
   Some M are S.
   Some S are P.

4. Some M are P.
   All S are M.
   No S are P.

5. All P are M.
   Some S are not M.
   Some S are not P.

6. No P are M.
   All M are S.
   Some S are not P.

7. All M are P.
   All S are M.
   All S are P.

8. No P are M.
   All S are M.
   Some S are not P.

9. Some M are not P.
   No M are S.
   Some S are P.

10. Some P are not M.
    No M are S.
    All S are P.

Part IV

1. No dogmatists are scholars who encourage free thinking.
   Some theologians are scholars who encourage free thinking.
   Some theologians are not dogmatists.

2. All lock step ideologues are persons incapable of objectivity.
   Some Supreme Court justices are lock step ideologues.
   Some Supreme Court justices are persons incapable of objectivity.

Exercise 5.2

3. All teenage suicides are tragic occurrences.
   No tragic occurrences are heroic episodes.
   No heroic episodes are teenage suicides.

4. Some viruses are not things capable of replicating by themselves.
   All viruses are structures that invade cells.
   Some structures that invade cells are not things capable of replicating by themselves.

5. No legally enforceable documents are guarantees of marital happiness.
   All prenuptial agreements are legally enforceable documents.
   No prenuptial agreements are guarantees of marital happiness.

Part V

1. False   6. False
2. False   7. True
3. True   8. True
4. False   9. True
5. True   10. True

Exercise 5.2
Part I

1. All C are U.
   Some U are I.
   Some I are C.
   AII-4
   Invalid

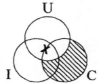

2. No A are P.
   Some K are A.
   Some K are not P.
   EIO-1
   Valid, Boolean and
   Aristotelian

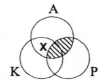

3. No I are P.
   All T are P.
   Some T are not I.
   EAO-2
   Invalid, Boolean;
   Valid, Aristotelian

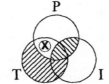

4. All H are D.
   Some D are not P.
   Some P are not H.
   AOO-4
   Invalid

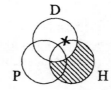

68

5. No C are S.
    <u>No S are Q.</u>
    No Q are C.
    EEE-4
    Invalid

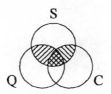

6. All D are E.
    <u>All C are D.</u>
    All C are E.
    AAA-1
    Valid, Boolean and
    Aristotelian

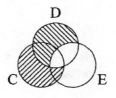

7. No P are I.
    <u>All F are I.</u>
    No F are P.
    EAE-2
    Valid, Boolean and
    Aristotelian

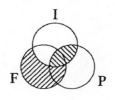

8. Some I are not M.
    <u>Some P are I.</u>
    Some P are not M.
    OIO-1
    Invalid

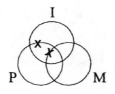

9. Some A are P.
    <u>All P are N.</u>
    Some N are A.
    IAI-4
    Valid, Boolean and
    Aristotelian

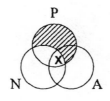

10. No C are O.
    <u>Some D are not O.</u>
    Some D are not C.
    EOO-2
    Invalid

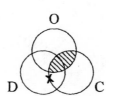

11. All C are P.
    <u>All C are T.</u>
    Some T are P.
    AAI-3
    Invalid

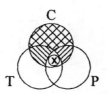

Exercise 5.2

12. All S are O.
   All Q are O.
   All Q are S.
   AAA-2
   Invalid

13. No P are W.
   All D are P.
   No D are W.
   EAE-1
   Valid, Boolean and
   Aristotelian

14. Some I are P.
   Some S are I.
   Some S are P.
   III-1
   Invalid

15. Some C are R.
   All C are D.
   Some D are R.
   IAI-3
   Valid, Boolean and
   Aristotelian

16. All C are G.
   All G are E.
   Some E are C.
   AAI-4
   Invalid

17. All S are P.
   No P are O.
   All O are S.
   AEA-4
   Invalid

18. No P are I.
   Some C are P.
   Some C are not I.
   EIO-1
   Valid, Boolean and
   Aristotelian

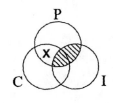

70

19. No A are I.
    <u>All A are N.</u>
    Some N are not I.
    EAO-3
    Invalid, Boolean;
    valid, Aristotelian

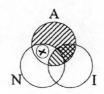

20. Some S are not U.
    <u>All S are C.</u>
    Some C are not U.
    OAO-3
    Valid, Boolean and
    Aristotelian

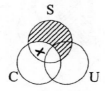

Part II

1. No P are M.
   <u>All S are M.</u>
   No S are P.

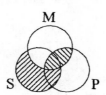

2. Some P are not M.
   <u>Some M are S.</u>
   No conclusion.

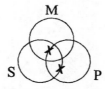

3. Some M are P.
   <u>All S are M.</u>
   No conclusion.

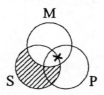

4. Some M are not P.
   <u>All M are S.</u>
   Some S are not P.

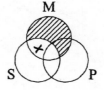

5. Some P are M.
   <u>All M are S.</u>
   Some S are P.

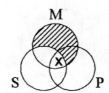

71

Exercise 5.3

6. No M are P.
   Some S are not M.
   No conclusion.

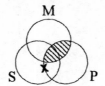

7. All M are P.
   All S are M.
   All S are P.

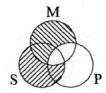

8. All P are M.
   All S are M.
   No conclusion.

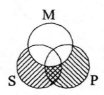

9. No P are M.
   Some M are S.
   Some S are not P.

10. No P are M.
    No M are S.
    No conclusion.

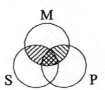

Part III
1. False   6. False
2. True   7. False
3. True   8. True
4. True   9. True
5. True   10. False

Exercise 5.3
Part I

1. All M are P.
   All M are S.
   All S are P.
   Invalid
   Illicit minor

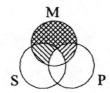

72

2. Some P are M
   <u>All S are M.</u>
   Some S are P.
   Invalid
   Undistributed middle

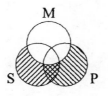

3. No M are P.
   <u>Some S are M.</u>
   Some S are not P.
   Valid, Boolean and
   Aristotelian
   No rules broken.

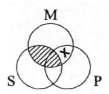

4. All P are M.
   <u>All S are M.</u>
   Some S are P.
   Invalid
   Undistributed middle

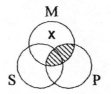

5. Some M are P.
   <u>No S are M.</u>
   Some S are not P.
   Invalid
   Illicit major

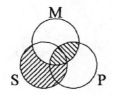

6. No P are M.
   <u>Some M are not S.</u>
   Some S are not P.
   Invalid
   Exclusive premises

7. No M are P.
   <u>All S are M.</u>
   All S are P.
   Invalid
   Drawing aff. concl.
   from neg. prem.

8. All M are P.
   <u>Some M are S.</u>
   Some S are P.
   Valid, Boolean and
   Aristotelian
   No rules broken.

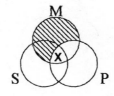

9. All P are M.
    <u>All M are S.</u>
    Some S are P.
    Invalid, Boolean
    Conditionally valid,
    Aristotelian (valid if P exists)
    Existential fallacy, Boolean

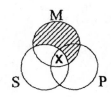

10. Some M are P.
    <u>All M are S.</u>
    Some S are not P.
    Invalid
    Illicit major; drawing
    neg. concl. from aff.
    premises

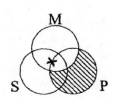

11. All P are M.
    <u>Some S are M.</u>
    Some S are P.
    Invalid
    Undistributed middle

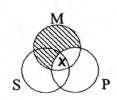

12. All M are P.
    <u>Some M are S.</u>
    Some S are not P.
    Invalid
    Illicit major; drawing
    neg. concl. from aff.
    premises

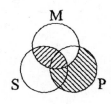

13 All P are M.
    <u>No M are S.</u>
    No S are P.
    Valid, Boolean and
    Aristotelian
    No rules broken.

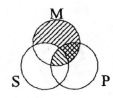

14. No P are M.
    <u>All M are S.</u>
    No S are P.
    Invalid
    Illicit minor

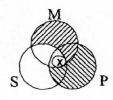

15. No M are P.
    All M are S.
    Some S are not P.
    Invalid, Boolean
    Conditionally valid,
    Aristotelian (valid if M exists)
    Existential fallacy, Boolean

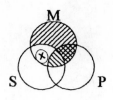

16. No M are P.
    No S are M.
    No S are P.
    Invalid
    Exclusive premises

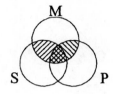

17. No M are P.
    All S are M.
    No S are P.
    Valid, Boolean and
    Aristotelian
    No rules broken.

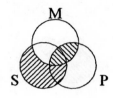

18. Some M are not P.
    All M are S.
    Some S are P.
    Invalid
    Drawing aff. concl.
    from a neg. premise

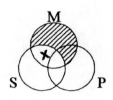

19. All P are M.
    Some S are not M.
    Some S are not P.
    Valid, Boolean and
    Aristotelian
    No rules broken.

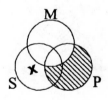

20. No M are P.
    All S are M.
    Some S are not P.
    Invalid, Boolean
    Conditionally valid,
    Aristotelian (valid if S exists)
    Existential fallacy, Boolean

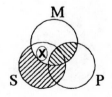

Exercise 5.3

Part II

1. Some N are C.
   <u>Some C are O.</u>
   Some O are N.
   Invalid
   Undistributed middle

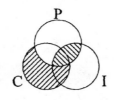

2. No I are P.
   <u>All C are P.</u>
   No C are I.
   Valid, Boolean and
   Aristotelian
   No rules broken.

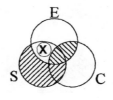

3. No E are C.
   <u>All S are E.</u>
   Some S are not C.
   Invalid, Boolean
   Valid, Aristotelian (since
   S exists). Existential
   fallacy, Boolean

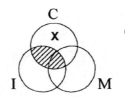

4. Some C are not M.
   <u>No C are I.</u>
   Some I are not M.
   Invalid
   Exclusive premises

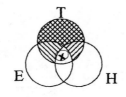

5. All T are H.
   <u>All T are E.</u>
   Some E are H.
   Invalid
   Existential fallacy,
   Boolean and Aristotelian

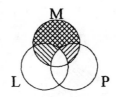

6. All M are P.
   <u>All M are L.</u>
   All L are P.
   Invalid
   Illicit minor

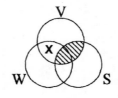

7. No S are V.
   <u>Some W are V.</u>
   Some W are not S.
   Valid, Boolean and
   Aristotelian
   No rules broken.

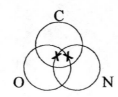

76

8. All W are P.
   Some P are I.
   Some I are W.
   Invalid
   Undistributed middle

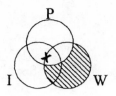

9. All I are P.
   Some E are not P.
   Some E are I.
   Invalid
   Drawing aff. concl.
   from a neg. premise

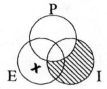

10. All S are M.
    All M are P.
    Some P are S.
    Invalid, Boolean
    Valid, Aristotelian (since
    S exists). Existential
    fallacy, Boolean

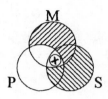

Part III

1. False	6. False
2. True	7. False
3. True	8. False
4. True	9. True
5. True	10. False

Exercise 5.4

1. Some non-T are M.   (conv., obv.)   Some M are not T.
   All non-I are non-M.   (contrapose)   All M are I.
   Some I are T.   Some I are T.
   Invalid
   Drawing affirmative conclusion from a negative premise

2. All S are R.   All S are R.
   Some non-R are C.   (conv., obv.)   Some C are not R.
   Some C are non-S.   (obvert)   Some C are not S.
   Valid

3. All non-S are non-W.   (contrapose)   All W are S.
   All P are W.   All P are W.
   All P are S.   All P are S.
   Valid

77

Exercise 5.5

4. Some I are C.   Some I are C.
   <u>All C are non-P.   </u>   <u>All C are non-P.   </u>
   Some non-I are not P.   (contrapose)   Some non-P are not I.
   Invalid
   Illicit major; drawing negative conclusion from affirmative premises

5. All W are non-D.   (obvert)   No W are D.
   <u>All D are non-S.</u>   (obvert)   <u>No D are S. </u>
   No non-W are S   (conv., obv.)   All S are W.
   Invalid.
   Exclusive premises; drawing affirmative conclusion from negative premises

6. No F are D.   No F are D.
   <u>No non-F are C.</u>   (conv., obv.)   <u>All C are F. </u>
   All C are non-D.   (obvert)   No C are D.
   Valid

7. All non-M are non-E.   (contrapose)   All E are M.
   <u>Some P are not M.   </u>   <u>Some P are not M.</u>
   Some P are non-E.   (obvert)   Some P are not E.
   Valid

8. All S are non-E.   (obvert)   No S are E.
   <u>Some non-S are U.</u>   (conv., obv.)   <u>Some U are not S.</u>
   Some U are not E.   Some U are not E.
   Invalid
   Exclusive premises

9. All D are non-I.   (obvert)   No D are I.
   <u>All non-D are non-C.</u>   (contrapose)   <u>All C are D.</u>
   No C are I.   No C are I.
   Valid

10. No D are V.   No D are V.
    <u>Some S are non-D.</u>   (obvert)   <u>Some S are not D.</u>
    Some non-V are S.   (conv., obv.)   Some S are not V.
    Invalid.
    Exclusive premises

Exercise 5.5

1. All scientists who theorize about the nature of time are physicists.
   All persons identical to Stephen Hawking are scientists who theorize about the
   nature of time.
   Therefore, all persons identical to Stephen Hawking are physicists.
   Valid

2. All times suicide rates decline are times people's lives are better adjusted.
   All recent years are times suicide rates decline.
   Therefore, all recent years are times people's lives are better adjusted.
   Valid

3. All cars purchased by environmentalists are fuel-efficient cars.
   No Hummers are cars purchased by environmentalists.
   Therefore, no Hummers are fuel-efficient cars.
   Invalid, illicit major

4. All persons who wrote the Declaration of Independence are persons who had a big impact on civilization.
   All persons identical to Thomas Jefferson are persons who had a big impact on civilization.
   Therefore, all persons identical to Thomas Jefferson are persons who wrote the Declaration of Independence.
   Invalid, undistributed middle

5. All institutions that teach secular humanism are institutions that teach religion.
   Some public schools are institutions that teach secular humanism.
   Therefore, some public schools are institutions that teach religion.
   Valid

6. All persons who led America into the Space age are persons who will live in history.
   All persons identical to John Glenn are persons who led America into the space age.
   Therefore, all persons identical to John Glenn are persons who will live in history.
   Valid

7. Some songs Shania Twain sings are country songs.
   All songs Shania Twain wants to sing are songs Shania Twain sings.
   Therefore, some songs Shania Twain wants to sing are country songs.
   Invalid, undistributed middle

8. Some interest expenses are not tax-deductible expenses.
   All home mortgage expenses are interest expenses.
   Therefore, no home mortgage expenses are tax-deductible expenses.
   Invalid, undistributed middle

9. All marriages that allow little room for growth are arrangements bound to fail.
   All marriages based on a meshing of neuroses are marriages that allow little room for growth.
   Therefore, all marriages based on a meshing of neuroses are arrangements bound to fail.
   Valid

10. All TV viewers who receive scrambled signals are viewers with a decoder.
    All persons who receive digital satellite signals are TV viewers who receive scrambled signals.
    Therefore, all persons who receive digital satellite signals are viewers with a decoder.
    Valid

11. All places icebergs are present are places threats to shipping exist.
    No places identical to the South Pacific are places icebergs are present.
    Therefore, no places identical to the South Pacific are places threats to shipping exist.
    Invalid, illicit major

12. All persons who think Africa is in North America are persons with no knowledge of geography.
    Some college students are persons who think Africa is in North America.
    Therefore, some college students are persons with no knowledge of geography.
    Valid

13. All diseases carried by recessive genes are diseases that can be inherited by offspring of two carriers.
    All diseases identical to cystic fibrosis are diseases carried by recessive genes.
    Therefore, all diseases identical to cystic fibrosis are diseases that can be inherited by offspring of two carriers.
    Valid

14. Since the first premise is an exceptive proposition, we have two arguments:
    No chick flicks are films that were exciting.
    No action films are chick flicks.
    Therefore, all action films are films that were exciting.
    Invalid, exclusive premises

    All films that are not chick flicks are films that were exciting.
    No action films are chick flicks.
    Therefore, all action films are films that were exciting.
        After obverting the second premise, we have:

    All films that are not chick flicks are films that were exciting.
    All action films are films that are not chick flicks.
    Therefore, all action films are films that were exciting.
    Valid
    Since one of the two arguments is valid, the original argument is valid.

15. Some times are times aversive therapy is inhumane.
    Some times are times autistic children are helped by aversive therapy.
    Therefore, some times autistic children are helped by aversive therapy are times aversive therapy is inhumane.
    Invalid, undistributed middle

Exercise 5.6
Part I

1. Premise missing: Some police chiefs fix parking tickets.

2. Conclusion missing: Plagiarism deserves to be punished.

3. Premise missing: Any film that wins 11 Oscars is a great film.

4. Conclusion missing: A few fraternities have no legitimate role in campus life.

5. Premise missing: Churches are nonprofit organizations.

6. Conclusion missing: Carmen was well performed.

7. Conclusion missing: Some phone calls are not from friends.

8. Premise missing: Higher life forms are organized beings.

9. Conclusion missing: *The Brothers Karamazov* is a timeless novel.

10. Premise missing: Whenever the humpback whale is overhunted, the humpback whale population decreases.

11. Conclusion missing: Human life can be sustained on the moon.

12. Conclusion missing: The Cleveland symphony has effective fund raisers.

13. Premise missing: No one who thinks that everything is governed by deterministic laws believes in free will.

14. Conclusion missing: Our client's contract to buy land is enforceable.

15. Conclusion missing: The Hubble telescope is unaffected by the atmosphere.

Part II.

1. All persons who fix parking tickets are persons who undermine the evenhanded enforcement of the law.
Some police chiefs are persons who fix parking tickets.
Therefore, some police chiefs are persons who undermine the evenhanded enforcement of the law.
Valid

2. All forms of cheating are incidents that deserve to be punished.
All cases of plagiarism are forms of cheating.
Therefore, all cases of plagiarism are incidents that deserve to be punished.
Valid

3. All films that won 11 Oscars are great films.
   All films identical to *Lord of the Rings* are films that won 11 Oscars.
   Therefore, all films identical to *Lord of the Rings* are great films.
   Valid

4. No groups that have dangerous initiation rites are groups that have a legitimate role in campus life.
   Some fraternities are groups that have dangerous initiation rites.
   Therefore, some fraternities are not groups that have a legitimate role in campus life.
   Valid

5. All organizations exempt from paying taxes are nonprofit organizations.
   All churches are nonprofit organizations.
   Therefore, all churches are organizations exempt from paying taxes.
   Invalid, undistributed middle

6. No Mozart operas are operas that were well performed.
   No operas identical to Carmen are Mozart operas.
   Therefore, all operas identical to Carmen are operas that were well performed.
   Invalid, exclusive premises and drawing affirmative conclusion from negative premises

   and

   All operas not written by Mozart are operas that were well performed.
   All operas identical to Carmen are operas not written by Mozart.
   Therefore, all operas identical to Carmen are operas that were well performed.
   Valid
   Since one of the two arguments is valid, the original argument is valid.

7. All calls from friends are calls that are welcome.
   Some phone calls are not calls that are welcome.
   Therefore, some phone calls are not calls from friends.
   Valid

8. No organized beings are things that could have evolved through merely random processes.
   All higher life forms are organized beings.
   Therefore, no higher life forms are things that could have evolved through merely random processes.
   Valid

9. All timeless novels are great novels.
   All novels identical to *The Brothers Karamazov* are great novels.
   Therefore, all novels identical to *The Brothers Karamazov* are timeless novels.
   Invalid, undistributed middle

10. All times the humpback whale is overhunted are times the humpback whale population decreases.
All recent years are times the humpback whale is overhunted.
Therefore, all recent years are times the humpback whale population decreases.
Valid

11. All places water exists are places human life can be sustained.
All places identical to the moon are places water exists.
Therefore, all places identical to the moon are places human life can be sustained.
Valid

12. All symphony orchestras with effective fund raisers are orchestras that survive.
All orchestras identical to the Cleveland symphony are orchestras that survive.
Therefore, all orchestras identical to the Cleveland symphony are orchestras with effective fund raisers.
Invalid, undistributed middle

13. No persons who think that everything is governed by deterministic laws are persons who believe in free will.
All mechanistic materialists are persons who think everything is governed by deterministic laws.
Therefore, no mechanistic materialists are persons who believe in free will.
Valid

14. All enforceable contracts to buy land are contracts in writing.
All contracts identical to our client's contract to buy land are contracts in writing.
Therefore, all contracts identical to our client's contract to buy land are enforceable contracts.
Invalid, undistributed middle

15. All telescopes unaffected by the atmosphere are orbiting telescopes.
All telescopes identical to the Hubble telescope are orbiting telescopes.
Therefore, all telescopes identical to the Hubble telescope are telescopes unaffected by the atmosphere.
Invalid

Part III

1. No organizations that make alcohol readily available and acceptable are organizations that are serious about fighting alcohol abuse.
All organizations identical to the Defense Department are organizations that make alcohol readily available and acceptable.
Therefore, no organizations identical to the Defense Department are organizations that are serious about fighting alcohol abuse.

2. All times in which American cities are practically broke and millions of people are out of work are times in which aid to Israel should be stopped.
All present times are times in which American cities are practically broke and millions of people are out of work.
Therefore, all present times are times in which aid to Israel should be stopped.

3. All times a person decides life is impossible are times a person has a right to end his/her life.
No times a person has a right to end his/her life are times suicide is immoral.
Therefore, no times a person decides life is impossible are times suicide is immoral.

4. All efforts to ban books are efforts that ensure those books will be read.
All efforts by the fundamentalist families in Church Hill, Tennessee to remove Macbeth, etc. from the libraries are efforts to ban books.
Therefore, all efforts by the fundamentalist families in Church Hill, Tennessee, to remove Macbeth, etc. from the libraries are efforts that ensure those books will be read.

5. No times in which elected officials in Washington fail to act courageously and responsibly are times the budget deficit will be brought under control.
All times in the foreseeable future are times elected officials in Washington fail to act courageously and responsibly.
Therefore, no times in the foreseeable future are times the budget deficit will be brought under control.

6. All laws that are so vague that men of common intelligence must guess at their meaning are laws banned by the Constitution.
All sexual harassment laws are laws so vague that men must guess at their meaning.
Therefore, all sexual harassment laws are laws banned by the constitution.

7. All policies that promote more college graduates tomorrow are policies that result in higher tax revenues tomorrow.
All policies that offer financial aid to college students today are policies that promote more college graduates tomorrow.
Therefore, all policies that offer financial aid to college students today are policies that result in higher tax revenues tomorrow.

and

All policies that result in higher tax revenues tomorrow are good investments in the future.
All policies that offer financial aid to college students today are policies that result in higher tax revenues tomorrow.
Therefore, all policies that offer financial aid to college students today are good investments in the future.

8. All beings in which genes and environment control destinies are beings that fail to act freely.
   All human beings are beings in which genes and environment control destinies.
   Therefore, all human beings are beings that fail to act freely.

   and

   No beings that fail to act freely are beings that should be sent to prison for their transgressions.
   All human beings are beings that fail to act freely.
   Therefore, no human beings are beings that should be sent to prison for their transgressions.

9. All times toy-gun play is encouraged are occasions in which children are sent the message that the best way to deal with frustration and conflict is with a gun.
   All occasions in which children are sent the massage that best way to deal with frustration and conflict is with a gun are occasions in which children are sent the wrong message.
   Therefore, all times toy-gun play is encouraged are occasions in which children are sent the wrong message.

10. All people who act in ways that decrease their chances of survival are people who will die out through natural selection.
    All smokers who continue smoking are people who act in ways that decrease their chances of survival.
    Therefore, all smokers who continue smoking are people who will die out through natural selection.

    and

    All people who act in ways that increase their chances of survival are people who will survive through natural selection.
    All smokers who quit are people who act in ways that increase their chances of survival.
    Therefore, all smokers who quit are people who will survive through natural selection.

Exercise 5.7
Part I

1. All A are B.
   No B are C.   No C are A.
   Some D are C. ─────────────→
   Some D are not A.

   Valid

85

Exercise 5.7

2. All A are B.
   Some C are not B.   Some C are not A.
   No C are D. ——————————→
   Some D are not A.

   Invalid

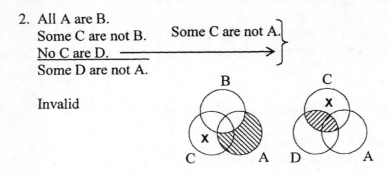

3. All E are F.
   All F are S.   All E are S.
   No S are M. ——————————→   No E are M.
   Some M are H. ——————————————————————→
   Some H are not E.

   Valid

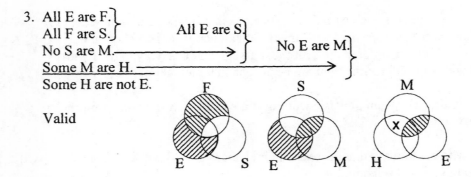

4. No K are N.
   Some T are K.   Some T are not N.
   All T are C. ——————————————————→   Some C are not N.
   Some C are Q. ——————————————————————————————→
   Some Q are not N.

   Invalid

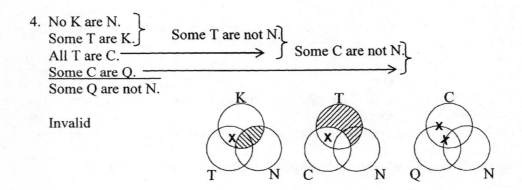

5. After obverting the first premise and contraposing the second premise, we have:

   No C are B.
   All A are B.   No C are A.
   All D are A. ——————————→
   No D are C.
   Valid

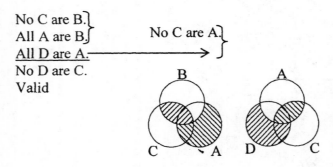

86

6. After obverting the first premise and contraposing the conclusion, we have,

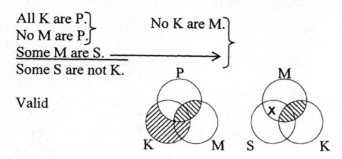

All K are P.⎤
No M are P.⎦   No K are M.⎤
Some M are S. ⟶   ⎦
Some S are not K.

Valid

7. After contraposing the first premise and obverting the second premise and the conclusion, we have,

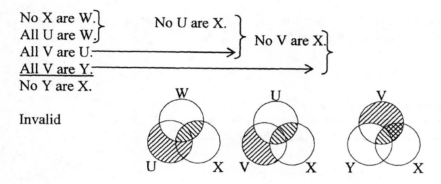

No X are W.⎤
All U are W.⎦   No U are X. ⎤
All V are U.⟶   ⎦ No V are X.⎤
All V are Y.⟶   ⎦
No Y are X.

Invalid

8. After obverting the first premise and contraposing the second premise and the conclusion, we have,

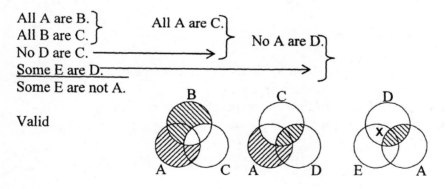

All A are B.⎤
All B are C.⎦   All A are C.⎤
No D are C. ⟶   ⎦ No A are D.⎤
Some E are D.⟶   ⎦
Some E are not A.

Valid

Exercise 5.7

9. After contraposing the first premise, obverting the third premise, converting and obverting the fourth premise, and obverting the fifth premise, we have,

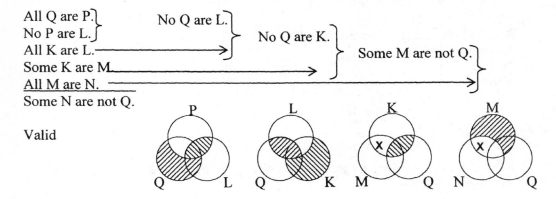

All Q are P.
No P are L.
All K are L.
Some K are M.
All M are N.
Some N are not Q.

No Q are L.
No Q are K.
Some M are not Q.

Valid

10. After converting and obverting the second and fourth premises, and obverting the third and fifth premises and the conclusion, we have:

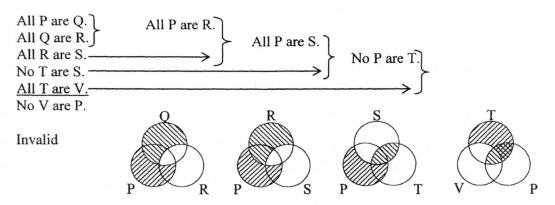

All P are Q.
All Q are R.
All R are S.
No T are S.
All T are V.
No V are P.

All P are R.
All P are S.
No P are T.

Invalid

Part II.

1. All things that produce oxygen are things that support human life.
   All rain forests are things that produce oxygen.
   No things that support human life are things that should be destroyed.
   Therefore, no rain forests are things that should be destroyed.

   All O are S.
   All R are O.
   No S are D.
   No R are D.

   No S are D.   No O are D.
   All O are S.
   All R are O.
   No R are D.

88

2. No restrictive trade pollicies are policies that fail to invite retaliation.
   All policies that lead to a trade war are policies that threaten our standard of living.
   Some Japanese trade policies are restrictive trade policies.
   Therefore, all policies that invite retaliation are policies that lead to a trade war.

   No R are non-I.   (obvert)
   All L are T.
   <u>Some J are R.</u>
   All I are L.

   All L are T.
   All I are L.
   All R are I.
   <u>Some J are R.</u>
   Some J are T.

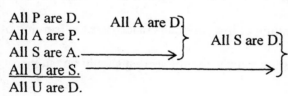

3. All things that poison drinking water are things that cause disease and death.
   All chemicals that percolate through the soil are things that contaminate aquifers.
   All dumped chemicals are chemicals that percolate through the soil.
   All things that contaminate aquifers are things that poison drinking water.
   Therefore, all dumped chemicals are things that cause disease and death.

   All P are D.
   All S are A.
   All U are S.
   <u>All A are P.</u>
   All U are D.

   All P are D.
   All A are P.
   All S are A.
   <u>All U are S.</u>
   All U are D.

   All A are D.
   All S are D.

4. No brittle things are ductile things.
   All superconductors are ceramics.
   All things that can be pulled into wires are ductile things.
   All ceramics are brittle things.
   Therefore, no superconductors are things that can be pulled into wires.

   No B are D.
   All S are C.
   All P are D.
   <u>All C are B.</u>
   No S are P.

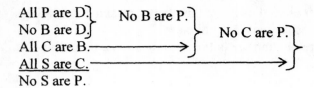

All P are D.⌉
No B are D.⌋   No B are P.⌉
All C are B.————————⟶ ⌋ No C are P.⌉
All S are C.————————————————⟶ ⌋
No S are P.

5   Some college students are persons who purchase their termpapers.
    All cheats are persons expelled from college.
    No persons who will achieve their career goals are persons expelled from college.
    No persons who purchase their termpapers are are non- cheats.
    Therefore, some college students are persons who will not achieve their career goals.

Some S are P.
All C are E.
No A are E.
No P are non-C.   (obvert)
Some S are non-A.   (obvert)

No A are E.⌉   No C are A.⌉
All C are E.⌋————————⟶ ⌋ No P are A.⌉
All P are C.————————⟶ ⌋
Some S are P. ————————————————⟶ ⌋
Some S are not A.

6. No things identical to creation science are things that favor the teaching of evolution.
    No things that frustrate the understanding of life are are things that should be taught.
    All things that oppose the teaching of evolution are things that impede the learning of
    biology.
    All things that enhance the understanding of life are things that foster the learning of
    biology.
    Therefore, no things identical to creation science are things that should be taught.

No C are T.
No non-U are S.   (convert, obvert)
All non-T are non-B. (contrapose)
All U are B.
No C are S.

All S are U.⌉   All S are B.⌉
All U are B.⌋————————⟶ ⌋ All S are T.⌉
All B are T.————————⟶ ⌋
No C are T.————————————————⟶ ⌋
No C are S.

7. All persons who give birth to crack babies are persons who increase future crime rates.
   Some pregnant women are pregnant crack users.
   All persons who increase future crime rates are criminals.
   No pregnant crack users are persons who fail to give birth to crack babies.
   Therefore, some pregnant women are criminals.

   All B are I.
   Some P are U.
   All I are C.
   <u>No U are non-B.</u>   (obvert)
   Some P are C.

   All I are C.⎤
   All B are I.⎦ All B are C.⎤
   All U are B. ⟶   ⎦ All U are C. ⎤
   <u>Some P are U.</u>————————————⟶   ⎦
   Some P are C.

8. All things that retard population growth are things that increase food availability.
   All things that prevent starvation are things that enhance life.
   No birth control measures are things that accelerate population growth.
   All things that enhance life are things that should be encouraged.
   All things that increase food availability are things that prevent starvation.
   Therefore, no birth control measures are things that should be discouraged.

   All non-I are non-R.
   All P are E.
   All B are R.
   No E are D.   (obvert)
   <u>All I are P.</u>
   No B are D.

   No E are D.⎤ No P are D.⎤
   All P are E.⎦   ⎦ No I are D.⎤
   All I are P. ⟶   ⎦   ⎦ No R are D.⎤
   All R are I. ——————⟶   ⎦   ⎦
   <u>All B are R.</u>————————————⟶   ⎦
   No B are D.

9. Some countries are countries that allow ivory trading.
   All countries that resist elephant killing are countries that discourage poachers.
   All countries that allow ivory trading are countries that encourage poachers.
   No countries that promote the extinction of elephants are countries that should escape the condemnation of the civilized world.
   All countries that support elephant killing are countries that promote the extinction of elephants.

91

Exercise 5.7

Therefore, some countries are countries that should be condemned by the civilized world.

Some C are I.
All non-K are non-E. (contrapose)
All I are E.
No P are non-S.   (obvert)
All K are P.
Some C are S.

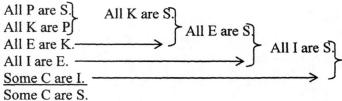

All P are S.⎤
All K are P.⎦
All E are K. ⟶ All K are S.⎤
All I are E. ⟶   ⎦ All E are S.⎤
Some C are I. ⟶   ⎦ All I are S.⎤
Some C are S.

10. All things that promote skin cancer are things that cause death.
    All things that preserve the ozone layer are things that prevent the release of CFCs.
    No things that resist skin cancer are things that increase UV radiation.
    All things that do not preserve the ozone layer are things that increase UV radiation.
    Some packaging materials are things that release CFCs.
    No things that cause death are things that should be legal.
    Therefore, some packaging materials are things that should not be legal.

All S are C.
All O are non-R.   (contrapose)
No non-S are U.   (convert, obvert)
All non-O are U.
Some M are R.
No C are L.
Some M are non-L.   (obvert)

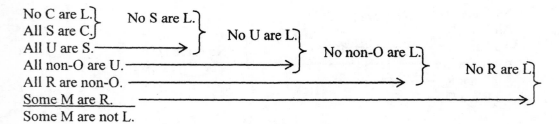

No C are L.⎤
All S are C.⎦
All U are S. ⟶ No S are L.⎤
All non-O are U. ⟶   ⎦ No U are L.⎤
All R are non-O. ⟶   ⎦ No non-O are L.⎤
Some M are R. ⟶   ⎦ No R are L.⎤
Some M are not L.

Part III

1. No ducks are waltzers.
   No officers are non-waltzers.
   All poultry of mine are ducks.
   Therefore, no poultry of mine are officers.

92

No D are W.
No O are non-W.   (obvert)
<u>All P are D.</u>
No P are O.

All O are W.   No D are O.⎤
No D are W.   ⎬
<u>All P are D.</u>────────→ ⎦
No P are O.

2. No experienced persons are incompetent persons.
   All persons identical to Jenkins are persons who are always blundering.
   No competent persons are persons who are always blundering.
   Therefore, all persons identical to Jenkins are inexperienced persons.

No E are non-C.   (obvert)
All J are B.
<u>No C are B.</u>
All J are non-E.   (obvert)

All E are C.⎤   No E are B.⎤
No C are B.⎦   ⎬
<u>All J are B.</u> ──────→ ⎦
No J are E.

3. No terriers are things that wander among the signs of the zodiac.
   No things that do not wander among the signs of the zodiac are comets.
   All things that have a curly tail are terriers.
   Therefore, no comets are things that have a curly tail.

No T are W.
No non-W are O.   (convert, obvert)
<u>All U are T.</u>
No O are U.

All U are T.⎤   No U are W.⎤
No T are W.⎦   ⎬
<u>All O are W.</u>──────→ ⎦
No O are U.

4. All hummingbirds are richly-colored birds.
   No large birds are birds that live on honey.
   All birds that do not live on honey are birds that are dull in color.
   Therefore, all hummingbirds are small birds.

All H are R.
No L are O.
All non-O are non-R. (contrapose)
All H are non-L.   (obvert)

No L are O.⌉
All R are O.⌡ No L are R.⌉
All H are R.————————→⌡
No H are L.

5. All non-ripe fruits are non-wholesome fruits.
   All apples identical to these are wholesome fruits.
   No fruits grown in the shade are ripe fruits.
   Therefore, all apples identical to these are apples not grown in the shade.

All non-R are non-W. (contrapose)
All A are W.
No S are R.
All A are non-S.   (obvert)

No S are R.⌉
All W are R.⌡ No W are S.⌉
All A are W.————————→⌡
No A are S.

6. All sons of mine are slim persons.
   No children of mine who do not exercise are healthy persons.
   All children of mine who are gluttons are fat persons.
   No daughters of mine are children of mine who exercise.
   Therefore, all children of mine who are gluttons are unhealthy persons.

All S are L.
No non-E are H.   (convert, obvert)
All G are non-L.   (obvert)
No non-S are E.   (convert, obvert)
All G are non-H.   (obvert)

All H are E.⌉
All E are S.⌡ All H are S.⌉
All S are L.————————→⌡ All H are L.⌉
No G are L.——————————————→⌡
No G are H.

7. All books in this library that I do not recommend are books that are unhealthy in tone.
   All the bound books are well-written books.
   All the romances are books that are healthy in tone.
   All the unbound books are books in this library that I do not recommend.
   Therefore, all the romances are well-written books.

94

All non-R are non-H. (contrapose)
All B are W.
All O are H.
<u>All non-B are non-R.</u> (contrapose)
All O are W.

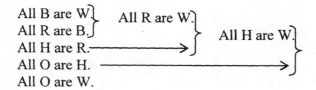

8. No interesting poems are unpopular poems among people of real taste.
   No modern poems are poems free from affection.
   All your poems are poems on the subject of soap bubbles.
   No affected poems are popular poems among people of real taste.
   No ancient poems are poems on the subject of soap bubbles.
   Therefore, all your poems are uninteresting poems.

   No I are non-P.   (obvert)
   No M are non-A.   (obvert)
   All Y are S.
   No A are P.
   <u>No non-M are S.</u>(convert, obvert)
   All Y are non-I.   (obvert)

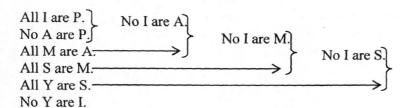

No Y are I.

9. All writers who understand human nature are clever persons.
   All true poets are persons who can stir the hearts of men.
   All persons identical to Shakespeare are persons who wrote Hamlet.
   No writers who do not understand human nature are persons who can stir the hearts of men.
   All persons who wrote Hamlet are true poets.
   Therefore, all persons identical to Shakespeare are clever persons.

   All U are C.
   All T are M.
   All S are H.
   No non-U are M.   (convert, obvert)
   <u>All H are T.</u>
   All S are C.

95

Exercise 6.1

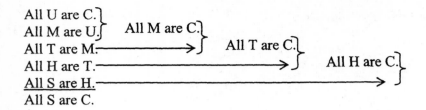

10. All animals that belong to me are animals I trust.
All dogs are animals that gnaw bones.
All animals I admit to my study are animals that beg when told to do so.
All the animals in the yard are animals that belong to me.
All animals I trust are animals I admit into my study.
All animals that are willing to beg when told to do so are dogs.
Therefore, all the animals in the yard are animals that gnaw bones.

All A are T.
All D are G.
All S are B.
All Y are A.
All T are S.
All B are D.
All Y are G.

All D are G.
All B are D.
All S are B.
All T are S.
All A are T.
All Y are A.
All Y are G.

All B are G.
All S are G.
All T are G.
All A are G.

Exercise 6.1
Part I

1. ~C

2. F • ~M

3. A ∨ L

4. F • U

5. N ⊃ S

6. S ⊃ N

7. M ≡ S

8. M ⊃ B

9. E ⊃ I

10. C ⊃ P

11. ~M ∨ A

12. A ⊃ (G • M)

96

13. P • (H ∨ S)

14. (P • H) ∨ S

15. ~(H • A)

16. ~H • ~A

17. M ∨ C

18. ~(M ∨ P)

19. ~(M ∨ P)

20. ~M ∨ ~P

21. C ⊃ (M ⊃ U)

22. (C ⊃ M) ⊃ U

23. D ≡ ~(C ∨ B)

24. I ⊃ (P ∨ B)

25. ~O ∨ (N ⊃ A)

26. (E ∨ D) ⊃ ~(B ∨ C)

27. (N • W) ⊃ (C ∨ M)

28. (~H • ~T) ⊃ (P ∨ S)

29. J • (B ∨ M)

30. (J • B) ∨ M

31. (Y • K) ∨ (~B • ~Z)

32. (M ⊃ J) • ~B

33. (A ∨ B) • ~(A • B)

34. ~M • [I ⊃ (D ∨ A)]

35. ~[B • (M ∨ H)]

36. ~[D ∨ (G • H)]

37. S ⊃ [D ⊃ (P • M)]

38. H ⊃ [S ⊃ (B ⊃ E)]

39. ~[(B • L) ∨ (E • K)]

40. ~[(M ∨ B) • (T ∨ K)]

41. M ⊃ C

42. C ⊃ M

43. M ≡ C

44. (O ⊃ W) ⊃ (S ⊃ J)

45. (N • A) ≡ (R ∨ C)

46. ~[(C ⊃ G) • (T ⊃ N)]

47. R ⊃ (P ⊃ D)

48. [Q ⊃ ~(N ∨ E)] ⊃ (V ⊃ A)

49. [G • A) ≡ O] ⊃ ~(N ∨ S)

50. (J ⊃ F) • [(W • D) ⊃ N]

Part II

1. R ∨ F

2. P ⊃ S

3. H • E

4. ~(H ∨ S)

5. ~(O • Y)

6. H ⊃ (P ∨ Q)

Exercise 6.2

7. S ⊃ G

8. C ⊃ (U • A)

9. O ⊃ I

10. A ⊃ (~N ⊃ M)

11. I ⊃ (M • N)

12. ~H ∨ (P ∨ L)

13. (C • K) ≡ P

14. (M ∨ C) ⊃ P

15. (C • O) ∨ (S • B)

16. [(T • L) ⊃ H] • (H ⊃ I)

17. E • [M ≡ (A • ~V)]

18. (E ⊃ H) • [H ⊃ (~D • P)]

19. (B ⊃ M) • [(M • I) ⊃ (C • P)]

20. [C ⊃ (T • B)] • [B ⊃ (~A • ~L)]

Part III

1. WFF
2. Not WFF
3. Not WFF
4. WFF
5. Not WFF

6. WFF
7. Not WFF
8. Not WFF
9. WFF
10. Not WFF

Exercise 6.2
Part I

1. Dot
2. Horseshoe
3. Tilde
4. Triple bar
5. Wedge

6. Tilde
7. Horseshoe
8. Triple bar
9. Dot
10. Wedge

Part II

1. ~H	False	7. W ⊃ E	True
2. N • L	True	8. L ≡ C	False
3. C ∨ L	True	9. ~(A ∨ W)	True
4. H • ~N	False	10. H ⊃ (C ∨ E)	True
5. E ∨ C	True	11. (L • E) ∨ (N • ~E)	True
6. N ⊃ A	False	12. (L ⊃ A) ≡ (C ⊃ W)	True

13. (~E • ~C) ⊃ (H • L)   True   15. C • [L ⊃ (W ∨ A)]   False

14. ~C ∨ (N • E)   False

Part III

1.	False	14.	True
2.	True	15.	False
3.	True	16.	True
4.	False	17.	True
5.	True	18.	True
6.	True	19.	True
7.	False	20.	False
8.	False	21.	False
9.	True	22.	True
10.	False	23.	True
11.	True	24.	False
12.	False	25.	True
13.	True		

Part IV

1.	True	9.	False
2.	Undetermined	10.	True
3.	False	11.	False
4.	Undetermined	12.	True
5.	True	13.	False
6.	True	14.	True
7.	Undetermined	15.	False
8.	False		

Exercise 6.3
Part I

1.	Tautologous	9.	Contingent
2.	Contingent	10.	Self-contradictory
3.	Self-contradictory	11.	Self-contradictory
4.	Contingent	12.	Tautologous
5.	Self-contradictory	13.	Self-contradictory
6.	Tautologous	14.	Tautologous
7.	Tautologous	15.	Contingent
8.	Contingent		

Exercise 6.4

Part II

1. Logically equivalent
2. Inconsistent
3. Consistent
4. Contradictory
5. Logically equivalent
6. Contradictory
7. Consistent
8. Inconsistent

9. Logically equivalent
10. Inconsistent
11. Contradictory
12. Consistent
13. Logically equivalent
14. Inconsistent
15. Contradictory

Part III

1. Carlson's prediction is false (self-contradictory).

2. Music is not dropped from the curriculum, and the students will become cultural philistines.

3. Thomas is not correct; the two statements are not logically equivalent.

4. It is possible that both astronomers are correct. If they are, a supernova will not occur within 10 light years of the earth.

5. Martinez's statement is tautologous; therefore, she has told us nothing about taxes, educational costs, or welfare.

6. It is possible that Goodbody is correct in his assessment. If so, Isuzu is not the lowest priced. We cannot conclude anything about Mitsubishi or Toyota.

7. It is possible that both stock brokers are correct. If they are, then Datapro will cut back its work force. We cannot conclude anything about Netmark and Compucel.

8. Eric's beliefs are inconsistent; therefore, they do not make sense.

9. It is possible that all three witnesses told the truth. If so, Lefty did not enter the bank, Howard pulled a gun, and Conrad collected the money.

10. It is possible that Nicole's philosophy makes sense. If it does, then the mind is not identical to the brain, personal freedom exists, and humans are responsible for their actions.

Exercise 6.4
Part I

1. $\underline{N \supset S}$
   $\sim N \supset \sim S$ (Invalid)

2. $\underline{B}$
   $B \lor A$ (Valid)

3. F ⊃ G
    G ⊃ W
    F ⊃ W   (Valid)

7. P ∨ S
    P___
    ~S   (Invalid)

4. D ⊃ W
    D___
    W   (Valid)

8. M ⊃ C
    ~C • M
    S   (Valid)

5. R ⊃ ~C
    W ⊃ ~C
    R ⊃ W   (Invalid)

9. ~A ∨ ~M
    ~(A ∨ M)   (Invalid)

10. (R ⊃ Q) • (~R ⊃ P)
    R ∨ ~R_____
    Q ∨ P   (Valid)

6. D_____
    P ⊃ (R ⊃ P)   (Valid)

Part II

1.	Valid	11.	Invalid
2.	Invalid	12.	Valid
3.	Valid	13.	Valid
4.	Valid	14.	Valid
5.	Invalid	15.	Invalid
6.	Valid	16.	Invalid
7.	Invalid	17.	Valid
8.	Invalid	18.	Invalid
9.	Valid	19.	Valid
10.	Invalid	20.	Invalid

Exercise 6.5
Part I

		8.	Invalid
1.	Valid	9.	Valid
2.	Invalid	10.	Invalid
3.	Valid	11.	Valid
4.	Invalid	12.	Valid
5.	Valid	13.	Valid
6.	Invalid	14.	Invalid
7.	Valid	15.	Invalid

Part II

1.	Inconsistent	6.	Inconsistent
2.	Consistent	7.	Inconsistent
3.	Inconsistent	8.	Consistent
4.	Consistent	9.	Inconsistent
5.	Consistent	10.	Consistent

Exercise 6.6
Part I

The exercises marked with an asterisk must be rewritten. See below.

1.	MT–valid	11.	Invalid
2.	HS–valid	12.	MP–valid
3.	Invalid	13.	DS–valid*
4.	CD–valid	14.	Invalid
5.	MP–valid	15.	DD–valid*
6.	DS–valid	16.	AC–invalid
7.	DD–valid*	17.	MT–valid*
8.	AC–invalid	18.	CD–valid*
9.	HS–valid	19.	Invalid
10.	DA–invalid	20.	DA–invalid*

7. (E ⊃ N) • (~L ⊃ ~K)
    ~N ∨ ~~K
    ‾‾‾‾‾‾‾‾‾‾‾‾‾‾‾‾‾‾
    ~E ∨ ~~L

17. K ⊃ ~C
    ~~C
    ‾‾‾‾‾‾‾
    ~K

13. ~S ∨ P
    ~~S
    ‾‾‾‾‾
    P

18. (I ⊃ M) • (~O ⊃ A)
    I ∨ ~O
    ‾‾‾‾‾‾‾‾‾‾‾‾‾‾‾‾‾
    M ∨ A

15. ~Q ∨ ~R
    (G ⊃ Q) • (H ⊃ R)
    ‾‾‾‾‾‾‾‾‾‾‾‾‾‾‾‾‾
    ~G ∨ ~H

20. ~L ⊃ U
    ~~L
    ‾‾‾‾‾
    ~U

Part II

1. F ⊃ T
    ~T
    ‾‾‾‾
    ~F   MT–valid

5. T ∨ ~D
    T
    ‾‾‾‾
    D   Invalid

2. M ⊃ F
    F
    ‾‾‾‾
    M   AC–valid

6. S ⊃ E
    E ⊃ G
    ‾‾‾‾‾
    S ⊃ G   HS–valid

3. (E ⊃ ~M) • (~E ⊃ ~T)
    E ∨ ~E
    ‾‾‾‾‾‾‾‾‾‾‾‾‾‾‾‾
    ~M ∨ ~T   CD–valid

7. T
    T ⊃ ~H
    ‾‾‾‾‾‾
    ~H   MP–valid

4. W ∨ ~M
    ~W
    ‾‾‾‾
    ~M   DS–valid

8. G ⊃ E
    ~G
    ‾‾‾‾
    ~E   DA–invalid

9. $(S \supset D) \cdot (I \supset \sim D)$
   $\underline{D \lor \sim D}$
   $\sim S \lor \sim I$
   Rewritten:
   $(S \supset D) \cdot (I \supset \sim D)$
   $\underline{\sim D \lor \sim\sim D}$
   $\sim S \lor \sim I$ DD–valid

10. $(L \supset \sim A) \cdot (C \supset F)$
    $\underline{\sim L \cdot \sim C}$
    $A \cdot \sim F$ Invalid.

11. $P \supset W$
    $\underline{\sim P}$
    $\sim W$ DA–invalid

12. $L \supset \sim C$
    $\underline{C}$
    $\sim L$
    Rewritten:
    $L \supset \sim C$
    $\underline{\sim\sim C}$
    $\sim L$ MT–valid

13. $(P \supset T) \cdot (A \supset \sim T)$
    $\underline{T \lor \sim T}$
    $\sim P \lor \sim A$
    Rewritten:
    $(P \supset T) \cdot (A \supset \sim T)$
    $\underline{\sim T \lor \sim\sim T}$
    $\sim P \lor \sim A$ DD–valid

14. $I \lor A$
    $\underline{I}$
    $\sim A$ Invalid

15. I
    $\underline{I \supset M}$
    M MP–valid

16. $\sim M \supset U$
    $\underline{U}$
    $\sim M$ AC–invalid

17. $\sim C \lor \sim A$
    $\underline{A}$
    $\sim C$
    Rewritten:
    $\sim A \lor \sim C$
    $\underline{\sim\sim A}$
    $\sim C$ DS–valid

18. $C \supset H$
    $\underline{\sim H \supset N}$
    $\sim C \supset N$ Invalid

19. $S \supset C$
    $\underline{I \supset S}$
    $I \supset C$ HS–valid

20. $(T \supset G) \cdot (\sim T \supset P)$
    $\underline{T \lor \sim T}$
    $G \lor P$ CD–valid

Part III

1. $(S \supset M) \cdot (\sim S \supset F)$
   $\underline{S \lor \sim S}$
   $M \lor F$ (CD)

Since the second premise is a tautology, it is impossible to escape between the horns. The two available strategies are therefore grasping by the horns and constructing a counterdilemma. If Melinda adequately prepares for the test before the party, then she does not spend the party night studying and she does not fail the test. This would falsify the right-hand conjunct of the first premise, thus falsifying the entire premise. Here is a counterdilemma:

If Melinda spends the night studying, she will pass the test tomorrow; and, if she does not spend the night studying, she will go to the party. She will either spend the night studying or not studying. Therefore, she will either pass the test or go to the party.

2. $(V \supset F) \cdot (H \supset L)$
   $\underline{V \vee H}$
   $F \vee L$ (CD)

Here it is easy to escape between the horns. If we build our home half way up the hillside, then it will neither be in the valley or on the hilltop, thus falsifying the disjunctive premise. It is also easy to grasp the dilemma by the horns: Build on the hilltop, but install a lightning rod. Here is a counterdilemma:

If we build our home in the valley, then it will not be hit by lightning; and, if we build it on the hilltop, then it will not be struck by floods. We must either build in the valley or on the hilltop. Therefore, either our home will not be hit by lightning or not be struck by floods.

3. $(C \supset {\sim}R) \cdot (W \supset R)$ Rewritten: $(C \supset {\sim}R) \cdot (W \supset R)$
   $\underline{R \vee {\sim}R}$ $\underline{{\sim}{\sim}R \vee {\sim}R}$
   ${\sim}C \vee {\sim}W$ ${\sim}C \vee {\sim}W$ (DD)

The disjunctive premise is a tautology, so it is impossible to escape between the horns. Grasping the dilemma by the horns is by no means easy, as numerous legislators and legal scholars have come to realize. Perhaps the psychotherapist could institute transactional therapy with the whole family, thus keeping tabs on the condition of the children and also preserving the confidentiality of the child-abusing primary client. Here is a counterdilemma:

If psychotherapists report child-abusing clients to the authorities, then they will maintain the welfare of children; but if they do not report them, then they will preserve their client's right to confidentiality. Psychotherapists must either report or not report. Therefore, either they will maintain the welfare of children or preserve their client's right to confidentiality.

4. $(C \supset {\sim}S) \cdot (E \supset S)$ Rewritten: $(C \supset {\sim}S) \cdot (E \supset S)$
   $\underline{S \vee {\sim}S}$ $\underline{{\sim}{\sim}S \vee {\sim}S}$
   ${\sim}C \vee {\sim}E$ ${\sim}C \vee {\sim}E$ (DD)

The second premise is a tautology, so it is impossible to escape between the horns. One could grasp the dilemma by the horns by arguing that corporations could share the cost of neutralizing toxic waste, thus preserving the competitive edge. Here is a constructive counterdilemma:

If corporations spend money to neutralize their toxic waste, then the environment will be preserved; but if corporations do not spend money to neutralize their toxic waste, then they will remain competitive. Corporations will do one or the other. Therefore, either the environment will be preserved or corporations will remain competitive.

5. $(P \supset M) \cdot (\sim P \supset S)$
    $\underline{P \vee \sim P}$
    $M \vee S$ (CD)

It is impossible to escape between the horns. One could grasp the dilemma by the horns by arguing that physicians should avail the terminally ill patient of the opportunity to pull the plug on himself. If the patient is in a coma, a living will could avoid the dilemma.

6. $(D \supset S) \cdot (M \supset T)$
    $\underline{D \vee M}$
    $S \vee T$ (CD)

If legal separation is considered to be an alternative to either getting a divorce or staying married, one can escape between the horns by posing that third alternative. If the disjunctive premise is considered to be tautologous, one might grasp the dilemma by the horns by attacking the right-hand horn: The Mitchells might stay married and arrange separate accommodations in the same dwelling. A counterdilemma:

If the Mitchells get a divorce, they will be happy; but if they stay married, they will have enough money to live. The Mitchells must either get a divorce or stay married. Therefore, either they will be happy or they will have enough money to live.

7. $(C \supset L) \cdot (J \supset B)$
    $\underline{\sim L \vee \sim B}$
    $\sim C \vee \sim J$ (DD)

Here the second premise is not a tautology, so it is possible to escape between the horns. Perhaps students could take a double major in liberal arts and business. One could also grasp the dilemma by the horns by arguing that students could major in a liberal arts field where a job would be available upon graduation. Here is a constructive counterdilemma:

If students major in liberal arts, then they will take courses that are interesting and rewarding; but if they major in business, then they will have a job when they graduate. Students will either major in liberal arts or business. Therefore, either they will take courses that are interesting and rewarding or they will have a job when they graduate.

8. $(A \supset F) \cdot (\sim A \supset L)$
   $\underline{A \vee \sim A}$
   $F \vee L$ (CD)

Since the second premise is a tautology, one cannot escape between the horns. One could grasp the dilemma by the horns by attacking the left hand horn: If the merchant can prove that detaining a suspected shop-lifter is reasonable under the circumstances, and if the merchant confines the search to the shopper's parcels, the merchant can accomplish his/her purpose and avoid charges of false arrest. A counterdilemma:

If merchants arrest suspected shop-lifters, they will avoid loss of merchandise; if they don't arrest them, they will avoid charges of false imprisonment. Merchants must either arrest or not arrest suspected shoplifters. Therefore, they will either avoid loss of merchandise or avoid charges of false imprisonment.

9. $(A \supset \sim R) \cdot (E \supset R)$ Rewritten: $(A \supset \sim R) \cdot (E \supset R)$
   $\underline{R \vee \sim R}$ $\underline{\sim\sim R \vee \sim R}$
   $\sim A \vee \sim E$ $\sim A \vee \sim E$ (DD)

It is impossible to escape between the horns. The left-hand horn could be attacked by arguing that women should study marshal arts and thereby overcome or avoid their assailant without risking serious bodily injury. A counterdilemma:

If women threatened with rape do not resist, then they will avoid being maimed or killed; but if they resist, then they will assist successful prosecution of the assailant. Since they must either resist or not resist, they will either avoid being maimed or killed or they will assist successful prosecution of the assailant.

10. $(P \supset R) \cdot (T \supset E)$
    $\underline{P \vee T}$
    $R \vee E$ (CD)

The second premise is not a tautology, so it is at least possible to escape between the horns. If we instructed counter-terrorist squads to execute terrorists on the spot, we would neither prosecute them nor release them. Here is a counter dilemma:

If we prosecute suspected terrorists, then we discourage terrorism; but if we release them, then we avoid the risk of retaliation by other terrorists. We must either prosecute or release suspected terrorists. Therefore, either we will discourage terrorism or we will avoid the risk of retaliation by other terrorists.

Part IV

1. If Oral Roberts actually receives messages from God, then he did not send the letter. Oral Roberts did send the letter. Therefore, Oral Roberts does not actually receive messages from God. (MT)

2. If we remain on standard time, then the grass will get one hour less sunlight. If the grass gets one hour less sunlight, then it will stay greener. Therefore, if we remain on standard time, then the grass will stay greener. (HS)

3. If the religious right is consistent in its opposition to killing, then it seeks to abolish the death penalty. The religious right does not seek to abolish the death penalty. Therefore, the religious right is not consistent in its opposition to killing. (MT)

   If the religious right gets its way, then there will be a constitutional amendment banning abortion. If there is a constitutional amendment banning abortion, then those caught performing an abortion will receive the death penalty. Therefore, if the religious right gets its way, then those caught performing an abortion will receive the death penalty. (HS)

4. If group problem solving is important, then we should not place emphasis on individual testing. Group problem solving is important. Therefore, we should not place emphasis on individual testing. (MP)

   If we should not place emphasis on individual testing, then the national math test is a mistake. We should not place emphasis on individual testing. Therefore, the national math test is a mistake. (MP)

5. If voluntary school prayer makes our children more moral, then mandatory church attendance on Sunday will do wonders for the rest of us. Mandatory church attendance on Sunday will not do wonders for the rest of us. Therefore, voluntary school prayer does not make our children more moral. (MT)

6. If America replaces the diseased hearts of old white men but refuses to feed school children, pay women adequately, or educate adolescents, then America is doomed. America does replace the diseased hearts of old white men but refuses to feed school children, pay women adequately, or educate adolescents. Therefore, America is doomed. (MP)

7. If we close the library at Central Juvenile Hall, then delinquents will be deprived of an opportunity to read. If delinquents are deprived of an opportunity to read, then they will not have access to ideas, dreams, and alternative ways of living. Therefore, if we close the library at Central Juvenile Hall, then delinquents will not have access to ideas, dreams, and alternative ways of living. (HS)

Exercise 7.1

If we close the library at Central Juvenile Hall, then delinquents will not have access to ideas, dreams, and alternative ways of living. Delinquents must have access to ideas, dreams, and alternative ways of living. Therefore, we must not close the library at Central Juvenile Hall. (MT)

8. If the death penalty deters at least one person form becoming a murderer, then it is justified. The death penalty does deter at least one person from becoming a murderer. Therefore, the death penalty is justified. (MP)

If the families and friends of innocent victims have the right to see effective retribution, then the death penalty is justified. The families and friends of innocent victims do have the right to see effective retribution. Therefore, the death penalty is justified. (MP)

If terminating the life of a killer is more economical than keeping him in jail at the taxpayer's expense, then the death penalty is justified. Terminating the life of a killer is more economical than keeping him in jail at the taxpayer's expense. Therefore, the death penalty is justified. (MP)

If everyone will have greater respect for the judicial system if the death penalty is imposed, then the death penalty is justified. Everyone will have greater respect for the judicial system if the death penalty is imposed. Therefore, the death penalty is justified. (MP)

9. If parents should be allowed to veto their minor daughter's abortion, then they should also be given the right to mandate it. Parents should not be given the right to mandate their minor daughter's abortion. Therefore, parents should not be allowed to veto their minor daughter's abortion. (MT)

10. If viewing adult video cassettes leads to violent sex crimes, then there are over a million violent sex crimes per week. It is not the case that there are over a million violent sex crimes per week. Therefore, viewing adult video cassettes does not lead to violent sex crimes. (MT)

Exercise 7.1
Part I

1.	~G	1, 2, MT		6.	~S	2, 3, MT
2.	M	1, 2, MP		7.	F ⊃ D	1, 3, HS
3.	E ⊃ D	1, 2, HS		8.	N	2, 3, DS
4.	C	1, 2, DS		9.	~N	2, 4, MT
5.	K	1, 3, MP		10.	G ⊃ A	1, 4, HS

11. A   2, 4, MP   16. ~P   1, 2, MP

12. S   2,3, DS   17. A ⊃ C   1, 4, DS

13. ~~C   1, 3, MT   18. (R ⊃ M) ⊃ (M ∨ E)   1, 3, HS

14. N   2, 4, DS   19. ~(S ∨ C)   1, 3, MT

15. C ⊃ ~T   1, 3, HS   20. A ∨ N   2, 4, MP

Part II

1. ~B   1, 2, DS   11. F ⊃ G   2, 4, HS

2. N   1, 2, MP   12. ~M   2, 4, DS

3. ~T   1, 2, MT   13. ~~S   3, 4, MT

4. R ⊃ C   1, 2, HS   14. ~F ⊃ ~J   2, 4, HS

5. ~N   1, 3, MT   15. ~~S   1, 4, DS

6. W ⊃ T   2, 3, HS   16. ~Z   3, 4, MP

7. Q   2, 3, MP   17. H ⊃ (E • R)   3, 4, HS

8. ~C   1, 3, DS   18. ~(M • G)   2, 4, MT

9. S   3, 4, MP   19. H ∨ G   2, 4, MP

10. ~A   1, 4, MT   20. ~(H • A)   1, 4, DS

Part III

(1) 1. ~C ⊃ (A ⊃ C)
     2. ~C   / ~A
     3. A ⊃ C   1, 2, MP
     4. ~A   2, 3, MT

(2) 1. F ∨ (D ⊃ T)
     2. ~F
     3. D   / T
     4. D ⊃ T   1, 2, DS
     5. T   3, 4, MP

Exercise 7.1

(3) 1. (K • B) ∨ (L ⊃ E)
     2 ~(K • B)
     3 ~E   / ~L
     4. L ⊃ E   1, 2, DS
     5. ~L   3, 4, MT

(4) 1. P ⊃ (G ⊃ T)
     2. Q ⊃ (T ⊃ E)
     3. P
     4. Q   / G ⊃ E
     5. G ⊃ T   1, 3, MP
     6. T ⊃ E   2, 4, MP
     7. G ⊃ E   5, 6, HS

(5) 1. ~W ⊃ [~W ⊃ (X ⊃ W)]
     2. ~W   / ~X
     3. ~W ⊃ (X ⊃ W)   1, 2, MP
     4. X ⊃ W   2, 3, MP
     5. ~X   2, 4, MT

(6) 1. J ⊃ (K ⊃ L)
     2. L ∨ J
     3. ~L   / ~K
     4. J   2, 3, DS
     5. K ⊃ L   1, 4, MP
     6. ~K   3, 5, MT

(7) 1. ~S ⊃ D
     2. ~S ∨ (~D ⊃ K)
     3. ~D   / K
     4. ~~S   1, 3, MT
     5. ~D ⊃ K   2, 4, DS
     6. K   3, 5, MP

(8) 1. A ⊃ (E ⊃ ~F)
     2. H ∨ (~F ⊃ M)
     3. A
     4. ~H   / E ⊃ M
     5. E ⊃ ~F   1, 3, MP
     6. ~F ⊃ M   2, 4, DS
     7. E ⊃ M   5, 6, HS

(9) 1. ~G ⊃ (G ∨ ~A)
     2. ~A ⊃ (C ⊃ A)
     3. ~G   /~C
     4. G ∨ ~A   1, 3, MP
     5. ~A   3, 4, DS
     6. C ⊃ A   2, 5, MP
     7. ~C   5, 6, MT

(10) 1. N ⊃ (J ⊃ P)
     2. (J ⊃ P) ⊃ (N ⊃ J)
     3. N   / P
     4. J ⊃ P   1, 3, MP
     5. N ⊃ J   2, 4, MP
     6. N ⊃ P   4, 5, HS
     7. P   3, 6, MP

(11) 1. G ⊃ [~O ⊃ (G ⊃ D)]
     2. O ∨ G
     3. ~O   / D
     4. G   2, 3, DS
     5. ~O ⊃ (G ⊃ D)   1, 4, MP
     6. G ⊃ D   3, 5, MP
     7. D   4, 6, MP

(12) 1. ~M ∨ (B ∨ ~T)
     2. B ⊃ W
     3. ~~M
     4. ~W   /~T
     5. B ∨ ~T   1, 3, DS
     6. ~B   2, 4, MT
     7. ~T   5, 6, DS

(13) 1. R ⊃ (G ∨ ~A)
     2. (G ∨ ~A) ⊃ ~S
     3. G ⊃ S
     4. R   /~A
     5. G ∨ ~A   1, 4, MP
     6. ~S   2, 5, MP
     7. ~G   3, 6, MT
     8. ~A   5, 7, DS

(14) 1. (L ≡ N) ⊃ C
     2. (L ≡ N) ∨ (P ⊃ ~E)
     3. ~E ⊃ C
     4. ~C   /~P

     5. ~(L ≡ N)   1, 4, MT
     6. P ⊃ ~E   2, 5, DS
     7. ~~E   3, 4, MT
     8. ~P   6, 7, MT

(15) 1. ~J ⊃ [~A ⊃ (D ⊃ A)]
     2. J ∨ ~A
     3. ~J   / ~D
     4. ~A ⊃ (D ⊃ A)   1, 3, MP
     5. ~A   2, 3, DS
     6. D ⊃ A   4, 5, MP
     7. ~D   5, 6, MT

(16) 1. (B ⊃ ~M) ⊃ (T ⊃ ~S)
     2. B ⊃ K
     3. K ⊃ ~M
     4. ~S ⊃ N   / T ⊃ N
     5. B ⊃ ~M   2, 3, HS
     6. T ⊃ ~S   1, 5, MP
     7. T ⊃ N   4, 6, HS

(17) 1. H ∨ (Q ∨ F)
     2. R ∨ (Q ⊃ R)
     3. R ∨ ~H
     4. ~R   / F
     5. ~H   3, 4, DS
     6. Q ∨ F   1, 5, DS
     7. Q ⊃ R   2, 4, DS
     8. ~Q   4, 7, MT
     9. F   6, 8, DS

(18) 1. ~A ⊃ (B ⊃ ~C)
     2. ~D ⊃ (~C ⊃ A)
     3. D ∨ ~A
     4. ~D   / ~B
     5. ~A   3, 4, DS
     6. B ⊃ ~C   1, 5, MP
     7. ~C ⊃ A   2, 4, MP
     8. B ⊃ A   6, 7, HS
     9. ~B   5, 8, MT

(19) 1. ~G ⊃ [G ∨ (S ⊃ G)]
     2. (S ∨ L) ⊃ ~G
     3. S ∨ L   / L
     4. ~G   2, 3, MP

5. G ∨ (S ⊃ G)   1, 4, MP
6. S ⊃ G   4, 5, DS
7. ~S   4, 6, MT
8. L   3, 7, DS

(20) 1. H ⊃ [~E ⊃ (C ⊃ ~D)]
    2. ~D ⊃ E
    3. E ∨ H
    4. ~E   / ~C
    5. H   3, 4, DS
    6. ~E ⊃ (C ⊃ ~D)   1, 5, MP
    7. C ⊃ ~D   4, 6, MP
    8. C ⊃ E   2, 7, HS
    9. ~C   4, 8, MT

(21) 1. ~B ⊃ [(A ⊃ K) ⊃ (B ∨ ~K)]
    2. ~J ⊃ K
    3. A ⊃ ~J
    4. ~B   / ~A
    5. (A ⊃ K) ⊃ (B ∨ ~K)   1, 4, MP
    6. A ⊃ K   2, 3, HS
    7. B ∨ ~K   5, 6, MP
    8. ~K   4, 7, DS
    9. ~A   6, 8, MT

(22) 1. (C ⊃ M) ⊃ (N ⊃ P)
    2. (C ⊃ N) ⊃ (N ⊃ M)
    3. (C ⊃ P) ⊃ ~M
    4. C ⊃ N   / ~C
    5. N ⊃ M   2, 4, MP
    6. C ⊃ M   4, 5, HS
    7. N ⊃ P   1, 6, MP
    8. C ⊃ P   4, 7, HS
    9. ~M   3, 8, MP
   10. ~C   6, 9, MT

(23) 1. (R ⊃ F) ⊃ [(R ⊃ ~G) ⊃ (S ⊃ Q)]
    2. (Q ⊃ F) ⊃ (R ⊃ Q)
    3. ~G ⊃ F
    4. Q ⊃ ~G   / S ⊃ F
    5. Q ⊃ F   3, 4, HS
    6. R ⊃ Q   2, 5, MP
    7. R ⊃ F   5, 6, HS
    8. (R ⊃ ~G) ⊃ (S ⊃ Q)   1, 7, MP
    9. R ⊃ ~G   4, 6, HS

     10. S ⊃ Q   8, 9, MP
     11. S ⊃ F   5, 10, HS

(24) 1. ~A ⊃ [A ∨ (T ⊃ R)]
     2. ~R ⊃ [R ∨ (A ⊃ R)]
     3. (T ∨ D) ⊃ ~R
     4. T ∨ D   / D
     5. ~R   3, 4, MP
     6. R ∨ (A ⊃ R)   2, 5, MP
     7. A ⊃ R   5, 6, DS
     8. ~A   5, 7, MT
     9. A ∨ (T ⊃ R)   1, 8, MP
    10. T ⊃ R   8, 9, DS
    11. ~T   5, 10, MT
    12. D   4, 11, DS

(25) 1. ~N ⊃ [(B ⊃ D) ⊃ (N ∨ ~E)]
     2. (B ⊃ E) ⊃ ~N
     3. B ⊃ D
     4. D ⊃ E   / ~D
     5. B ⊃ E   3, 4, HS
     6. ~N   2, 5, MP
     7. (B ⊃ D) ⊃ (N ∨ ~E)   1, 6, MP
     8. N ∨ ~E   3, 7, MP
     9. ~E   6, 8, DS
    10. ~D   4, 9, MT

Part IV

(1) 1. W ⊃ (P ∨ C)
    2. ~P
    3. W   / C
    4. P ∨ C   1, 3, MP
    5. C   2, 4, DS

(2) 1. E ⊃ O
    2. R ∨ ~O
    3. ~R   / ~E
    4. ~O   2, 3, DS
    5. ~E   1, 4, MT

(3) 1. (Q ⊃ ~J) ⊃ (M ⊃ ~D)
    2. Q ⊃ M
    3. M ⊃ ~J   / Q ⊃ ~D

4. Q ⊃ ~J   2, 3, HS
5. M ⊃ ~D   1, 4, MP
6. Q ⊃ ~D   2, 5, HS

(4)   1. (R ⊃ L) ⊃ (L ⊃ ~F)
      2. ~F ∨ (R ⊃ L)
      3. ~~F   / ~R
      4. R ⊃ L   2, 3, DS
      5. L ⊃ ~F   1, 4, MP
      6. ~L   3, 5, MT
      7. ~R   4, 6, MT

(5)   1. C ∨ (H ⊃ R)
      2. S ∨ (R ⊃ E)
      3. ~C
      4. ~S   / H ⊃ E
      5. H ⊃ R   1, 3, DS
      6. R ⊃ E   2, 4, DS
      7. H ⊃ E   5, 6, HS

(6)   1. ~D ∨ (L ⊃ ~F)
      2. ~D ⊃ ~F
      3. ~~F   / ~L
      4. ~~D   2, 3, MT
      5. L ⊃ ~F   1, 4, DS
      6. ~L   2, 5, MT

(7)   1. H ⊃ (D ≡ A)
      2. V ∨ (R ⊃ V)
      3. R ∨ H
      4. ~V   / D ≡ A
      5. R ⊃ V   2, 4, DS
      6. ~R   4, 5, MT
      7. H   3, 6, DS
      8. D ≡ A   1, 7, MP

(8)   1. R ∨ B
      2. (I ⊃ H) ⊃ ~R
      3. L ⊃ (I ⊃ T)
      4. T ⊃ H
      5. L   / B
      6. I ⊃ T   3, 5, MP
      7. I ⊃ H   4, 6, HS
      8. ~R   2, 7, MP
      9. B   1, 8, DS

Exercise 7.2

(9) 1. $(D \supset C) \supset (N \lor W)$
     2. $D \supset S$
     3. $S \supset C$
     4. $\sim N$ / W
     5. $D \supset C$ 2, 3, HS
     6. $N \lor W$ 1, 5, MP
     7. W   4, 6, DS

(10) 1. $\sim C \supset [C \lor (J \supset D)]$
     2. $C \supset (C \cdot U)$
     3. $\sim(C \cdot U)$
     4. $\sim D$ / $\sim J$
     5. $\sim C$ 2, 3, MT
     6. $C \lor (J \supset D)$ 1, 5, MP
     7. $J \supset D$ 5, 6, DS
     8. $\sim J$ 4, 7, MT

Exercise 7.2
Part I

1.	B	2	6.	$A \lor \sim N$	1, 3
2.	$T \lor Q$	1, 3	7.	$Q \lor K$	1
3.	$D \cdot W$	1, 2	8.	$(E \cdot G) \lor T$	1
4.	$H \lor F$	1	9.	$\sim B \cdot (F \lor N)$	1, 2
5.	R	1	10.	$\sim L \lor M$	1, 2

Part II

1.	G	2, Simp 3, Add	6.	$N \lor F$	1, Add 3, 4, CD
2.	E	1, 2, DS 1, 3, Conj	7.	$\sim F$	2, 3, MT 1, 4, Conj
3.	$(B \supset N) \cdot (K \supset R)$	1, 3, Conj 2, 4, CD	8.	$E \supset B$	1, Simp 3, 4, HS
4.	$T \lor U$	1, Add 3, 4, MP	9.	$H \cdot R$	2, 3, MP Simp
5.	$S \cdot P$	2, 3, DS 4, Simp	10.	$M \cdot E$	1, 3, Conj 2, 4, MP

Part III

(1) 1. ~M ⊃ Q
     2. R ⊃ ~T
     3. ~M ∨ R   / Q ∨ ~T
     4. (~M ⊃ Q) • (R ⊃ ~T)   1, 2, Conj
     5. Q ∨ ~T   3, 4, CD

(2) 1. N ⊃ (D • W)
     2. D ⊃ K
     3. N   / N • K
     4. D • W   1, 3, MP
     5. D   4, Simp
     6. K   2, 5, MP
     7. N • K   3, 6, Conj

(3) 1. E ⊃ (A • C)
     2. A ⊃ (F • E)
     3. E   / F
     4. A • C   1, 3, MP
     5. A   4, Simp
     6. F • E   2, 5, MP
     7. F   6, Simp

(4) 1. (H ∨ ~B) ⊃ R
     2. (H ∨ ~M) ⊃ P
     3. H   / R • P
     4. H ∨ ~B   3, Add
     5. R   1, 4, MP
     6. H ∨ ~M   3, Add
     7. P   2, 6, MP
     8. R • P   5, 7, Conj

(5) 1. G ⊃ (S • T)
     2. (S ∨ T) ⊃ J
     3. G   / J
     4. S • T   1, 3, MP
     5. S   4, Simp
     6. S ∨ T   5, Add
     7. J   2, 6, MP

(6) 1. (L ∨ T) ⊃ (B • G)
     2. L • (K ≡ R)   / L • B
     3. L   2, Simp
     4. L ∨ T   3, Add
     5. B • G   1, 4, MP
     6. B   5, Simp

7. L • B   3, 6, Conj

(7) 1. (~F ∨ X) ⊃ (P ∨ T)
    2. F ⊃ P
    3. ~P   / T
    4. ~F   2, 3, MT
    5. ~F ∨ X   4, Add
    6. P ∨ T   1, 5, MP
    7. T   3, 6, DS

(8) 1. (N ⊃ B) • (O ⊃ C)
    2. Q ⊃ (N ∨ O)
    3. Q   / B ∨ C
    4. N ∨ O   2, 3, MP
    5. B ∨ C   1, 4, CD

(9) 1. (U ∨ W) ⊃ (T ⊃ R)
    2. U • H
    3. ~R • ~J   / U • ~T
    4. U   2, Simp
    5. U ∨ W   4, Add
    6. T ⊃ R   1, 5, MP
    7. ~R   3, Simp
    8. ~T   6, 7, MT
    9. U • ~T   4, 8, Conj

(10) 1. (D ∨ E) ⊃ (G • H)
    2. G ⊃ ~D
    3. D • F   / M
    4. D   3, Simp
    5. D ∨ E   4, Add
    6. G • H   1, 5, MP
    7. G   6, Simp
    8. ~D   2, 7, MP
    9. D ∨ M   4, Add
  10. M   8, 9, DS

(11) 1. (B ∨ F) ⊃ (A ⊃ G)
    2. (B ∨ F) ⊃ (G ⊃ K)
    3. B • ~H   / A ⊃ K
    4. B   3, Simp
    5. B ∨ F   4, Add
    6. A ⊃ G   1, 5, MP
    7. B ∨ E   4, Add
    8. G ⊃ K   2, 7, MP
    9. A ⊃ K   6, 8, HS

(12) 1. (P ⊃ R) ⊃ (M ⊃ P)
    2. (P ∨ M) ⊃ (P ⊃ R)
    3. P ∨ M   / R ∨ P
    4. P ⊃ R   2, 3, MP
    5. M ⊃ P   1, 4, MP
    6. (P ⊃ R) • (M ⊃ P)   4, 5, Conj
    7. R ∨ P   3, 6, CD

(13) 1. (C ⊃ N) • E
    2. D ∨ (N ⊃ D)
    3. ~D   / ~C ∨ P
    4. N ⊃ D   2, 3, DS
    5. ~N   3, 4, MT
    6. C ⊃ N   1, Simp
    7. ~C   5, 6, MT
    8. ~C ∨ P   7, Add

(14) 1. F ⊃ (~T • A)
    2. (~T ∨ G) ⊃ (H ⊃ T)
    3. F • O   / ~H • ~T
    4. F   3, Simp
    5. ~T • A   1, 4, MP
    6. ~T   5, Simp
    7. ~T ∨ G   6, Add
    8. H ⊃ T   2, 7, MP
    9. ~H   6, 8, MT
   10. ~H • ~T   6, 9, Conj

(15) 1. (~S ∨ B) ⊃ (S ∨ K)
    2. (K ∨ ~D) ⊃ (H ⊃ S)
    3. ~S • W   / ~H
    4. ~S   3, Simp
    5. ~S ∨ B   4, Add
    6. S ∨ K   1, 5, MP
    7. K   4, 6, DS
    8. K ∨ ~D   7, Add
    9. H ⊃ S   2, 8, MP
   10. ~H   4, 9, MT

(16) 1. (C ∨ ~G) ⊃ (~P • L)
    2. (~P • C) ⊃ (C ⊃ D)
    3. C • ~R   / D ∨ R
    4. C   3, Simp
    5. C ∨ ~G   4, Add
    6. ~P • L   1, 5, MP

7. ~P   6, Simp
8. ~P • C   4, 7, Conj
9. C ⊃ D   2, 8, MP
10. D   4, 9, MP
11. D ∨ R   10, Add

(17) 1. [A ∨ (K • J)] ⊃ (~E • ~F)
     2. M ⊃ [A • (P ∨ R)]
     3. M • U   / ~E • A
     4. M   3, Simp
     5. A • (P ∨ R)   2, 4, MP
     6. A   5, Simp
     7. A ∨ (K • J)   6, Add
     8. ~E • ~F   1, 7, MP
     9. ~E   8, Simp
     10. ~E • A   6, 9, Conj

(18) 1. ~H ⊃ (~T ⊃ R)
     2. H ∨ (E ⊃ F)
     3. ~T ∨ E
     4. ~H • D   / R ∨ F
     5. ~H   4, Simp
     6. ~T ⊃ R   1, 5, MP
     7. E ⊃ F   2, 5, DS
     8. (~T ⊃ R) • (E ⊃ F) 6, 7, Conj
     9. R ∨ F   3, 8, CD

(19) 1. (U • ~~P) ⊃ Q
     2. ~O ⊃ U
     3. ~P ⊃ O
     4. ~O • T   / Q
     5. ~O   4, Simp
     6. U   2, 5, MP
     7. ~~P   3, 5, MT
     8. U • ~~P   6, 7, Conj
     9. Q   1, 8, MP

(20) 1. (M ∨ N) ⊃ (F ⊃ G)
     2. D ⊃ ~C
     3. ~C ⊃ B
     4. M • H
     5. D ∨ F   / B ∨ G
     6. D ⊃ B   2, 3, HS
     7. M   4, Simp
     8. M ∨ N   7, Add

    9. F ⊃ G   1, 8, MP
  10. (D ⊃ B) • (F ⊃ G)   6, 9, Conj
  11. B ∨ G   5, 10, CD

(21) 1. (F • M) ⊃ (S ∨ T)
     2. (~S ∨ A) ⊃ F
     3. (~S ∨ B) ⊃ M
     4. ~S • G   / T
     5. ~S   4, Simp
     6. ~S ∨ A   5, Add
     7. F   2, 6, MP
     8. ~S ∨ B   5, Add
     9. M   3, 8, MP
   10. F • M   7, 9, Conj
   11. S ∨ T   1, 10, MP
   12. T   5, 11, DS

(22) 1. (~K • ~N) ⊃ [(~P ⊃ K) • (~R ⊃ G)]
     2. K ⊃ N
     3. ~N • B
     4. ~P ∨ ~R   / G
     5. ~N   3, Simp
     6. ~K   2, 5, MT
     7. ~K • ~N   5, 6, Conj
     8. (~P ⊃ K) • (~R ⊃ G)   1, 7, MP
     9. K ∨ G   4, 8, CD
   10. G   6, 9, DS

(23) 1. (~A ∨ D) ⊃ (B ⊃ F)
     2. (B ∨ C) ⊃ (A ⊃ E)
     3. A ∨ B
     4. ~A   / E ∨ F
     5. ~A ∨ D   4, Add
     6. B ⊃ F   1, 5, MP
     7. B   3, 4, DS
     8. B ∨ C   7, Add
     9. A ⊃ E   2, 8, MP
   10. (A ⊃ E) • (B ⊃ F)   8, 9, Conj
   11. E ∨ F   3, 10, CD

(24) 1. (J ⊃ K) • (~O ⊃ ~P)
     2. (L ⊃ J) • (~M ⊃ ~O)
     3. ~K ⊃ (L ∨ ~M)
     4. ~K • G   / ~P
     5. ~K   4, Simp

   6. L ∨ ~M   3, 5, MP
   7. J ∨ ~O   2, 6, CD
   8. K ∨ ~P   1, 7, CD
   9. ~P   5, 8, DS

(25) 1. (~M • ~N) ⊃ [(~M ∨ H) ⊃ (K • L)]
     2. ~M • (C ⊃ D)
     3. ~N • (F ≡ G)   / K • ~N
     4. ~M   2, Simp
     5. ~N   3, Simp
     6. ~M • ~N   4, 5, Conj
     7. (~M ∨ H) ⊃ (K • L) 1, 6, MP
     8. ~M ∨ H   4, Add
     9. K • L   7, 8, MP
    10. K   9, Simp
    11. K • ~N   5, 10, Conj

(26) . (P ∨ S) ⊃ (E ⊃ F)
     2. (P ∨ T) ⊃ (G ⊃ H)
     3. (P ∨ U) ⊃ (E ∨ G)
     4. P   / F ∨ H
     5. P ∨ S   4, Add
     6. E ⊃ F   1, 5, MP
     7. P ∨ T   4, Add
     8. G ⊃ H   2, 7, MP
     9. P ∨ U   4, Add
    10. E ∨ G   3, 9, MP
    11. (E ⊃ F) • (G ⊃ H)   6, 8, Conj
    12. F ∨ H   10, 11, CD

(27) 1. (S ⊃ Q) • (Q ⊃ ~S)
     2. S ∨ Q
     3. ~Q   / P • R
     4. Q ∨ ~S   1, 2, CD
     5. ~S   3, 4, DS
     6. Q   2, 5, DS
     7. Q ∨ (P • R)   6, Add
     8. P • R   3, 7, DS

(28) 1. (D ⊃ B) • (C ⊃ D)
     2. (B ⊃ D) • (E ⊃ C)
     3. B ∨ E   / D ∨ B
     4. D ∨ C   2, 3, CD
     5. B ∨ D   1, 4, CD
     6. B ⊃ D   2, Simp

7. D ⊃ B   1, Simp
8. (B ⊃ D) • (D ⊃ B) 6, 7, Conj
9. D ∨ B   5, 8, CD

(29) 1. (R ⊃ H) • (S ⊃ I)
  2. (~H • ~L) ⊃ (R ∨ S)
  3. ~H • (K ⊃ T)
  4. H ∨ ~L   / I ∨ M
  5. ~H   3, Simp
  6. ~L   4, 5, DS
  7. ~H • ~L   5, 6, Conj
  8. R ∨ S   2, 7, MP
  9. H ∨ I   1, 8, CD
 10. I   5, 9, DS
 11. I ∨ M   10, Add

(30) 1. (W • X) ⊃ (Q ∨ R)
  2. (S ∨ F) ⊃ (Q ∨ W)
  3. (S ∨ G) ⊃ (~Q ⊃ X)
  4. Q ∨ S
  5. ~Q • H   / R
  6. ~Q   5, Simp
  7. S   4, 6, DS
  8. S ∨ F   7, Add
  9. Q ∨ W   2, 8, MP
 10. W   6, 9, DS
 11. S ∨ G   7, Add
 12. ~Q ⊃ X   3, 11, MP
 13. X   6, 12, MP
 14. W • X   10, 13, Conj
 15. Q ∨ R   1, 14, MP
 16. R   6, 15, DS

Part IV

(1) 1. T ⊃ (Q • F)
  2. T • C   / Q ∨ O
  3. T   2, Simp
  4. Q • F   1, 3, MP
  5. Q   4, Simp
  6. Q ∨ O   5, Add

(2) 1. (C • ~E) ⊃ (E ∨ T)
  2. C
  3. ~E   / T

    4. C • ~E   2, 3, Conj
    5. E ∨ T   1, 4, MP
    6. T   3, 5, DS

(3) 1. (R ∨ P) ⊃ (G ∨ M)
     2. R • U
     3. (G ⊃ E) • (M ⊃ F)
     4. (E ∨ F) ⊃ C   / C
     5. R   2, Simp
     6. R ∨ P   5, Add
     7. G ∨ M   1, 6, MP
     8. E ∨ F   3, 7, CD
     9. C   4, 8, MP

(4) 1. M ∨ P
     2. (P ∨ S) ⊃ (R • D)
     3. ~M   / R
     4. P   1, 3, DS
     5. P ∨ S   4, Add
     6. R • D   2, 5, MP
     7. R   6, Simp

(5) 1. H ⊃ [(I ∨ P) ⊃ E]
     2. (H ∨ W) ⊃ ~E
     3. H   / ~(I ∨ P)
     4. H ∨ W   3, Add
     5. ~E   2, 4, MP
     6. (I ∨ P) ⊃ E   1, 3, MP
     7. ~(I ∨ P)   5, 6, MT

(6) 1. (P ∨ S) ⊃ [(L ⊃ R) • (I ⊃ M)]
     2. (P ∨ N) ⊃ (L ∨ I)
     3. P • W   / R ∨ M
     4. P   3, Simp
     5. P ∨ N   4, Add
     6. L ∨ I   2, 5, MP
     7. P ∨ S   4, Add
     8. (L ⊃ R) • (I ⊃ M)   1, 7, MP
     9. R ∨ M   6, 8, CD

(7) 1. (~C ∨ ~M) ⊃ (~C ⊃ T)
     2. C ∨ ~T
     3. ~C   / B
     4. ~C ∨ ~M   3, Add
     5. ~C ⊃ T   1, 4, MP
     6. T   3, 5, MP

```
7. T ∨ B          6, Add
8. ~T             2, 3, DS
9. B              7, 8, DS
```

```
(8)  1. (F ∨ A) ⊃ (H • P)
     2. L ⊃ A
     3. D ⊃ F
     4. (D ∨ L) • I          / H
     5. (D ⊃ F) • (L ⊃ A)    2, 3, Conj
     6. D ∨ L                4, Simp
     7. F ∨ A                5, 6, CD
     8. H • P                1, 7, MP
     9. H                    8, Simp
```

```
(9)  1. L ⊃ G
     2. C ⊃ A
     3. (G ∨ A) ⊃ (~L • ~M)
     4. L ∨ C
     5. C ⊃ I                / I
     6. (L ⊃ G) • (C ⊃ A)    1, 2, Conj
     7. G ∨ A                4, 6, CD
     8. ~L • ~M              3, 7, MP
     9. ~L                   8, Simp
    10. C                    4, 9, DS
    11. I                    5, 10, MP
```

```
(10) 1. (V • ~E) ⊃ (P ⊃ E)
     2. V ⊃ ~E
     3. V • I
     4. ~E ⊃ (P ∨ J)         / J • ~E
     5. V                    3, Simp
     6. ~E                   2, 5, MP
     7. V • ~E               5, 6, Conj
     8. P ⊃ E                1, 7, MP
     9. ~P                   6, 8, MT
    10. P ∨ J                4, 6, MP
    11. J                    9, 10, DS
    12. J • ~E               6, 11, Conj
```

Exercise 7.3
Part I

1. ~N • ~G	2	3. (M ∨ G) ∨ T	1
2. (S • T) ∨ (S • U)	3	4. A • S	3

Exercise 7.3

5.	R ∨ T	1	11.	~B ∨ ~~E	1
6.	H • (Z ∨ W)	2	12.	(~Q ∨ T) • (~Q ∨ R)	3
7.	~G ∨ ~~Q	1	13.	H ⊃ ~(L ∨ D)	2
8.	J ⊃ (~N ∨ S)	3	14.	(M • R) • ~T	3
9.	E • (H • Q)	3	15.	D ∨ (~K • ~W)	1
10.	~(R • P)	1			

Part II

1. C ∨ K 1, Com 2, 3, DS

2. ~(R ∨ N) 2, DM 1, 3, MT

3. T • H 1, Com 2, Simp

4. L • (S • F) 1, Assoc 2, Simp

5. ~B ∨ ~~K 1, DN 2, DM

6. ~~A 2, DN 1, 3, MT

7. D • (M ∨ N) 1, Dist 2, Simp

8. U ∨ T 2, Com 1, 3, MP

Or

(T ∨ U) ⊃ R 1, Com 2, 3, MP

9. ~~L 2, DN 1, 3, DS

10. (D ∨ N) • (D ∨ H) 1, Dist 2, Simp

11. K ∨ (E • G) 1, Dist 2, 3, DS

12. N ∨ F 2, Com 1, 3, CD

13. M ∨ (G ∨ T) 1, Assoc 2, 3, DS

14. ~A ∨ ~S 2, DM 1, 3, CD

15. ~R ∨ ~T 1, Add 2, DM

Part III

(1) 1. (~M ⊃ P) • (~N ⊃ Q)
    2. ~(M • N) / P ∨ Q
    3. ~M ∨ ~N 2, DM
    4. P ∨ Q 1, 3, CD

(2) 1. ~S / ~(F • S)
    2. ~S ∨ ~F 1, Add
    3. ~F ∨ ~S 2, Com
    4. ~(F • S) 3, DM

(3) 1. J ∨ (K • L)
     2. ~K   / J
     3. (J ∨ K) • (J ∨ L)   1, Dist
     4. J ∨ K   3, Simp
     5. K ∨ J   4, Com
     6. J   2, 5, DS

(4) 1. ~(N • T)
     2. T   / ~N
     3. ~N ∨ ~T   2, DM
     4. ~T ∨ ~N   3, Com
     5. ~~T   2, DN
     6. ~N   4, 5, DS

(5) 1. H ⊃ ~A
     2. A   / ~(H ∨ ~A)
     3. ~~A   2, DN
     4. ~H   1, 3, MT
     5. ~H • ~~A   3, 4, Conj
     6. ~(H ∨ ~A)   5, DM

(6) 1. R ⊃ ~B
     2. D ∨ R
     3. B   / D
     4. ~~B   3, DN
     5. ~R   1, 4, MT
     6. R ∨ D   2, Com
     7. D   5, 6, DS

(7) 1. T ⊃ (B ∨ E)
     2. ~E • T   / B
     3. T • ~E   2, Com
     4. T   3, Simp
     5. B ∨ E   1, 4, MP
     6. E ∨ B   5, Com
     7. ~E   2, Simp
     8. B   6, 7, DS

(8) 1. (O ∨ M) ⊃ S
     2. ~S   / ~M
     3. ~(O ∨ M)   1, 2, MT
     4. ~O • ~M   3, DM
     5. ~M • ~O   4, Com
     6. ~M   5, Simp

127

Exercise 7.3

(9) 1. Q ∨ (L ∨ C)
   2. ~C   / L ∨ Q
   3. (Q ∨ L) ∨ C   1, Assoc
   4. C ∨ (Q ∨ L)   3, Com
   5. Q ∨ L   2, 4, DS
   6. L ∨ Q   5, Com

(10) 1. (K • H) ∨ (K • L)
    2. ~L   / H
    3. K • (H ∨ L)   1, Dist
    4. (H ∨ L) • K   3, Com
    5. H ∨ L   4, Simp
    6. L ∨ H   5, Com
    7. H   2, 6, DS

(11) 1. ~(~E • ~N) ⊃ T
    2. G ⊃ (N ∨ E)   / G ⊃ T
    3. (~~E ∨ ~~N) ⊃ T 1, DM
    4. (E ∨ ~~N) ⊃ T   3, DN
    5. (E ∨ N) ⊃ T   4, DN
    6. (N ∨ E) ⊃ T   5, Com
    7. G ⊃ T   2, 6, HS

(12) 1. H • (C • T)
    2. ~(~F • T)   / F
    3. ~~F ∨ ~T   2, DM
    4. F ∨ ~T   3, DN
    5. ~T ∨ F   4, Com
    6. (H • C) • T   1, Assoc
    7. T • (H • C)   6, Com
    8. T   7, Simp
    9. ~~T   8, DN
   10. F   5, 9, DS

(13) 1. (E • I) ∨ (M • U)
    2. ~E   / ~(E ∨ ~M)
    3. ~E ∨ ~I   2, Add
    4. ~(E • I)   3, DM
    5. M • U   1, 4, DS
    6. M   5, Simp
    7. ~~M   6, DN
    8. ~E • ~~M   2, 7, Conj
    9. ~(E ∨ ~M)   8, DM

(14) 1. ~(J ∨ K)
      2. B ⊃ K
      3. S ⊃ B   / ~S • ~J
      4. ~J • ~K   1, DM
      5. ~K • ~J   4, Com
      6. ~K   5, Simp
      7. ~B   2, 6, MT
      8. ~S   3, 7, MT
      9. ~J   4, Simp
      10. ~S • ~J   8, 9, Conj

(15) 1. (G • H) ∨ (M • G)
      2. G ⊃ (T • A)   / A
      3. (G • H) ∨ (G • M)   1, Com
      4. G • (H ∨ M)   3, Dist
      5. G   4, Simp
      6. T • A   2, 5, MP
      7. A • T   6, Com
      8. A   7, Simp

(16) 1. (Q • N) ∨ (N • T)
      2. (Q ∨ C) ⊃ ~N   / T
      3. (N • Q) ∨ (N • T)   1, Com
      4. N • (Q ∨ T)   3, Dist
      5. N   4, Simp
      6. ~~N   5, DN
      7. ~(Q ∨ C)   2, 6, MT
      8. ~Q • ~C   7, DM
      9. ~Q   8, Simp
      10. (Q ∨ T) • N   4, Com
      11. Q ∨ T   10, Simp
      12. T   9, 11, DS

(17) 1. ~(U ∨ R)
      2. (~R ∨ N) ⊃ (P • H)
      3. Q ⊃ ~H   / ~Q
      4. ~U • ~R   1, DM
      5. ~R • ~U   4, Com
      6. ~R   5, Simp
      7. ~R ∨ N   6, Add
      8. P • H   2, 7, MP
      9. H • P   8, Com
      10. H   9, Simp
      11. ~~H   10, DN
      12. ~Q   3, 11, MT

Exercise 7.3

(18) 1. ~(F • A)
    2. ~(L ∨ ~A)
    3. D ⊃ (F ∨ L)   / ~D
    4. ~L • ~~A   2, DM
    5. ~~A • ~L   4, Com
    6. ~~A   5, Simp
    7. ~F ∨ ~A   1, DM
    8. ~A ∨ ~F   7, Com
    9. ~F   6, 8, DS
    10. ~L   4, Simp
    11. ~F • ~L   9, 10, Conj
    12. ~(F ∨ L)   11, DM
    13. ~D   3, 12, MT

(19) 1. [(I ∨ M) ∨ G] ⊃ ~G
    2. M ∨ G   / M
    3. (M ∨ G) ∨ I   2, Add
    4. I ∨ (M ∨ G)   3, Com
    5. (I ∨ M) ∨ G   4, Assoc
    6. ~G   1, 5, MP
    7. G ∨ M   2, Com
    8. M   6, 7, DS

(20) 1. E ⊃ ~B
    2. U ⊃ ~C
    3. ~(~E • ~U)   / ~(B • C)
    4. (E ⊃ ~B) • (U ⊃ ~C)   1, 2, Conj
    5. ~~E ∨ ~~U   3, DM
    6. E ∨ ~~U   5, DN
    7. E ∨ U   6, DN
    8. ~B ∨ ~C   4, 7, CD
    9. ~(B • C)   8, DM

(21) 1. ~(K ∨ F)
    2. ~F ⊃ (K ∨ C)
    3. (G ∨ C) ⊃ ~H   / ~(K ∨ H)
    4. ~K • ~F   1, DM
    5. ~F • ~K   4, Com
    6. ~F   5, Simp
    7. K ∨ C   2, 6, MP
    8. ~K   4, Simp
    9. C   7, 8, DS
    10. C ∨ G   9, Add
    11. G ∨ C   10, Com
    12. ~H   3, 11, MP

13. ~K • ~H   8, 12, Conj
14. ~(K ∨ H)   13, DM

(22) 1. S ∨ (I • ~J)
      2. S ⊃ ~R
      3. ~J ⊃ ~Q   / ~(R • Q)
      4. (S ∨ I) • (S ∨ ~J)   1, Dist
      5. (S ∨ ~J) • (S ∨ I)   4, Com
      6. S ∨ ~J   5, Simp
      7. (S ⊃ ~R) • (~J ⊃ ~Q)   2, 3, Conj
      8. ~R ∨ ~Q   6, 7, CD
      9. ~(R • Q)   8, DM

(23) 1. (J ∨ F) ∨ M
      2. (J ∨ M) ⊃ ~P
      3. ~F   / ~(F ∨ P)
      4. (F ∨ J) ∨ M   1, Com
      5. F ∨ (J ∨ M)   4, Assoc
      6. J ∨ M   3, 5, DS
      7. ~P   2, 6, MP
      8. ~F • ~P   3, 7, Conj
      9. ~(F ∨ P)   8, DM

(24) 1. (K • P) ∨ (K • Q)
      2. P ⊃ ~K   / Q ∨ T
      3. K • (P ∨ Q)   1, Dist
      4. K   3, Simp
      5. ~~K   4, DN
      6. ~P   2, 5, MT
      7. (P ∨ Q) • K   3, Com
      8. P ∨ Q   7, Simp
      9. Q   6, 8, DS
    10. Q ∨ T   9, Add

(25) 1. E ∨ ~(D ∨ C)
      2. (E ∨ ~D) ⊃ C   / E
      3. E ∨ (~D • ~C)   1, DM
      4. (E ∨ ~D) • (E ∨ ~C)   3, Dist
      5. E ∨ ~D   4, Simp
      6. C   2, 5, MP
      7. (E ∨ ~C) • (E ∨ ~D)   4, Com
      8. E ∨ ~C   7, Simp
      9. ~C ∨ E   8, Com
    10. ~~C   6, DN
    11. E   9, 10, DS

Exercise 7.3

(26) 1. A • (F • L)
    2. A ⊃ (U ∨ W)
    3. F ⊃ (U ∨ X)   / U ∨ (W • X)
    4. (A • F) • L   1, Assoc
    5. A • F   4, Simp
    6. A   5, Simp
    7. U ∨ W   2, 6, MP
    8. F • A   5, Com
    9. F   8, Simp
    10. U ∨ X   3, 9, MP
    11. (U ∨ W) • (U ∨ X)   7, 10, Conj
    12. U ∨ (W • X)   11, Dist

(27) 1. (T • R) ⊃ P
    2. (~P • R) • G
    3. (~T ∨ N) ⊃ H   / H
    4. ~P • (R • G)   2, Assoc
    5. ~P   4, Simp
    6. ~(T • R)   1, 5, MT
    7. ~T ∨ ~R   6, DM
    8. ~R ∨ ~T   7, Com
    9. (R • ~P) • G   2, Com
    10. R • (~P • G)   9, Assoc
    11. R   10, Simp
    12. ~~R   11, DN
    13. ~T   8, 12, DS
    14. ~T ∨ N   13, Add
    15. H   3, 14, MP

(28) 1. P ∨ (I • L)
    2. (P ∨ I) ⊃ ~(L ∨ C)
    3. (P • ~C) ⊃ (E • F)   / F ∨ D
    4. (P ∨ I) • (P ∨ L)   1, Dist
    5. P ∨ I   4, Simp
    6. ~(L ∨ C)   2, 5, MP
    7. ~L • ~C   6, DM
    8. ~L   7, Simp
    9. (P ∨ L) • (P ∨ I)   4, Com
    10. P ∨ L   9, Simp
    11. L ∨ P   10, Com
    12. P   8, 11, DS
    13. ~C • ~L   7, Com
    14. ~C   13, Simp
    15. P • ~C   12, 14, Conj
    16. E • F   3, 15, MP
    17. F • E   16, Com

18. F	17, Simp
19. F ∨ D	18, Add

(29) 1. B ∨ (S • N)
   2. B ⊃ ~S
   3. S ⊃ ~N   / B ∨ W
   4. (B ∨ S) • (B ∨ N)   1, Dist
   5. B ∨ S   4, Simp
   6. (B ⊃ ~S) • (S ⊃ ~N)   2, 3, Conj
   7. ~S ∨ ~N   5, 6, CD
   8. ~(S • N)   7, DM
   9. (S • N) ∨ B   1, Com
  10. B   8, 9, DS
  11. B ∨ W   10, Add

(30) 1. (~M ∨ E) ⊃ (S ⊃ U)
   2. (~Q ∨ E) ⊃ (U ⊃ H)
   3. ~(M ∨ Q)   / S ⊃ H
   4. ~M • ~Q   3, DM
   5. ~M   4, Simp
   6. ~M ∨ E   5, Add
   7. S ⊃ U   1, 6, MP
   8. ~Q • ~M   4, Com
   9. ~Q   8, Simp
  10. ~Q ∨ E   9, Add
  11. U ⊃ H   2, 10, MP
  12. S ⊃ H   7, 11, HS

(31) 1. (~R ∨ D) ⊃ ~(F • G)
   2. (F • R) ⊃ S
   3. F • ~S   / ~(S ∨ G)
   4. ~S • F   3, Com
   5. ~S   4, Simp
   6. ~(F • R)   2, 5, MT
   7. ~F ∨ ~R   6, DM
   8. F   3, Simp
   9. ~~F   8, DN
  10. ~R   7, 9, DS
  11. ~R ∨ D   10, Add
  12. ~(F • G)   1, 11, MP
  13. ~F ∨ ~G   12, DM
  14. ~G   9, 13, DS
  15. ~S • ~G   5, 14, Conj
  16. ~(S ∨ G)   15, DM

Exercise 7.3

(32) 1. ~Q ⊃ (C • B)
    2. ~T ⊃ (B • H)
    3. ~(Q • T)   / B
    4. ~Q ∨ ~T   3, DM
    5. [~Q ⊃ (C • B)] • [~T ⊃ (B • H)]   1, 2, Conj
    6. (C • B) ∨ (B • H)   4, 5, CD
    7. (B • C) ∨ (B • H)   6, Com
    8. B • (C ∨ H)   7, Dist
    9. B   8, Simp

(33) 1. ~(A • G)
    2. ~(A • E)
    3. G ∨ E   / ~(A • F)
    4. ~A ∨ ~G   1, DM
    5. ~A ∨ ~E   2, DM
    6. (~A ∨ ~G) • (~A ∨ ~E)   4, 5, Conj
    7. ~A ∨ (~G • ~E)   6, Dist
    8. ~A ∨ ~(G ∨ E)   7, DM
    9. ~(G ∨ E) ∨ ~A   8, Com
    10. ~~(G ∨ E)   3, DN
    11. ~A   9, 10, DS
    12. ~A ∨ ~F   11, Add
    13. ~(A • F)   12, DM

(34) 1. (M • N) ∨ (O • P)
    2. (N ∨ O) ⊃ ~P   / N
    3. [(M • N) ∨ O] • [(M • N) ∨ P]   1, Dist
    4. (M • N) ∨ O   3, Simp
    5. O ∨ (M • N)   4, Com
    6. (O ∨ M) • (O ∨ N)   5, Dist
    7. (O ∨ N) • (O ∨ M)   6, Com
    8. O ∨ N   7, Simp
    9. N ∨ O   8, Com
    10. ~P   2, 9, MP
    11. [(M • N) ∨ P] • [(M • N) ∨ O]   3, Com
    12. (M • N) ∨ P   11, Simp
    13. P ∨ (M • N)   12, Com
    14. M • N   10, 13, DS
    15. N • M   14, Com
    16. N   15, Simp

(35) 1. (T • K) ∨ (C • E)
    2. K ⊃ ~E
    3. E ⊃ ~C   / T • K
    4. [(T • K) ∨ C] • [(T • K) ∨ E]   1, Dist

5. [(T • K) ∨ E] • [(T • K) ∨ C]	4, Com
6. (T • K) ∨ E	5, Simp
7. E ∨ (T • K)	6, Com
8. (E ∨ T) • (E ∨ K)	7, Dist
9. (E ∨ K) • (E ∨ T)	8, Com
10. E ∨ K	9, Simp
11. K ∨ E	10, Com
12. (K ⊃ ~E) • (E ⊃ ~C)	2, 3, Conj
13. ~E ∨ ~C	11, 12, CD
14. ~C ∨ ~E	13, Com
15. ~(C • E)	14, DM
16. (C • E) ∨ (T • K)	1, Com
17. T • K	15, 16, DS

Part IV

(1)
1. (S • D) ∨ (S • H)	
2. S ⊃ (I • R)	/ S • R
3. S • (D ∨ H)	1, Dist
4. S	3, Simp
5. I • R	2, 4, MP
6. R • I	5, Com
7. R	6, Simp
8. S • R	4, 7, Conj

(2)
1. (C • I) ∨ (H • I)	
2. B ⊃ ~I	/ ~B
3. (I • C) ∨ (I • H)	1, Com
4. I • (C ∨ H)	3, Dist
5. I	4, Simp
6. ~~I	5, DN
7. ~B	2, 6, MT

(3)
1. ~(S ∨ C)	
2. ~(S • R) ⊃ (C ∨ D)	/ D
3. ~S • ~C	1, DM
4. ~S	3, Simp
5. ~S ∨ ~R	4, Add
6. ~(S • R)	5, DM
7. C ∨ D	2, 6, MP
8. ~ C • ~S	3, Com
9. ~C	8, Simp
10. D	7, 9, DS

Exercise 7.3

(4) 1. G ∨ (R • E)
    2. (G ∨ E) ⊃ ~R   / G ∨ M
    3. (G ∨ R) • (G ∨ E)   1, Dist
    4. (G ∨ E) • (G ∨ R)   3, Com
    5. G ∨ E   4, Simp
    6. ~R   2, 5, MP
    7. G ∨ R   3, Simp
    8. R ∨ G   7, Com
    9. G   6, 8, DS
    10. G ∨ M   9, Add

(5) 1. E • (P • B)
    2. (E • B) ⊃ ~(P • ~M)   / E • M
    3. E • (B • P)   1, Com
    4. (E • B) • P   3, Assoc
    5. E • B   4, Simp
    6. ~(P • ~M)   2, 5, MP
    7. ~P ∨ ~~M   6, DM
    8. P • (E • B)   4, Com
    9. P   8, Simp
    10. ~~P   9, DN
    11. ~~M   7, 10, DS
    12. M   11, DN
    13. E   3, Simp
    14. E • M   12, 13, Conj

(6) 1. F ⊃ (U • R)
    2. ~F ⊃ (P • J)
    3. F ∨ ~F   / U ∨ P
    4. [F ⊃ (U • R)] • [~F ⊃ (P • J)]   1, 2, Conj
    5. (U • R) ∨ (P • S)   3, 4, CD
    6. [(U • R) ∨ P] • [(U • R) ∨ S]   5, Dist
    7. (U • R) ∨ P   6, Simp
    8. P ∨ (U • R)   7, Com
    9. (P ∨ U) • (P ∨ R)   8, Dist
    10. P ∨ U   9, Simp
    11. U ∨ P   10, Com

(7) 1. R ⊃ (C ∨ M)
    2. ~(I ∨ C)
    3. ~(A ∨ M)   / ~R
    4. ~I • ~C   2, DM
    5. ~A • ~M   3, DM
    6. ~C • ~I   4, Com
    7. ~C   6, Simp

8. ~M • ~A	5, Com
9. ~M	8, Simp
10. ~C • ~M	7, 9, Conj
11. ~(C ∨ M)	10, DM
12. ~R	1, 11, MT

(8)
1. (P ∨ U) ⊃ ~L	
2. (I ∨ W) ⊃ ~K	
3. L • K	/ ~(U ∨ W)
4. L	3, Simp
5. ~~L	4, DN
6. ~(P ∨ U)	1, 5, MT
7. ~P • ~U	6, DM
8. ~U • ~P	7, Com
9. ~U	8, Simp
10. K • L	3, Com
11. K	10, Simp
12. ~~K	11, DN
13. ~(I ∨ W)	2, 12, MT
14. ~I • ~W	13, DM
15. ~W • ~I	14, Com
16. ~W	15, Simp
17. ~U • ~W	9, 16, Conj
18. ~(U ∨ W)	17, DM

(9)
1. ~(S ∨ E)	
2. (~S • M) ⊃ E	/ ~M
3. ~S • ~E	1, DM
4. ~E • ~S	3, Com
5. ~E	4, Simp
6. ~(~S • M)	2, 5, MT
7. ~~S ∨ ~M	6, DM
8. S ∨ ~M	7, DN
9. ~S	3, Simp
10. ~M	8, 9, DS

(10)
1. ~E ∨ (B • P)	
2. ~E ∨ (G • W)	
3. ~P ∨ ~W	/ ~E
4. (~E ∨ B) • (~E ∨ P)	1, Dist
5. (~E ∨ P) • (~E ∨ B)	4, Com
6. ~E ∨ P	5, Simp
7. (~E ∨ G) • (~E ∨ W)	2, Dist
8. (~E ∨ W) • (~E ∨ G)	7, Com
9. ~E ∨ W	8, Simp

Exercise 7.4

10. (~E ∨ P) • (~E ∨ W)   6, 9, Conj
11. ~E ∨ (P • W)   10, Dist
12. (P • W) ∨ ~E   11, Com
13. ~(P • W)   3, DM
14. ~E   12, 13, DS

Exercise 7.4
Part I

1. G ⊃ Q   3   9. D ≡ H   1

2. (R • S) ⊃ N   1   10. S ⊃ G   3

3. ~P ⊃ ~H   2   11. J ⊃ F   2

4. B ≡ N   1   12. (C • H) ⊃ A   3

5. A   2   13. W ≡ ~T   2

6. ~Q ⊃ ~~L   3   14. (K ⊃ M) ≡ S   1

7. ~~C ∨ ~F   1   15. S ⊃ D   1

8. G ⊃ (N ⊃ Z)   2

Part II

1. J ⊃ M   1, Impl   9. (K • A) ⊃ F   1, Exp
                   2, 3, HS   2, 3, MT
2. J ⊃ (F ⊃ N)   1, Exp   10. ~H ∨ ~H   1, Impl
                   2, 3, MP   2, Taut
3. (C ⊃ A) • (A ⊃ C) 1, 2, Conj 11. ~S ∨ K   1, Add
                   3, Equiv   2, Impl
4. K ∨ K   1, 2, CD   12. (M • M) ⊃ D   1, Exp
                   3, Taut   2, Taut
5. (G ⊃ B) • (H ⊃ C) 1, Trans   13. (N ⊃ A) • (A ⊃ N) 1, Trans
                   2, 3, CD   2, Equiv
6. (J • M) ⊃ Q   1, Exp   14. (E • R) ∨ (~E • ~R) 1, Add
                   2, 3, MP   2, Equiv
7. H ⊃ (C ⊃ R)   1, Impl   15. Q ⊃ (G ⊃ W)   1, Trans
                   2, Exp   2, Exp
8. T ⊃ G   1, Trans
                   2, 3, HS

Part III

(1) 1. (S • K) ⊃ R
     2. K   / S ⊃ R
     3. (K • S) ⊃ R   1, Com
     4. K ⊃ (S ⊃ R)   3, Exp
     5. S ⊃ R   2, 5, MP

(2) 1. T ⊃ (F ∨ F)
     2. ~(F • F)   / ~T
     3. T ⊃ F   1, Taut
     4. ~F   2, Taut
     5. ~T   3, 4, MT

(3) 1. G ⊃ E
     2. H ⊃ ~E   / G ⊃ ~H
     3. ~~E ⊃ ~H   2, Trans
     4. E ⊃ ~H   3, DN
     5. G ⊃ ~H   1, 4, HS

(4) 1. S ≡ Q
     2. ~S   / ~Q
     3. (S ⊃ Q) • (Q ⊃ S)   1, Equiv
     4. (Q ⊃ S) • (S ⊃ Q)   3, Com
     5. Q ⊃ S   4, Simp
     6. ~Q   2, 5, MT

(5) 1. ~N ∨ P
     2. (N ⊃ P) ⊃ T   / T
     3. N ⊃ P   1, Impl
     4. T   2, 3, MP

(6) 1. F ⊃ B
     2. B ⊃ (B ⊃ J)   / F ⊃ J
     3. (B • B) ⊃ J   2, Exp
     4. B ⊃ J   3, Taut
     5. F ⊃ J   1, 4, HS

(7) 1. (B ⊃ M) • (D ⊃ M)
     2. B ∨ D   / M
     3. M ∨ M   1, 2, CD
     4. M   3, Taut

139

Exercise 7.4

(8) 1. Q ⊃ (F ⊃ A)
     2. R ⊃ (A ⊃ F)
     3. Q • R   / F ≡ A
     4. Q   3, Simp
     5. F ⊃ A   1, 4, MP
     6. R • Q   3, Com
     7. R   6, Simp
     8. A ⊃ F   2, 7, MP
     9. (F ⊃ A) • (A ⊃ F)   5, 8, Conj
     10. F ≡ A   9, Equiv

(9) 1. T ⊃ (~T ∨ G)
     2. ~G   / ~T
     3. T ⊃ (T ⊃ G)   1, Impl
     4. (T • T) ⊃ G   3, Exp
     5. T ⊃ G   4, Taut
     6. ~T   2, 5, MT

(10) 1. (B ⊃ G) • (F ⊃ N)
     2. ~(G • N)   / ~(B • F)
     3. ~G ∨ ~N   2, DM
     4. (~G ⊃ ~B) • (F ⊃ N)   1, Trans
     5. (~G ⊃ ~B) • (~N ⊃ ~F)   4, Trans
     6. ~B ∨ ~F   3, 5, CD
     7. ~(B • F)   6, DM

(11) 1. (J • R) ⊃ H
     2. (R ⊃ H) ⊃ M
     3. ~(P ∨ ~J)   / M • ~P
     4. J ⊃ (R ⊃ H)   1, Exp
     5. J ⊃ M   2, 4, HS
     6. ~P • ~~J   3, DM
     7. ~P • J   6, DN
     8. ~P   7, Simp
     9. J • ~P   7, Com
     10. J   9, Simp
     11. M   5, 10, MP
     12. M • ~P   8, 11, Conj

(12) 1. T   / S ⊃ T
     2. T ∨ ~S   1, Add
     3. ~S ∨ T   2, Com
     4. S ⊃ T   3, Impl

140

(13) 1. K ⊃ (B ⊃ ~M)
    2. D ⊃ (K • M)   / D ⊃ ~B
    3. K ⊃ (~~M ⊃ ~B)   1, Trans
    4. K ⊃ (M ⊃ ~B)   3, DN
    5. (K • M) ⊃ ~B   4, Exp
    6. D ⊃ ~B   2, 5, HS

(14) 1. (O ⊃ C) • (~S ⊃ ~D)
    2. (E ⊃ D) • (~E ⊃ ~C)   / O ⊃ S
    3. O ⊃ C   1, Simp
    4. (~S ⊃ ~D) • (O ⊃ C)   1, Com
    5. ~S ⊃ ~D   4, Simp
    6. D ⊃ S   5, Trans
    7. E ⊃ D   2, Simp
    8. (~E ⊃ ~C) • (E ⊃ D)   2, Com
    9. ~E ⊃ ~C   8, Simp
   10. C ⊃ E   9, Trans
   11. O ⊃ E   7, 10, HS
   12. O ⊃ D   7, 11, HS
   13. O ⊃ S   6, 12, HS

(15) 1. ~(U • W) ⊃ X
    2. U ⊃ ~U   / ~(U ∨ ~X)
    3. ~U ∨ ~U   2, Impl
    4. ~U   3, Taut
    5. ~U ∨ ~W   4, Add
    6. ~(U • W)   5, DM
    7. X   1, 6, MP
    8. ~U • X   4, 7, Conj
    9. ~U • ~~X   8, DN
   10. ~(U ∨ ~X)   9, DM

(16) 1. T ⊃ R
    2. T ⊃ ~R   / ~T
    3. ~~R ⊃ ~T   2, Trans
    4. R ⊃ ~T   3, DN
    5. T ⊃ ~T   1, 4, HS
    6. ~T ∨ ~T   5, Impl
    7. ~T   6, Taut

(17) 1. S ∨ ~N
    2. ~S ∨ Q   / N ⊃ Q
    3. ~N ∨ S   1, Com
    4. N ⊃ S   3, Impl
    5. S ⊃ Q   2, Impl

Exercise 7.4

    6. N ⊃ Q   4, 5, HS

(18) 1. M ⊃ (U ⊃ H)
    2. (H ∨ ~U) ⊃ F   / M ⊃ F
    3. (~U ∨ H) ⊃ F   2, Com
    4. (U ⊃ H) ⊃ F   3, Impl
    5. M ⊃ F   1, 4, HS

(19) 1. ~R ∨ P
    2. R ∨ ~P   / R ≡ P
    3. R ⊃ P   1, Impl
    4. ~P ∨ R   2, Com
    5. P ⊃ R   4, Impl
    6. (R ⊃ P) • (P ⊃ R)   3, 5, Conj
    7. R ≡ P   6, Equiv

(20) 1. ~H ⊃ B
    2. ~H ⊃ D
    3. ~(B • D)   / H
    4. ~B ⊃ ~~H   1, Trans
    5. ~B ⊃ H   4, DN
    6. ~D ⊃ ~~H   2, Trans
    7. ~D ⊃ H   6, DN
    8. ~B ∨ ~D   3, DM
    9. (~B ⊃ H) • (~D ⊃ H)   5, 7, Conj
    10. H ∨ H   8, 9, CD
    11. H   10, Taut

(21) 1. J ⊃ (G ⊃ L)   / G ⊃ (J ⊃ L)
    2. (J • G) ⊃ L   1, Exp
    3. (G • J) ⊃ L   2, Com
    4. G ⊃ (J ⊃ L)   3, Exp

(22) 1. S ⊃ (L • M)
    2. M ⊃ (L ⊃ R)   / S ⊃ R
    3. (M • L) ⊃ R   2, Exp
    4. (L • M) ⊃ R   3, Com
    5. S ⊃ R   1, 4, HS

(23) 1. F ⊃ (A • K)
    2. G ⊃ (~A • ~K)
    3. F ∨ G   / A ≡ K
    4. [F ⊃ (A • K)] • [G ⊃ (~A • ~K)]   1, 2, Conj
    5. (A • K) ∨ (~A • ~K)   3, 4, CD
    6. A ≡ K   5, Equiv

(24) 1. (I ⊃ E) ⊃ C
    2. C ⊃ ~C   / I
    3. ~C ∨ ~C   2, Impl
    4. ~C   3, Taut
    5. ~(I ⊃ E)   1, 4, MT
    6. ~(~I ∨ E)   5, Impl
    7. ~~I • ~E   6, DM
    8. I • ~E   7, DN
    9. I   8, Simp

(25) 1. T ⊃ G
    2. S ⊃ G   / (T ∨ S) ⊃ G
    3. ~T ∨ G   1, Impl
    4. ~S ∨ G   2, Impl
    5. G ∨ ~T   3, Com
    6. G ∨ ~S   4, Com
    7. (G ∨ ~T) • (G ∨ ~S)   5, 6, Conj
    8. G ∨ (~T • ~S)   7, Dist
    9. (~T • ~S) ∨ G   8, Com
  10. ~(T ∨ S) ∨ G   9, DM
  11. (T ∨ S) ⊃ G   10, Impl

(26) 1. H ⊃ U   / H ⊃ (U ∨ T)
    2. ~H ∨ U   1, Impl
    3. (~H ∨ U) ∨ T   2, Add
    4. ~H ∨ (U ∨ T)   3, Assoc
    5. H ⊃ (U ∨ T)   4, Impl

(27) 1. Q ⊃ (W • D)   / Q ⊃ W
    2. ~Q ∨ (W • D)   1, Impl
    3. (~Q ∨ W) • (~Q ∨ D)   2, Dist
    4. ~Q ∨ W   3, Simp
    5. Q ⊃ W   4, Impl

(28) 1. P ⊃ (~E ⊃ B)
    2. ~(B ∨ E)   / ~P
    3. ~(E ∨ B)   2, Com
    4. ~(~~E ∨ B)   3, DN
    5. ~(~E ⊃ B)   4, Impl
    6. ~P   1, 5, MT

(29) 1. (G ⊃ J) ⊃ (H ⊃ Q)
    2. J • ~Q   / ~H
    3. J   2, Simp
    4. J ∨ ~G   3, Add

5. ~G ∨ J	4, Com
6. G ⊃ J	5, Impl
7. H ⊃ Q	1, 6, MP
8. ~Q • J	2, Com
9. ~Q	9, Simp
10. ~H	7, 9, MT

(30) 1. I ∨ (N • F)

2. I ⊃ F	/ F
3. (I ∨ N) • (I ∨ F)	1, Dist
4. (I ∨ F) • (I ∨ N)	3, Com
5. I ∨ F	4, Simp
6. ~~I ∨ F	5, DN
7. ~I ⊃ F	6, Impl
8. ~F ⊃ ~I	2, Trans
9. ~F ⊃ F	7, 8, HS
10. ~~F ∨ F	9, Impl
11. F ∨ F	10, DN
12. F	11, Taut

(31) 1. K ≡ R

2. K ⊃ (R ⊃ P)

3. ~P	/ ~R
4. (K • R) ∨ (~K • ~R)	1, Equiv
5. (K • R) ⊃ P	2, Exp
6. ~(K • R)	3, 5, MT
7. ~K • ~R	4, 6, DS
8. ~R • ~K	7, Com
9. ~R	8, Simp

(32) 1. C ⊃ (~L ⊃ Q)

2. L ⊃ ~C

3. ~Q	/ ~C
4. (C • ~L) ⊃ Q	1, Exp
5. ~(C • ~L)	3, 4, MT
6. ~C ∨ ~~L	5, DM
7. ~C ∨ L	6, DN
8. C ⊃ L	7, Impl
9. C ⊃ ~C	2, 8, HS
10. ~C ∨ ~C	9, Impl
11. ~C	10, Taut

(33) 1. (E ⊃ A) • (F ⊃ A)

2. E ∨ G

3. F ∨ ~G	/ A

144

4. ~~E ∨ G   2, DN
5. ~E ⊃ G   4, Impl
6. ~~F ∨ ~G   3, DN
7. ~F ⊃ ~G   6, Impl
8. G ⊃ F   7, Trans
9. ~E ⊃ F   5, 8, HS
10. ~~E ∨ F   9, Impl
11. E ∨ F   10, DN
12. A ∨ A   1, 11, CD
13. A   12, Taut

(34) 1. (F • H) ⊃ N
2. F ∨ S
3. H   / N ∨ S
4. (H • F) ⊃ N   1, Com
5. H ⊃ (F ⊃ N)   4, Exp
6. F ⊃ N   3, 5, MP
7. ~N ⊃ ~F   6, Trans
8. ~~F ∨ S   2, DN
9. ~F ⊃ S   8, Impl
10. ~N ⊃ S   7, 9, HS
11. ~~N ∨ S   10, Impl
12. N ∨ S   11, DN

(35) 1. T ⊃ (H • J)
2. (H ∨ N) ⊃ T   / T ≡ H
3. ~T ∨ (H • J)   1, Impl
4. (~T ∨ H) • (~T ∨ J) 3, Dist
5. ~T ∨ H   4, Simp
6. T ⊃ H   5, Impl
7. ~(H ∨ N) ∨ T   2, Impl
8. (~H • ~N) ∨ T   7, DM
9. T ∨ (~H • ~N)   8, Com
10. (T ∨ ~H) • (T ∨ ~N) 9, Dist
11. (~H ∨ T) • (T ∨ ~N) 10, Com
12. ~H ∨ T   11, Simp
13. H ⊃ T   12, Impl
14. (T ⊃ H) • (H ⊃ T)   6, 13, Conj
15. T ≡ H   14, Equiv

(36) 1. T ⊃ ~(A ⊃ N)
2. T ∨ N   / T ≡ ~N
3. ~T ∨ ~(A ⊃ N)   1, Impl
4. ~T ∨ ~(~A ∨ N)   3, Impl
5. ~T ∨ (~~A • ~N)   4, DM

145

6. ~T ∨ (A • ~N)	5, DN
7. (~T ∨ A) • (~T ∨ ~N)	6, Dist
8. (~T ∨ ~N) • (~T ∨ A)	7, Com
9. ~T ∨ ~N	8, Simp
10. T ⊃ ~N	9, Impl
11. N ∨ T	2, Com
12. ~~N ∨ T	11, DN
13. ~N ⊃ T	12, Impl
14. (T ⊃ ~N) • (~N ⊃ T)	10, 13, Conj
15. T ≡ ~N	14, Equiv

(37)		
1. (D ⊃ E) ⊃ (E ⊃ D)	
2. (D ≡ E) ⊃ ~(G • ~H)	
3. E • G	/ G • H
4. E	3, Simp
5. E ∨ ~D	4, Add
6. ~D ∨ E	5, Com
7. D ⊃ E	6, Impl
8. E ⊃ D	1, 7, MP
9. (D ⊃ E) • (E ⊃ D)	7, 8, Conj
10. D ≡ E	9, Equiv
11. ~(G • ~H)	2, 10, MP
12. ~G ∨ ~~H	11, DM
13. ~G ∨ H	12, DN
14. G • E	3, Com
15. G	14, Simp
16. ~~G	15, DN
17. H	13, 16, DS
18. G • H	15, 17, Conj

(38)	
1. (O ⊃ R) ⊃ S	
2. (P ⊃ R) ⊃ ~S	/ ~R
3. ~~S ⊃ ~(P ⊃ R)	2, Trans
4. S ⊃ ~(P ⊃ R)	3, DN
5. (O ⊃ R) ⊃ ~(P ⊃ R)	1, 4, HS
6. ~(O ⊃ R) ∨ ~(P ⊃ R)	5, Impl
7. ~(~O ∨ R) ∨ ~(~P ∨ R)	6, Impl
8. (~~O • ~R) ∨ ~(~P ∨ R)	7, DM
9. (O • ~R) ∨ ~(~P ∨ R)	8, DN
10. (~R • O) ∨ ~(~P ∨ R)	9, Com
11. (~R • O) ∨ (~~P • ~R)	10, DM
12. (~R • O) ∨ (P • ~R)	11, DN
13. (~R • O) ∨ (~R • P)	12, Com
14. ~R • (O ∨ P)	13, Dist
15. ~R	14, Simp

(39) 1. (L ∨ P) ⊃ U
    2. (M ⊃ U) ⊃ I
    3. P   / I
    4. P ∨ L   3, Add
    5. L ∨ P   4, Com
    6. U   1, 5, MP
    7. U ∨ ~M   6, Add
    8. ~M ∨ U   7, Com
    9. M ⊃ U   8, Impl
   10. I   2, 9, MP

(40) 1. A ≡ W
    2. ~A ∨ ~W
    3. R ⊃ A   / ~(W ∨ R)
    4. (A • W) ∨ (~A • ~W)   1, Equiv
    5. ~(A • W)   2, DM
    6. ~A • ~W   4, 5, DS
    7. ~A   6, Simp
    8. ~R   3, 7, MT
    9. ~W • ~A   6, Com
   10. ~W   9, Simp
   11. ~W • ~R   8, 10, Conj
   12. ~(W ∨ R)   11, DM

(41) 1. (S ∨ T) ⊃ (S ⊃ ~T)
    2. (S ⊃ ~T) ⊃ (T ⊃ K)
    3. S ∨ T   / S ∨ K
    4. S ⊃ ~T   1, 3, MP
    5. T ⊃ K   2, 4, MP
    6. ~~S ∨ T   3, DN
    7. ~S ⊃ T   6, Impl
    8. ~S ⊃ K   5, 7, HS
    9. ~~S ∨ K   8, Impl
   10. S ∨ K   9, DN

(42) 1. G ≡ M
    2. G ∨ M
    3. G ⊃ (M ⊃ T)   / T
    4. (G • M) ∨ (~G • ~M)   1, Equiv
    5. ~~G ∨ M   2, DN
    6. ~~G ∨ ~~M   5, DN
    7. ~(~G • ~M)   6, DM
    8. (~G • ~M) ∨ (G • M)   4, Com
    9. G • M   7, 8, DS

    10. (G • M) ⊃ T   3, Exp
    11. T   9, 10, MP

(43) 1. O ⊃ (Q • N)
     2. (N ∨ E) ⊃ S   / O ⊃ S
     3. ~O ∨ (Q • N)   1, Impl
     4. (~O ∨ Q) • (~O ∨ N)   3, Dist
     5. (~O ∨ N) • (~O ∨ Q)   4, Com
     6. ~O ∨ N   5, Simp
     7. O ⊃ N   6, Impl
     8. ~(N ∨ E) ∨ S   2, Impl
     9. (~N • ~E) ∨ S   8, DM
     10. S ∨ (~N • ~E)   9, Com
     11. (S ∨ ~N) • (S ∨ ~E)   10, Dist
     12. S ∨ ~N   11, Simp
     13. ~N ∨ S   12, Com
     14. N ⊃ S   13, Impl
     15. O ⊃ S   7, 14, HS

(44) 1. H ≡ I
     2. H ⊃ (I ⊃ F)
     3. ~(H ∨ I) ⊃ F   / F
     4. (H • I) ∨ (~H • ~I)   1, Equiv
     5. (H • I) ⊃ F   2, Exp
     6. (~H • ~I) ⊃ F   3, DM
     7. [(H • I) ⊃ F] • [(~H • ~I) ⊃ F]   5, 6, Conj
     8. F ∨ F   4, 7, CD
     9. F   8, Taut

(45) 1. P ⊃ A
     2. Q ⊃ B   / (P ∨ Q) ⊃ (A ∨ B)
     3. ~P ∨ A   1, Impl
     4. ~Q ∨ B   2, Impl
     5. (~P ∨ A) ∨ B   3, Add
     6. (~Q ∨ B) ∨ A   4, Add
     7. ~P ∨ (A ∨ B)   5, Assoc
     8. ~Q ∨ (B ∨ A)   6, Assoc
     9. ~Q ∨ (A ∨ B)   8, Com
     10. (A ∨ B) ∨ ~P   7, Com
     11. (A ∨ B) ∨ ~Q   8, Com
     12. [(A ∨ B) ∨ ~P] • [(A ∨ B) ∨ ~Q]   10, 11, Conj
     13. (A ∨ B) ∨ (~P • ~Q)   12, Dist
     14. (~P • ~Q) ∨ (A ∨ B)   13, Com
     15. ~(P ∨ Q) ∨ (A ∨ B)   14, DM
     16. (P ∨ Q) ⊃ (A ∨ B)   15 Impl

Part IV

(1) 1. D ⊃ C
    2. ~(C • ~S)   / D ⊃ S
    3. ~C ∨ ~~S   2, DM
    4. C ⊃ ~~S   3, Impl
    5. C ⊃ S   4, DN
    6. D ⊃ S   1, 5, HS

(2) 1. C ⊃ (D • M)
    2. ~M   / ~C
    3. ~M ∨ ~D   2, Add
    4. ~D ∨ ~M   3, Com
    5. ~(D • M)   4, DM
    6. ~C   1, 5, MP

(3) 1. ~(M ∨ S)   / S ⊃ U
    2. ~M • ~S   1, DM
    3. ~S • ~M   2, Com
    4. ~S   3, Simp
    5. ~S ∨ U   4, Add
    6. S ⊃ U   5, Impl

(4) 1. D ⊃ P   / (I • D) ⊃ P
    2. ~D ∨ P   1, Impl
    3. (~D ∨ P) ∨ ~I   2, Add
    4. ~I ∨ (~D ∨ P)   3, Com
    5. (~I ∨ ~D) ∨ P   4, Assoc
    6. ~(I • D) ∨ P   5, DM
    7. (I • D) ⊃ P   6, Impl

(5) 1. (E ∨ P) ⊃ U   / E ⊃ U
    2. ~(E ∨ P) ∨ U   1, Impl
    3. (~E • ~P) ∨ U   2, DM
    4. U ∨ (~E • ~P)   3, Com
    5. (U ∨ ~E) • (U ∨ ~P) 4, Dist
    6. U ∨ ~E   5, Simp
    7. ~E ∨ U   6, Com
    8. E ⊃ U   7, Impl

(6) 1. (W • C) ⊃ ~S
    2. W   / C ⊃ ~S
    3. W ⊃ (C ⊃ ~S)   1, Exp
    4. C ⊃ ~S   2, 3, MP

Exercise 7.4

(7) 1. G ⊃ A
     2. G ⊃ L   / G ⊃ (A • L)
     3. ~G ∨ A   1, Impl
     4. ~G ∨ L   2, Impl
     5. (~G ∨ A) • (~G ∨ L)   3, 4, Conj
     6. ~G ∨ (A • L)   5, Dist
     7. G ⊃ (A • L)   6, Impl

(8) 1. S ⊃ (D • I)
     2. S ∨ (U • D)   / D
     3. ~S ∨ (D • I)   1, Impl
     4. (~S ∨ D) • (~S ∨ I)   3, Dist
     5. ~S ∨ D   4, Simp
     6. S ⊃ D   5, Impl
     7. (S ∨ U) • (S ∨ D)   2, Dist
     8. (S ∨ D) • (S ∨ U)   7, Com
     9. S ∨ D   8, Simp
    10. ~~S ∨ D   9, DN
    11. ~S ⊃ D   10, Impl
    12. ~D ⊃ ~S   6, Trans
    13. ~D ⊃ D   11, 12, HS
    14. ~~D ∨ D   13, Impl
    15. D ∨ D   14, DN
    16. D   15, Taut

(9) 1. T ⊃ (G ⊃ R)   / ~R ⊃ (G ⊃ ~T)
     2. ~T ∨ (G ⊃ R)   1, Impl
     3. ~T ∨ (~G ∨ R)   2, Impl
     4. (~T ∨ ~G) ∨ R   3, Assoc
     5. R ∨ (~T ∨ ~G)   4, Com
     6. R ∨ (~G ∨ ~T)   5, Com
     7. ~~R ∨ (~G ∨ ~T)   6, DN
     8. ~R ⊃ (~G ∨ ~T)   7, Impl
     9. ~R ⊃ (G ⊃ ~T)   8, Impl

(10) 1. (A • U) ≡ ~R
     2. ~(~R ∨ ~A)   / ~U
     3. [(A • U) ⊃ ~R] • [~R ⊃ (A • U)] 1, Equiv
     4. (A • U) ⊃ ~R   3, Simp
     5. ~~R • ~~A   2, DM
     6. ~~R   5, Simp
     7. ~(A • U)   4, 6, MT
     8. ~A ∨ ~U   7, DM
     9. ~~A • ~~R   5, Com

10. ~~A	9, Simp
11. ~U	8, 10, DS

Exercise 7.5
Part I

(1) 1. N ⊃ O
    2. N ⊃ P   / N ⊃ (O • P)
       3. N   ACP
       4. O   1, 3, MP
       5. P   2, 3, MP
       6. O • P   4, 5, Conj
    7. N ⊃ (O • P)   3-6, CP

(2) 1. F ⊃ E
    2. (F • E) ⊃ R   / F ⊃ R
       3. F   ACP
       4. E   1, 3, MP
       5. F • E   3, 4, Conj
       6. R   2, 5, MP
    7. F ⊃ R   3-6, CP

(3) 1. G ⊃ T
    2. (T ∨ S) ⊃ K   / G ⊃ K
       3. G   ACP
       4. T   1, 3, MP
       5. T ∨ S   4, Add
       6. K   2, 5, MP
    7. G ⊃ K   3-6, CP

(4) 1. (G ∨ H) ⊃ (S • T)
    2. (T ∨ U) ⊃ (C • D)   / G ⊃ C
       3. G   ACP
       4. G ∨ H   3, Add
       5. S • T   1, 4, MP
       6. T • S   5, Com
       7. T   6, Simp
       8. T ∨ U   7, Add
       9. C • D   2, 8, MP
      10. C   9, Simp
    11. G ⊃ C   3-10, CP

(5) 1. A ⊃ ~(A ∨ E)   / A ⊃ F
    2. A   ACP
    3. ~(A ∨ E)   1, 2, MP
    4. ~A • ~E   3, DM
    5. ~A   4, Simp

6. A ∨ F	2, Add
7. F	5, 6, DS
8. A ⊃ F	2-7, CP

(6) 1. J ⊃ (K ⊃ L)
    2. J ⊃ (M ⊃ L)

3. ~L	/ J ⊃ ~(K ∨ M)
4. J	ACP
5. K ⊃ L	1, 4, MP
6. M ⊃ L	2, 4, MP
7. ~K	3, 5, MT
8. ~M	3, 6, MT
9. ~K • ~M	7, 8, Conj
10. ~(K ∨ M)	9, DM
11. J ⊃ ~(K ∨ M)	4-10, CP

(7) 1. M ∨ (N • O)

	/ ~N ⊃ M
2. ~M	ACP
3. N • O	1, 2, DS
4. N	3, Simp
5. ~M ⊃ N	2-4, CP
6. ~M ⊃ ~~N	5, DN
7. ~N ⊃ M	6, Trans

(8) 1. P ⊃ (Q ∨ R)
    2. (P ⊃ R) ⊃ (S • T)

3. Q ⊃ R	/ T
4. P	ACP
5. Q ∨ R	1, 4, MP
6. R ∨ Q	5, Com
7. ~~R ∨ Q	6, DN
8. ~R ⊃ Q	7, Impl
9. ~R ⊃ R	3, 8, HS
10. ~~R ∨ R	9, Impl
11. R ∨ R	10, DN
12. R	11, Taut
13. P ⊃ R	4-12, CP
14. S • T	2, 13, MP
15. T • S	14, Com
16. T	14, Simp

(9) 1. H ⊃ (I ⊃ N)
    2. (H ⊃ ~I) ⊃ (M ∨ N)

3. ~N	/ M
4. H	ACP
5. I ⊃ N	1, 4, MP

      6. ~I   3, 5, MT
      7. H ⊃ ~I   4-6, CP
      8. M ∨ N   2, 7, MP
      9. N ∨ M   8, Com
   10. M   3, 9, DS

(10) 1. C ⊃ (A • D)
     2. B ⊃ (A • E)   / (C ∨ B) ⊃ A
       3. C ∨ B   ACP
       4. [C ⊃ (A • D)] • [B ⊃ (A • E)]   1, 2, Conj
       5. (A • D) ∨ (A • E)   3, 4, CD
       6. A • (D ∨ E)   5, Dist
       7. A   6, Simp
      8. (C ∨ B) ⊃ A   3-7, CP

(11) 1. M ⊃ (K ⊃ L)
     2. (L ∨ N) ⊃ J   / M ⊃ (K ⊃ J)
       3. M   ACP
         4. K   ACP
         5. K ⊃ L   1, 3, MP
         6. L   4, 5, MP
         7. L ∨ N   6, Add
         8. J   2, 7, MP
       9. K ⊃ J   4-8, CP
   10. M ⊃ (K ⊃ J)   3-9, CP

(12) 1. F ⊃ (G • H)   / (A ⊃ F) ⊃ (A ⊃ H)
       2. A ⊃ F   ACP
         3. A   ACP
         4. F   2, 3, MP
         5. G • H   1, 4, MP
         6. H • G   5, Com
         7. H   6, Simp
       8. A ⊃ H   3-7, CP
      9. (A ⊃ F) ⊃ (A ⊃ H)   2-8, CP

(13) 1. R ⊃ B
     2. R ⊃ (B ⊃ F)
     3. B ⊃ (F ⊃ H)   / R ⊃ H
       4. R   ACP
       5. B   1, 4, MP
       6. B ⊃ F   2, 4, MP
       7. F   5, 6, MP
       8. F ⊃ H   3, 5, MP
       9. H   7, 8, MP
   10. R ⊃ H   4-9, CP

Exercise 7.5

(14) 1. $(F \cdot G) \equiv H$
  2. $F \supset G$ $/ F \equiv H$
  3. $[(F \cdot G) \supset H] \cdot [H \supset (F \cdot G)]$ 1, Equiv
    4. F   ACP
    5. G   2, 4, MP
    6. $F \cdot G$ 4, 5, Conj
    7. $(F \cdot G) \supset H$ 3, Simp
    8. H   6, 7, MP
  9. $F \supset H$ 4-8, CP
    10. H   ACP
    11. $[H \supset (F \cdot G)] \cdot [(F \cdot G) \supset H]$ 3, Com
    12. $H \supset (F \cdot G)$ 11, Simp
    13. $F \cdot G$ 10, 12, MP
    14. F   13, Simp
  15. $H \supset F$ 10-14, CP
  16. $(F \supset H) \cdot (H \supset F)$ 9, 15, Conj
  17. $F \equiv H$ 16, Equiv

(15) 1. $C \supset (D \vee {\sim}E)$
  2. $E \supset (D \supset F)$ $/ C \supset (E \supset F)$
    3. C   ACP
      4. E   ACP
      5. $D \vee {\sim}E$ 1, 3, MP
      6. ${\sim}E \vee D$ 5, Com
      7. ${\sim}{\sim}E$ 4, DN
      8. D   6, 7, DS
      9. $D \supset F$ 2, 4, MP
      10. F   8, 9, MP
    11. $E \supset F$ 4-10, CP
  12. $C \supset (E \supset F)$ 3-11, CP

(16) 1. $Q \supset (R \supset S)$
  2. $Q \supset (T \supset {\sim}U)$
  3. $U \supset (R \vee T)$ $/ Q \supset (U \supset S)$
    4. Q   ACP
      5. U   ACP
      6. $R \supset S$ 1, 4, MP
      7. $T \supset {\sim}U$ 2, 4, MP
      8. ${\sim}{\sim}U$ 5, DN
      9. ${\sim}T$ 7, 8, MT
      10. $R \vee T$ 3, 5, MP
      11. $T \vee R$ 10, Com
      12. R   9, 11, DS
      13. S   6, 12, MP
    14. $U \supset S$ 5-13, CP
  15. $Q \supset (U \supset S)$ 4-14, CP

(17) 1. N ⊃ (O • P)
  2. Q ⊃ (R • S)   / (P ⊃ Q) ⊃ (N ⊃ S)
    3. P ⊃ Q   ACP
      4. N   ACP
        5. O • P   1, 4, MP
        6. P • O   5, Com
        7. P   6, Simp
        8. Q   3, 7, MP
        9. R • S   2, 8, MP
        10. S • R   9, Com
        11. S   10, Simp
      12. N ⊃ S   4-11, CP
  13. (P ⊃ Q) ⊃ (N ⊃ S) 3-12, CP

(18) 1. E ⊃ (F ⊃ G)
  2. H ⊃ (G ⊃ I)
    3. (F ⊃ I) ⊃ (J ∨ ~H)   / (E • H) ⊃ J
      4. E • H   ACP
      5. E   4, Simp
      6. F ⊃ G   1, 5, MP
      7. H • E   4, Com
      8. H   7, Simp
      9. G ⊃ I   2, 8, MP
      10. F ⊃ I   6, 9, HS
      11. J ∨ ~H   3, 10, MP
      12. ~H ∨ J   11, Com
      13. ~~H   8, DN
      14. J   12, 13, DS
  15. (E • H) ⊃ J   4-14, CP

(19) 1. P ⊃ [(L ∨ M) ⊃ (N • O)]
  2. (O ∨ T) ⊃ W   / P ⊃ (M ⊃ W)
    3. P   ACP
      4. M   ACP
        5. (L ∨ M) ⊃ (N • O)   1, 3, MP
        6. M ∨ L   4, Add
        7. L ∨ M   6, Com
        8. N • O   5, 7, MP
        9. O • N   8, Com
        10. O   9, Simp
        11. O ∨ T   10, Add
        12. W   2, 11, MP
      13. M ⊃ W   4-12, CP
  14. P ⊃ (M ⊃ W)   3-13, CP

Exercise 7.5

(20) 1. A ⊃ [B ⊃ (C • ~D)]
    2. (B ∨ E) ⊃ (D ∨ E)   / (A • B) ⊃ (C • E)
      3. A • B   ACP
      4. A   3, Simp
      5. B ⊃ (C • D)   1, 4, MP
      6. B • A   3, Com
      7. B   6, Simp
      8. C • ~D   5, 7, MP
      9. C   8, Simp
    10. ~D • C   8, Com
    11. ~D   10, Simp
    12. B ∨ E   7, Add
    13. D ∨ E   2, 12, MP
    14. E   11, 13, DS
    15. C • E   9, 14, Conj
  16. (A • B) ⊃ (C • E)   3-15, CP

Part II

(1) 1. H ⊃ D
    2. U ⊃ S   / (H • U) ⊃ (S • D)
      3. H • U   ACP
      4. H   3, Simp
      5. D   1, 4, MP
      6. U • H   3, Com
      7. U   6, Simp
      8. S   2, 7, MP
      9. S • D   5, 8, Conj
  10. (H • U) ⊃ (S • D)   3-9, CP

(2) 1. P ⊃ (I ⊃ W)
    2. I ⊃ (W ⊃ ~S)   / P ⊃ (I ⊃ ~S)
      3. P   ACP
         4. I   ACP
         5. I ⊃ W   1, 3, MP
         6. W ⊃ ~S   2, 4, MP
         7. I ⊃ ~S   5, 6, HS
         8. ~S   4, 7, MP
      9. I ⊃ ~S   4-8, CP
  10. P ⊃ (I ⊃ ~S)   3-9, CP

(3) 1. D ≡ (S ⊃ F)
    2. R ⊃ (D • P)
    3. S   / R ⊃ F
      4. R   ACP

5. D • P	2, 4, MP
6. D	5, Simp
7. [D ⊃ (S ⊃ F)] • [(S ⊃ F) ⊃ D]	1, Equiv
8. D ⊃ (S ⊃ F)	7, Simp
9. S ⊃ F	6, 8, MP
10. F	3, 9, MP
11. R ⊃ F	4-10, CP

(4)
1. J ⊃ D		
2. (J • D) ⊃ C		
3. (N • C) ⊃ I	/ J ⊃ (N ⊃ I)	
4. J	ACP	
5. N	ACP	
6. D	1, 4, MP	
7. J • D	4, 6, Conj	
8. C	2, 7, MP	
9. N • C	5, 8, Conj	
10. I	3, 9, MP	
11. N ⊃ I	5-10, CP	
12. J ⊃ (N ⊃ I)	4-11, CP	

(5)
1. A ⊃ H	
2. (F ∨ W) ⊃ L	/ (H ⊃ F) ⊃ (A ⊃ L)
3. H ⊃ F	ACP
4. A	ACP
5. H	1, 4, MP
6. F	3, 5, MP
7. F ∨ W	6, Add
8. L	2, 7, MP
9. A ⊃ L	4-8, CP
10. (H ⊃ F) ⊃ (A ⊃ L)	3-9, CP

Exercise 7.6
Part I

(1)
1. (S ∨ T) ⊃ ~S	/ ~S
2. S	AIP
3. S ∨ T	2, Add
4. ~S	1, 3, MP
5. S • ~S	2, 4, Conj
6. ~S	2-5, IP

(2)
1. (K ⊃ K) ⊃ R	
2. (R ∨ M) ⊃ N	/ N
3. ~N	AIP

157

4.	~(R ∨ M)	2, 3, MT
5.	~R • ~M	4, DM
6.	~R	5, Simp
7.	~(K ⊃ K)	1, 6, MT
8.	~(~K ∨ K)	7, Impl
9.	~~K • ~K	8, DM
10.	K • ~K	9, DN
11.	~~N	3-10, IP
12.	N	11, DN

(3)
1.	(C • D) ⊃ E	
2.	(D • E) ⊃ F	/ (C • D) ⊃ F
3.	C • D	ACP
4.	E	1, 3, MP
5.	D • C	3, Com
6.	D	5, Simp
7.	D • E	4, 6, Conj
8.	F	2, 7, MP
9.	(C • D) ⊃ F	3-8, CP

(4)
1.	H ⊃ (L ⊃ K)	
2.	L ⊃ (K ⊃ ~L)	/ ~H ∨ ~L
3.	H • L	AIP
4.	H	3 Simp
5.	L ⊃ K	1, 4, MP
6.	L • H	3, Com
7.	L	6, Simp
8.	K ⊃ ~L	2, 7, MP
9.	K	5, 7, MP
10.	~L	8, 9, MP
11.	L • ~L	7, 10, Conj
12.	~(H • L)	3-11, IP
13.	~H ∨ ~L	12, DM

(5)
1.	S ⊃ (T ∨ ~U)	
2.	U ⊃ (~T ∨ R)	
3.	(S • U) ⊃ ~R	/ ~S ∨ ~U
4.	~(~S ∨ ~U)	AIP
5.	~~S • ~~U	4, DM
6.	S • ~~U	5, DN
7.	S • U	6, DN
8.	~R	3, 7, MP
9.	S	7, Simp
10.	U • S	7, Com
11.	U	10, Simp
12.	T ∨ ~U	1, 9, MP

13. ~T ∨ R	2, 11, MP
14. R ∨ ~T	13, Com
15. ~T	8, 14, DS
16. ~U	12, 15, DS
17. U • ~U	11, 16, Conj
18. ~~(~S ∨ ~U)	4-17, IP
19. ~S ∨ ~U	18, DN

(6) 1. ~A ⊃ (B • C)

2. D ⊃ ~C	/ D ⊃ A
3. D	ACP
4. ~C	2, 3, MP
5. ~C ∨ ~B	4, Add
6. ~B ∨ ~C	5, Com
7. ~(B • C)	6, DM
8. ~~A	1, 7, MT
9. A	8, DN
10. D ⊃ A	3-9, CP

(7) 1. (E ∨ F) ⊃ (C • D)

2. (D ∨ G) ⊃ H	
3. E ∨ G	/ H
4. ~H	AIP
5. ~(D ∨ G)	2, 4, MT
6. ~D • ~G	5, DM
7. ~D	6, Simp
8. ~D ∨ ~C	7, Add
9. ~C ∨ ~D	8, Com
10. ~(C • D)	9, DM
11. ~(E ∨ F)	1, 10, MT
12. ~E • ~F	11, DM
13. ~E	12, Simp
14. G	3, 13, DS
15. ~G • ~D	6, Com
16. ~G	15, Simp
17. G • ~G	14, 16, Conj
18. ~~H	4-17, IP
19. H	18, DN

(8) 1. ~M ⊃ (N • O)

2. N ⊃ P	
3. O ⊃ ~P	/ M
4. ~M	AIP
5. N • O	1, 4, MP
6. N	5, Simp

159

Exercise 7.6

7. P	2, 6, MP
8. O • N	5, Com
9. O	8, Simp
10. ~P	3, 9, MP
11. P • ~P	7, 10, Conj
12. ~~M	4-11, IP
13. M	12, DN

(9)
1. (R ∨ S) ⊃ T	
2. (P ∨ Q) ⊃ T	
3. R ∨ P	/ T
4. R	ACP
5. R ∨ S	4, Add
6. T	1, 5, MP
7. R ⊃ T	4-6, CP
8. P	ACP
9. P ∨ Q	8, Add
10. T	2, 9, MP
11. P ⊃ T	8-10, CP
12. (R ⊃ T) • (P ⊃ T)	7, 11, Conj
13. T ∨ T	3, 12, CD
14. T	13, Taut

(10)
1. K	/ S ⊃ (T ⊃ S)
2. S	ACP
3. S ∨ ~T	2, Add
4. ~T ∨ S	3, Com
5. T ⊃ S	4, Impl
6. S ⊃ (T ⊃ S)	2-5, CP

(11)
1. (A ∨ B) ⊃ C	
2. (~A ∨ D) ⊃ E	/ C ∨ E
3. ~C	ACP
4. ~(A ∨ B)	1, 3, MT
5. ~A • ~B	4, DM
6. ~A	5, Simp
7. ~A ∨ D	6, Add
8. E	2, 7, MP
9. ~C ⊃ E	3-8, CP
10. ~~C ∨ E	9, Impl
11. C ∨ E	10, DN

(12)
1. (K ∨ L) ⊃ (M • N)	
2. (N ∨ O) ⊃ (P • ~K)	/ ~K
3. K	AIP
4. K ∨ L	3, Add

160

	5. M • N	1, 4, MP
	6. N • M	5, Com
	7. N	6, Simp
	8. N ∨ O	7, Add
	9. P • ~K	2, 8, MP
	10. ~K • P	9, Com
	11. ~K	10, Simp
	12. K • ~K	3, 11, Conj
13. ~K		3-12, IP

(13)	1. [C ⊃ (D ⊃ C)] ⊃ E	/ E
	2. C	ACP
	3. C ∨ ~D	2, Add
	4. ~D ∨ C	3, Com
	5. D ⊃ C	4, Impl
	6. C ⊃ (D ⊃ C)	2-5, CP
	7. E	1, 6, MP

(14)	1. F	/ (G ⊃ H) ∨ (~G ⊃ J)
	2. G • ~H	ACP
	3. G	2, Simp
	4. G ∨ J	3, Add
	5. ~~G ∨ J	4, DN
	6. ~G ⊃ J	5, Impl
	7. (G • ~H) ⊃ (~G ⊃ J)	2-6, CP
	8. ~(G • ~H) ∨ (~G ⊃ J)	7, Impl
	9. (~G ∨ ~~H) ∨ (~G ⊃ J)	8, DM
	10. (~G ∨ H) ∨ (~G ⊃ J)	9, DN
	11. (G ⊃ H) ∨ (~G ⊃ J)	10, Impl

(15)	1. B ⊃ (K • M)	
	2. (B • M) ⊃ (P ≡ ~P)	/ ~B
	3. B	AIP
	4. K • M	1, 3, MP
	5. M • K	4, Com
	6. M	5, Simp
	7. B • M	3, 6, Conj
	8. P ≡ ~P	2, 7, MP
	9. (P • ~P) ∨ (~P • ~~P)	8, Equiv
	10. (P • ~P) ∨ (~P • P)	9, DN
	11. (P • ~P) ∨ (P • ~P)	10, Com
	12. P • ~P	11, Taut
13. ~B		3-12, IP

Exercise 7.6

(16) 1. $(N \lor O) \supset (C \cdot D)$
   2. $(D \lor K) \supset (P \lor \sim C)$
   3. $(P \lor G) \supset \sim(N \cdot D)$ / $\sim N$
     4. N AIP
     5. $N \lor O$ 4, Add
     6. $C \cdot D$ 1, 5, MP
     7. $D \cdot C$ 6, Com
     8. D 7, Simp
     9. $D \lor K$ 8, Add
     10. $P \lor \sim C$ 2, 9, MP
     11. C 6, Simp
     12. $\sim\sim C$ 11, DN
     13. $\sim C \lor P$ 10, Com
     14. P 12, 13, DS
     15. $P \lor G$ 14, Add
     16. $\sim(N \cdot D)$ 3, 15, MP
     17. $\sim N \lor \sim D$ 16, DM
     18. $\sim\sim N$ 4, DN
     19. $\sim D$ 17, 18, DS
     20. $D \cdot \sim D$ 8, 19, Conj
   21. $\sim N$ 4-20, IP

(17) 1. $(R \cdot S) \equiv (G \cdot H)$
   2. $R \supset S$
   3. $H \supset G$ / $R \equiv H$
   4. $[(R \cdot S) \supset (G \cdot H)] \cdot [(G \cdot H) \supset (R \cdot S)]$ 1, Equiv
     5. R ACP
     6. S 2, 5, MP
     7. $R \cdot S$ 5, 6, Conj
     8. $(R \cdot S) \supset (G \cdot H)$ 4, Simp
     9. $G \cdot H$ 7, 8, MP
     10. $H \cdot G$ 9, Com
     11. H 10, Simp
   12. $R \supset H$ 5-11, CP
     13. H ACP
     14. G 3, 13, MP
     15. $G \cdot H$ 13, 14, Conj
     16. $[(G \cdot H) \supset (R \cdot S)] \cdot [(R \cdot S) \supset (G \cdot H)]$ 4, Com
     17. $(G \cdot H) \supset (R \cdot S)$ 16, Simp
     18. $R \cdot S$ 15, 17, MP
     19. R 18, Simp
   20. $H \supset R$ 13-19, CP
   21. $(R \supset H) \cdot (H \supset R)$ 12, 20, Conj
   22. $R \equiv H$ 21, Equiv

(18) 1. K ⊃ [(M ∨ N) ⊃ (P • Q)]
  2. L ⊃ [(Q ∨ R) ⊃ (S • ~N)] / (K • L) ⊃ ~N
   3. K • L   ACP
   4. K   3, Simp
   5. (M ∨ N) ⊃ (P • Q) 1, 4, MP
   6. L • K   3, Com
   7. L   6, Simp
   8. (Q ∨ R) ⊃ (S • ~N) 2, 7, MP
    9. N   AIP
    10. N ∨ M   9, Add
    11. M ∨ N   10, Com
    12. P • Q   5, 11, MP
    13. Q • P   12, Com
    14. Q   13, Simp
    15. Q ∨ R   14, Add
    16. S • ~N   8, 15, MP
    17. ~N • S   16, Com
    18. ~N   17, Simp
    19. N • ~N   9, 18, Conj
   20. ~N   9-19, IP
  21. (K • L) ⊃ ~N   3-20, CP

(19) 1. A ⊃ [(N ∨ ~N) ⊃ (S ∨ T)]
  2. T ⊃ ~(F ∨ ~F)   / A ⊃ S
   3. A • ~S   AIP
   4. A   3, Simp
   5. (N ∨ ~N) ⊃ (S ∨ T) 1, 4, MP
    6. N   ACP
    7. N ∨ N   6, Add
    8. N   7, Taut
   9. N ⊃ N   6-8, CP
   10. ~N ∨ N   9, Impl
   11. N ∨ ~N   10, Com
   12. S ∨ T   5, 11, MP
   13. ~S • A   3, Com
   14. ~S   13, Simp
   15. T   12, 14, DS
   16. ~(F ∨ ~F)   2, 15, MP
   17. ~F • ~~F   16, DM
  18. ~(A • ~S)   3-17, IP
  19. ~A ∨ ~~S   18, DM
  20. ~A ∨ S   19, DN
  21. A ⊃ S   20, Impl

Exercise 7.6

(20) 1. F ⊃ [(C ⊃ C) ⊃ G]
       2. G ⊃ {[H ⊃ (E ⊃ H)] ⊃ (K • ~K)}   / ~F
          3. F   AIP
          4. (C ⊃ C) ⊃ G   1, 3, MP
             5. C   ACP
                6. C ∨ C   5, Add
                7. C   6, Taut
             8. C ⊃ C   5-7, CP
          9. G   4, 8, MP
          10. [H ⊃ (E ⊃ H)] ⊃ (K • ~K)   2, 9, MP
             11. H   ACP
                12. H ∨ ~E   11, Add
                13. ~E ∨ H   12, Com
                14. E ⊃ H   13, Impl
             15. H ⊃ (E ⊃ H)   11-14, CP
          16. K • ~K   10, 15, MP
       17. ~F   3-16, IP

Part II

(1) 1. (C • R) ⊃ (I • D)
      2. R ⊃ ~D   / ~C ∨ ~R
         3. C • R   AIP
         4. I • D   1, 3, MP
         5. D • I   4, Com
         6. D   5, Simp
         7. R • C   3, Com
         8. R   7, Simp
         9. ~D   2, 8, MP
         10. D • ~D   6, 9, Conj
      11. ~(C • R)   3-10, IP
      12. ~C ∨ ~R   11, DM

(2) 1. (C ∨ R) ⊃ (N • I)
      2. (N ∨ P) ⊃ (I ⊃ ~C)   / ~C
         3. C   AIP
         4. C ∨ R   3, Add
         5. N • I   1, 4, MP
         6. N   5, Simp
         7. N ∨ P   6, Add
         8. I ⊃ ~C   2, 7, MP
         9. I • N   5, Com
         10. I   9, Simp
         11. ~C   8, 10, MP
         12. C • ~C   3, 11, Conj
      13. ~C   3-12, IP

164

(3)　1. S ⊃ (P ⊃ B)
　　　2. S ⊃ P
　　　3. C ⊃ (S ∨ B)　　　　　/ ~C ∨ B
　　　　　4. C • ~B　　　　　AIP
　　　　　5. C　　　　　　　　4, Simp
　　　　　6. S ∨ B　　　　　　3, 5, MP
　　　　　7. B ∨ S　　　　　　6, Com
　　　　　8. ~B • C　　　　　4, Com
　　　　　9. ~B　　　　　　　8, Simp
　　　　10. S　　　　　　　　7, 9, DS
　　　　11. P ⊃ B　　　　　1, 10, MP
　　　　12. S ⊃ B　　　　　2, 11, HS
　　　　13. B　　　　　　　10, 12, MP
　　　　14. B • ~B　　　　9, 13, Conj
　　　15. ~(C • ~B)　　　4-14, IP
　　　16. ~C ∨ ~~B　　　15, DM
　　　17. ~C ∨ B　　　　16, DN

(4)　1. (Z ⊃ C) ⊃ B
　　　2. (V ⊃ Z) ⊃ B　　　　/ B
　　　　　3. ~B　　　　　　　AIP
　　　　　4. ~(Z ⊃ C)　　　1, 3, MT
　　　　　5. ~(~Z ∨ C)　　　4, Impl
　　　　　6. ~~Z • ~C　　　5, DM
　　　　　7. ~~Z　　　　　　6, Simp
　　　　　8. ~(V ⊃ Z)　　　2, 3, MT
　　　　　9. ~(~V ∨ Z)　　　8, Impl
　　　　10. ~~V • ~Z　　　9, DM
　　　　11. ~Z • ~~V　　　10, Com
　　　　12. ~Z　　　　　　　11, Simp
　　　　13. ~Z • ~~Z　　　7, 12, Conj
　　　14. ~~B　　　　　　　3-13, IP
　　　15. B　　　　　　　　14, DN

(5)　1. (B • S) ∨ (H • C)
　　　2. (P ∨ H) ⊃ S　　　　/ S
　　　　　3. ~S　　　　　　　AIP
　　　　　4. ~(P ∨ H)　　　2, 3, MT
　　　　　5. ~P • ~H　　　4, DM
　　　　　6. ~H • ~P　　　5, Com
　　　　　7. ~H　　　　　　6, Simp
　　　　　8. ~H ∨ ~C　　　7, Add
　　　　　9. ~(H • C)　　　8, DM
　　　　10. (H • C) ∨ (B • S)　1, Com

Exercise 7.7

11. B • S	9, 10, DS
12. S • B	11, Com
13. S	12, Simp
14. S • ~S	3, 13, Conj
15. ~~S	3-14, IP
16. S	15, DN

Exercise 7.7

(1)   / P ⊃ [(P ⊃ Q) ⊃ Q]

1. P	ACP
2. P ⊃ Q	ACP
3. Q	1, 2, MP
4. (P ⊃ Q) ⊃ Q	2-3, CP
5. P ⊃ [(P ⊃ Q) ⊃ Q]	1-4, CP

(2)   / (~P ⊃ Q) ∨ (P ⊃ R)

1. ~[(~P ⊃ Q) ∨ (P ⊃ R)]	AIP
2. ~(~P ⊃ Q) • ~(P ⊃ R)	1, DM
3. ~(~P ⊃ Q)	2, Simp
4. ~(~~P ∨ Q)	3, Impl
5. ~(P ∨ Q)	4, DN
6. ~P • ~Q	5, DM
7. ~P	6, Simp
8. ~(P ⊃ R) • ~(~P ⊃ Q)	2, Com
9. ~(P ⊃ R)	8, Simp
10. ~(~P ∨ R)	9, Impl
11. ~~P • ~R	10, DM
12. ~~P	11, Simp
13. ~P • ~~P	7, 12, Conj
14. ~~[(~P ⊃ Q) ∨ (P ⊃ R)]	1-13, IP
15. (~P ⊃ Q) ∨ (P ⊃ R)	14, DN

(3)   / P ≡ [P ∨ (Q • P)]

1. P	ACP
2. P ∨ (Q • P)	1, Add
3. P ⊃ [P ∨ (Q • P)]	1-2, CP
4. P ∨ (Q • P)	ACP
5. (P ∨ Q) • (P ∨ P)	4, Dist
6. (P ∨ P) • (P ∨ Q)	5, Com
7. P ∨ P	6, Simp
8. P	7, Taut
9. [P ∨ (Q • P)] ⊃ P	4-7, CP
10. {line 3} • {line 9}	3, 9, Conj
11. P ≡ [P ∨ (Q • P)]	10, Equiv

166

(4)   / (P ⊃ Q) ⊃ [(P • R) ⊃ (Q • R)]

1. P ⊃ Q   ACP
2. P • R   ACP
3. P   2, Simp
4. Q   1, 3, MP
5. R • P   2, Com
6. R   5, Simp
7. Q • R   4, 6, Conj
8. (P • R) ⊃ (Q • R)   2-7, CP
9. (P ⊃ Q) ⊃ [(P • R) ⊃ (Q • R)]   1-8, CP

(5)   / (P ∨ ~Q) ⊃ [(~P ∨ R) ⊃ (Q ⊃ R)]

1. P ∨ ~Q   ACP
2. ~P ∨ R   ACP
3. ~Q ∨ P   1, Com
4. Q ⊃ P   3, Impl
5. P ⊃ R   2, Impl
6. Q ⊃ R   4, 5, HS
7. (~P ∨ R) ⊃ (Q ⊃ R)   2-6, CP
8. (P ∨ ~Q) ⊃ [(~P ∨ R) ⊃ (Q ⊃ R)]   1-7, CP

(6)   / P ≡ [P • (Q ∨ ~Q)]

1. P   ACP
2. Q   ACP
3. Q ∨ Q   2, Add
4. Q   3, Taut
5. Q ⊃ Q   2-4, CP
6. ~Q ∨ Q   5, Impl
7. Q ∨ ~Q   6, Com
8. P • (Q ∨ ~Q)   1, 7, Conj
9. P ⊃ [P • (Q ∨ ~Q)]   1-8, CP
10. P • (Q ∨ ~Q)   ACP
11. P   10, Simp
12. [P • (Q ∨ ~Q)] ⊃ P   10-11, CP
13. {line 9} • {line 12}   9, 12, Conj
14. P ≡ [P • (Q ∨ ~Q)]   13, Equiv

(7)   / (P ⊃ Q) ∨ (~Q ⊃ P)]

1. ~[(P ⊃ Q) ∨ (~Q ⊃ P)]   AIP
2. ~(P ⊃ Q) • ~(~Q ⊃ P)   1, DM
3. ~(P ⊃ Q)   2, Simp
4. ~(~P ∨ Q)   3, Impl
5. ~~P • ~Q   4, DM
6. ~~P   5, Simp
7. ~(~Q ⊃ P) • ~(P ⊃ Q)   2, Com

Exercise 7.7

8. ~(~Q ⊃ P)		7, Simp
9. ~(~~Q ∨ P)		8, Impl
10. ~(Q ∨ P)		9, DN
11. ~Q • ~P		10, DM
12. ~P • ~Q		11, Com
13. ~P		12, Simp
14. ~P • ~~P		6, 13, Conj
15. ~~[(P ⊃ Q) ∨ (~Q ⊃ P)]		1-14, IP
16. (P ⊃ Q) ∨ (~Q ⊃ P)		15, DN

(8)   / (P ⊃ Q) ≡ [P ⊃ (P • Q)]

1. P ⊃ Q		ACP
2. P		ACP
3. Q		1, 2, MP
4. P • Q		2, 3, Conj
5. P ⊃ (P • Q)		2-4, CP
6. (P ⊃ Q) ⊃ [P ⊃ (P • Q)]		1-5, CP
7. P ⊃ (P • Q)		ACP
8. P		ACP
9. P • Q		7, 8, MP
10. Q • P		9, Com
11. Q		10, Simp
12. P ⊃ Q		8-11, CP
13. [P ⊃ (P • Q)] ⊃ (P ⊃ Q)		7-12, CP
14. {line 6]} • {line 13}		6, 13, Conj
15. (P ⊃ Q) ≡ [P ⊃ (P • Q)]		14, Equiv

(9)   / [(P ⊃ Q) • (P ⊃ R)] ⊃ [P ⊃ (Q • R)]

1. (P ⊃ Q) • (P ⊃ R)		ACP
2. P		ACP
3. P ⊃ Q		1, Simp
4. Q		2, 3, MP
5. (P ⊃ R) • (P ⊃ Q)		1, Com
6. P ⊃ R		5, Simp
7. R		2, 6, MP
8. Q • R		4, 7, Conj
9. P ⊃ (Q • R)		2-8, CP
10. [(P ⊃ Q) • (P ⊃ R)] ⊃ [P ⊃ (Q • R)]		1-9, CP

(10)   / [~(P • ~Q) • ~Q] ⊃ ~P

1. ~(P • ~Q) • ~Q		ACP
2. ~(P • ~Q)		1, simp
3. ~P ∨ ~~Q		2, DM
4. ~P ∨ Q		3, DN
5. Q ∨ ~P		4, Com
6. ~Q • ~(P • ~Q)		1, Com

168

7. ~Q	6, Simp
8. ~P	5, 7, DS
9. [~(P • ~Q) • ~Q] ⊃ ~P	1-8, CP

(11)   / (P ⊃ Q) ∨ (Q ⊃ P)

1. ~[(P ⊃ Q) ∨ (Q ⊃ P)]	AIP
2. ~(P ⊃ Q) • ~(Q ⊃ P)	1, DM
3. ~(P ⊃ Q)	2, Simp
4. ~(~P ∨ Q)	3, Impl
5. ~~P • ~Q	4, DM
6. ~~P	5, Simp
7. ~(Q ⊃ P) • ~(P ⊃ Q)	2, Com
8. ~(Q ⊃ P)	7, Simp
9. ~(~Q ∨ P)	8, Impl
10. ~~Q • ~P	9, DM
11. ~P • ~~Q •	10, Com
12. ~P	11, Simp
13. ~P •~~P	6, 12, Conj
14. ~~[(P ⊃ Q) ∨ (Q ⊃ P)]	1-13, IP
15. (P ⊃ Q) ∨ (Q ⊃ P)	14, DN

(12)   / [P ⊃ (Q ⊃ R)] ≡ [Q ⊃ (P ⊃ R)]

1. P ⊃ (Q ⊃ R)	ACP
2. Q	ACP
3. P	ACP
4. Q ⊃ R	1, 3, MP
5. R	2, 4, MP
6. P ⊃ R	3-5, CP
7. Q ⊃ (P ⊃ R)	2-6, CP
8. [P ⊃ (Q ⊃ R)] ⊃ [Q ⊃ (P ⊃ R)]	1-7, CP
9. Q ⊃ (P ⊃ R)	ACP
10. P	ACP
11. Q	ACP
12. P ⊃ R	9, 11, MP
13. R	10, 12, MP
14. Q ⊃ R	11-13, CP
15. P ⊃ (Q ⊃ R)	10-14, CP
16. [Q ⊃ (P ⊃ R)] ⊃ [P ⊃ (Q ⊃ R)]	9-15, CP
17. {line 8} • {line 16}	8, 16, Conj
18. [P ⊃ (Q ⊃ R)] ≡ [Q ⊃ (P ⊃ R)]	17, Equiv

(13)   / (P ⊃ Q) ⊃ [(P ⊃ ~Q) ⊃ ~P]

1. P ⊃ Q	ACP
2. P ⊃ ~Q	ACP
3. ~~Q ⊃ ~P	2, Trans

169

4. Q ⊃ ~P	3, DN
5. P ⊃ ~P	1, 4, HS
6. ~P ∨ ~P	5, Impl
7. ~P	6, Taut
8. (P ⊃ ~Q) ⊃ ~P	2-7, CP
9. (P ⊃ Q) ⊃ [(P ⊃ ~Q) ⊃ ~P]	1-8, CP

(14) / [(P ⊃ Q) ⊃ R] ⊃ [(R ⊃ ~R) ⊃ P]

1. (P ⊃ Q) ⊃ R	ACP
2. R ⊃ ~R	ACP
3. ~R ∨ ~R	2, Impl
4. ~R	3, Taut
5. ~(P ⊃ Q)	1, 4, MT
6. ~(~P ∨ Q)	5, Impl
7. ~~P • ~Q	6, DM
8. ~~P	7 Simp
9. P	8, DN
10. (R ⊃ ~R) ⊃ P	2-9, CP
11. [(P ⊃ Q) ⊃ R] ⊃ [(R ⊃ ~R) ⊃ P]	1-10, CP

(15) / (~P ∨ Q) ⊃ [(P ∨ ~Q) ⊃ (P ≡ Q)]

1. ~P ∨ Q	ACP
2. P ∨ ~Q	ACP
3. P ⊃ Q	1, Impl
4. ~Q ∨ P	2, Com
5. Q ⊃ P	4, Impl
6. (P ⊃ Q) • (Q ⊃ P)	3, 5, Conj
7. P ≡ Q	6, Equiv
8. (P ∨ ~Q) ⊃ (P ≡ Q)	2-7, CP
9. (~P ∨ Q) ⊃ [(P ∨ ~Q) ⊃ (P ≡ Q)]	1-8, CP

(16) / ~[(P ⊃ ~P) • (~P ⊃ P)]

1. (P ⊃ ~P) • (~P ⊃ P)	AIP
2. (~P ∨ ~P) • (~P ⊃ P)	1, Impl
3. ~P • (~P ⊃ P)	2, Taut
4. ~P • (~~P ∨ P)	3, Impl
5. ~P • (P ∨ P)	4, DN
6. ~P • P	5, Taut
7. P • ~P	6, Com
8. ~[(P ⊃ ~P) • (~P ⊃ P)]	1-4, IP

(17) / P ⊃ [(Q • ~Q) ⊃ R]

1. P	ACP
2. Q • ~Q	ACP
3. Q	2, Simp

4. Q ∨ R	3, Add
5. ~Q • Q	2, Com
6. ~Q	5, Simp
7. R	4, 6, DS
8. (Q • ~Q) ⊃ R	2-7, CP
9. P ⊃ [(Q • ~Q) ⊃ R]	1-8, CP

(18)   / [(P • Q) ∨ R] ⊃ [(~R ∨ Q) ⊃ (P ⊃ Q)]

1. (P • Q) ∨ R	ACP
2. ~R ∨ Q	ACP
3. P	ACP
4. R ∨ (P • Q)	1, Com
5. (R ∨ P) • (R ∨ Q)	4, Dist
6. (R ∨ Q) • (R ∨ P)	5, Com
7. R ∨ Q	6, Simp
8. Q ∨ R	7, Com
9. ~~Q ∨ R	8, DN
10. ~Q ⊃ R	9, Impl
11. R ⊃ Q	2, Impl
12. ~Q ⊃ Q	10, 11, HS
13. ~~Q ∨ Q	12, Impl
14. Q ∨ Q	13, DN
15. Q	14, Taut
16. P ⊃ Q	3-15, CP
17. (~R ∨ Q) ⊃ (P ⊃ Q)	2-16, CP
18. [(P • Q) ∨ R] ⊃ [(~R ∨ Q) ⊃ (P ⊃ Q)]	1-17, CP

(19)   / P ≡ [P ∨ (Q • ~Q)]

1. P	ACP
2. P ∨ (Q • ~Q)	1, Add
3. P ⊃ [P ∨ (Q • ~Q)]	1-2, CP
4. P ∨ (Q • ~Q)	ACP
5. ~P	AIP
6. Q • ~Q	4, 5, DS
7. ~~P	5-6, IP
8. P	7, DN
9. [P ∨ (Q • ~Q)] ⊃ P	4-8, CP
10. {line 3} • {line 9}	3, 9, Conj
11. P ≡ [P ∨ (Q • ~Q)]	10, Equiv

(20)   / P ⊃ [Q ≡ (P ⊃ Q)]

1. P	ACP
2. Q	ACP
3. Q ∨ ~P	2, Add
4. ~P ∨ Q	3, Com

Exercise 8.1

5. P ⊃ Q		4, Impl
6. Q ⊃ (P ⊃ Q)		2-5, CP
7. P ⊃ Q		ACP
8. Q		1, 7, MP
9. (P ⊃ Q) ⊃ Q		7-8, CP
10. [Q ⊃ (P ⊃ Q)] • [(P ⊃ Q) ⊃ Q]		6, 9, Conj
11. Q ≡ (P ⊃ Q)		10, Equiv
12. P ⊃ [Q ≡ (P ⊃ Q)]		1-11, CP

Exercise 8.1

1. Ce

2. ~Sn

3. ~(Iw ∨ Is)

4. Jr ∨ Nr

5. Di ⊃ Dm

6. (Sb • Sf) ⊃ (Ea ∨ Eg)

7. (x)(Mx ⊃ Tx)

8. (∃x)(Gx • Sx)

9. (x)(Nx ⊃ ~Bx)

10. (∃x)(Hx • ~Rx)

11. Cg ⊃ Mt

12. ~Cg ⊃ Gt

13. (∃x)Tx

14. (x)(Lx ⊃ Wx)

15. (∃x)(Ax • Px)

16. (∃x)(Sx • ~Gx)

17. (x)(Px ⊃ Lx)

18. (∃x)(Tx • Rx)

172

19. (x)(Sx ⊃ Vx)

20. (x)[(Cx • Mx) ⊃ (Vx • Nx)]

21. (x)[Tx ⊃ ~(Rx ∨ Ex)]

22. (x)(Cx ⊃ ~Hx)

23. (x)Ix

24. (x)~Gx

25. (x)(Tx ⊃ Hx)

26. (∃x)(Tx • Wx)

27. (∃x)(Mx • ~Ex)

28. (x)(Hx ⊃ ~Ex)

29. (∃x)(Gx • Ax)

30. (x)(Px ⊃ Gx)

31. (∃x)[Cx • ~(Sx ∨ Bx)]

32. (x)(Cx ⊃ ~Tx)

33. (x)[Sx ⊃ (Hx ∨ Fx)]

34. (∃x)[(Dx • Bx) ≡ Tx]

35. (x)[Ax ⊃ (Sx ≡ Px)]

36. (∃x)[Cx • (Sx ⊃ Bx)]

37. (∃x)[Cx • (Ax ⊃ Tx)]

38. (x)[(Mx • Ax) ⊃ Tx]

39. (x)[(Mx • Px) ⊃ Tx]

40. (x)[(Wx • Cx) ⊃ Rx]

41   (∃x)[(Fx • Cx) • ~Rx]

Exercise 8.2

42. (x)[(Gx • Vx) ⊃ (Rx • Ex)]

43. (x)[(Vx ∨ Cx) ⊃ (Sx • Ix)]

44. (∃x)[(Rx • Vx) • Ax]

45. (x)[(Rx • Vx) ⊃ Ex]

46 (∃x)[(Fx • Rx) • Ex]

47. (∃x)[(Fx • Cx) • ~Rx]

48. (x)[(Hx ∨ Ex) ⊃ (Vx • Dx)]

49. Gt ≡ (x)(Wx ⊃ Cx)

50. (∃x)(Wx • Tx) ⊃ (Gp ∨ Gh)

51. (x)(Mx ⊃ Ix) ⊃ Ir

52. (∃x)(Ix • Mx) ⊃ Ir

53. (x)[(Sx ∨ Dx) ⊃ (Ix • Ex)]

54. (x)[(Sx • Wx) ⊃ (~Ex ∨ Mx)]

55. (x)[(Bx • Mx) ⊃ Sx] ⊃ Sc

56. (x)[(Ex • Mx) ⊃ Wx] ⊃ (x)[(Mx • ~Ex) ⊃ Lx]

57. (x)[(Sx • Bx) ⊃ ~Cx] ∨ (x)[(Sx • Ox) ⊃ Tx]

58. (∃x)(Ex • Rx) ≡ (∃x)(Mx • Ox)

59. (x){[(Px ∨ Ax) • Sx] ⊃ [(Cx ∨ Rx) ⊃ Lx]}

60. (x)[(Sx ∨ Tx) ⊃ (Cx • Ex)] ⊃ (∃x)[Mx • (Px ∨ Dx)]

Exercise 8.2
Part I

(1) 1. (x)(Ax ⊃ Bx)
     2. (x)(Bx ⊃ Cx)   / (x)(Ax ⊃ Cx)
     3. Ax ⊃ Bx   1, UI
     4. Bx ⊃ Cx   2, UI

5. Ax ⊃ Cx   3, 4, HS
6. (x)(Ax ⊃ Cx)   5, UG

(2) 1. (x)(Bx ⊃ Cx)
    2. (∃x)(Ax • Bx)   / (∃x)(Ax • Cx)
    3. Am • Bm   2, EI
    4. Bm ⊃ Cm   1, UI
    5. Bm • Am   3, Com
    6. Bm   5, Simp
    7. Cm   4, 6, MP
    8. Am   3, Simp
    9. Am • Cm   7, 8, Conj
  10. (∃x)(Ax • Cx)   9, EG

(3) 1. (x)(Ax ⊃ Bx)
    2. ~Bm   / (∃x)~Ax
    3. Am ⊃ Bm   1, UI
    4. ~Am   2, 3, MT
    5. (∃x)~Ax   4, EG

(4) 1. (x)[Ax ⊃ (Bx ∨ Cx)]
    2. Ag • ~Bg   / Cg
    3. Ag ⊃ (Bg ∨ Cg)   1, UI
    4. Ag   2, Simp
    5. Bg ∨ Cg   3, 4, MP
    6. ~Bg • Ag   2, Com
    7. ~Bg   6, Simp
    8. Cg   5, 7, DS

(5) 1. (x)[(Ax ∨ Bx) ⊃ Cx]
    2. (∃y)(Ay • Dy)   / (∃y)Cy
    3. Am • Dm   2, EI
    4. Am   3, Simp
    5. (Am ∨ Bm) ⊃ Cm   1, UI
    6. Am ∨ Bm   4, Add
    7. Cm   5, 6, MP
    8. (∃y)Cy   7, EG

(6) 1. (x)[Jx ⊃ (Kx • Lx)]
    2. (∃y)~Ky   / (∃z)~Jz
    3. ~Km   2, EI
    4. Jm ⊃ (Km • Lm)   1, UI
    5. ~Km ∨ ~Lm   3, Add
    6. ~(Km • Lm)   5, DM
    7. ~Jm   4, 6, MT
    8. (∃z)~Jz   7, EG

Exercise 8.2

(7) 1. (x)[Ax ⊃ (Bx ∨ Cx)]
    2. (∃x)(Ax • ~Cx)   / (∃x)Bx
    3. Am • ~Cm   2, EI
    4. Am ⊃ (Bm ∨ Cm)   1, UI
    5. Am   3, Simp
    6. Bm ∨ Cm   4, 5, MP
    7. ~Cm • Am   3, Com
    8. ~Cm   7, Simp
    9. Cm ∨ Bm   6, Com
  10. Bm   8, 9, DS
  11. (∃x)Bx   10, EG

(8) 1. (x)(Ax ⊃ Bx)
    2. Am • An   / Bm • Bn
    3. Am ⊃ Bm   1, UI
    4. Am   2, Simp
    5. Bm   3, 4, MP
    6. An ⊃ Bn   1, UI
    7. An • Am   2, Com
    8. An   7, Simp
    9. Bn   6, 8, MP
  10. Bm • Bn   5, 9, Conj

(9) 1. (x)(Ax ⊃ Bx)
    2. Am ∨ An   / Bm ∨ Bn
    3. Am ⊃ Bm   1, UI
    4. An ⊃ Bn   1, UI
    5. (Am ⊃ Bm) • (An ⊃ Bn)   3, 4, Conj
    6. Bm ∨ Bn   2, 5, CD

(10) 1. (x)(Bx ∨ Ax)
    2. (x)(Bx ⊃ Ax)   / (x)Ax
    3. Bx ∨ Ax   1, UI
    4. Bx ⊃ Ax   2, UI
    5. Ax ∨ Bx   3, Com
    6. ~~Ax ∨ Bx   5, DN
    7. ~Ax ⊃ Bx   6, Impl
    8. ~Ax ⊃ Ax   4, 7, HS
    9. ~~Ax ∨ Ax   8, Impl
  10. Ax ∨ Ax   9, DN
  11. Ax   10, Taut
  12. (x)Ax   11, UG

(11) 1. (x)[(Ax • Bx) ⊃ Cx]
    2. (∃x)(Bx • ~Cx)   / (∃x)~Ax
    3. Bm • ~Cm   2, EI

4. (Am • Bm) ⊃ Cm   1, UI
5. ~Cm • Bm   3, Com
6. ~Cm   5, Simp
7. ~(Am • Bm)   4, 6, MT
8. ~Am ∨ ~Bm   7, DM
9. Bm   3, Simp
10. ~~Bm   9, DN
11. ~Bm ∨ ~Am   8, Com
12. ~Am   10, 11, DS
13. (∃x)~Ax   12, EG

(12) 1. (∃x)Ax ⊃ (x)(Bx ⊃ Cx)
2. Am • Bm   / Cm
3. Am   2, Simp
4. (∃x)Ax   3, EG
5. (x)(Bx ⊃ Cx)   1, 4, MP
6. Bm ⊃ Cm   5, UI
7. Bm • Am   2, Com
8. Bm   7, Simp
9. Cm   6, 8, MP

(13) 1. (∃x)Ax ⊃ (x)Bx
2. (∃x)Cx ⊃ (∃x)Dx
3. An • Cn   / (∃x)(Bx • Dx)
4. An   2, Simp
5. (∃x)Ax   4, EG
6. (x)Bx   1, 5, MP
7. Cn • An   3, Com
8. Cn   7, Simp
9. (∃x)Cx   8, EG
10. (∃x)Dx   2, 9, MP
11. Dm   10, EI
12. Bm   6, UI
13. Bm • Dm   11, 12, Conj
14. (∃x)(Bx • Dx)   13, EG

(14) 1. (∃x)Ax ⊃ (x)(Cx ⊃ Bx)
2. (∃x)(Ax ∨ Bx)
3. (x)(Bx ⊃ Ax)   / (x)(Cx ⊃ Ax)
4. Am ∨ Bm   2, EI
5. Bm ⊃ Am   3, UI
6. ~~Am ∨ Bm   4, DN
7. ~Am ⊃ Bm   6, Impl
8. ~Am ⊃ Am   5, 7, HS
9. ~~Am ∨ Am   8, Impl
10. Am ∨ Am   9, DN

177

11. Am	10, Taut
12. (∃x)Ax	11, EG
13. (x)(Cx ⊃ Bx)	1, 12, MP
14. Cx ⊃ Bx	13, UI
15. Bx ⊃ Ax	3, UI
16. Cx ⊃ Ax	14, 15, HS
17. (x)(Cx ⊃ Ax)	16, UG

(15)
1. (∃x)Ax ⊃ (x)(Bx ⊃ Cx)	
2. (∃x)Dx ⊃ (∃x)~Cx	
3. (∃x)(Ax • Dx)	/ (∃x)~Bx
4. Am • Dm	3, EI
5. Am	4, Simp
6. Dm • Am	4, Com
7. Dm	6, Simp
8. (∃x)Ax	7, EG
9. (∃x)Dx	7, EG
10. (x)(Bx ⊃ Cx)	1, 8, MP
11. (∃x)~Cx	2, 9, MP
12. ~Cn	11, EI
13. Bn ⊃ Cn	10, UI
14. ~Bn	12, 13, MT
15. (∃x)~Bx	14, EG

Part II

(1)
1. (x)(Ox ⊃ Sx)	
2. (x)(Ox ⊃ Fx)	/ (x)[Ox ⊃ (Sx • Fx)]
3. Ox ⊃ Sx	1, UI
4. OX ⊃ Fx	2, UI
5. ~Ox ∨ Sx	3, Impl
6. ~Ox ∨ Fx	4, Impl
7. (~Ox ∨ Sx) • (~Ox ∨ Fx)	5, 6, Conj
8. ~Ox ∨ (Sx • Fx)	7, Dist
9. Ox ⊃ (Sx • Fx)	8, Impl
10. (x)[Ox ⊃ (Sx • Fx)	9, UG

(2)
1. (x)(Tx ⊃ Vx)	/ (x)[(Tx • Gx) ⊃ Vx]
2. Tx ⊃ Vx	1, UI
3. ~Tx ∨ Vx	2, Impl
4. Vx ∨ ~Tx	3, Com
5. (Vx ∨ ~Tx) ∨ ~Gx	4, Add
6. Vx ∨ (~Tx ∨ ~Gx)	5, Assoc
7. Vx ∨ ~(Tx • Gx)	6, DM

8. ~(Tx • Gx) ∨ Vx   7, Com
9. (Tx • Gx) ⊃ Vx   8, Impl
10. (x)[(Tx • Gx) ⊃ Vx]   9, UG

(3)   1. (x)[(Ax ∨ Px) ⊃ Gx]   / (x)(Ax ⊃ Gx)
     2. (Ax ∨ Px) ⊃ Gx   1, UI
     3. ~(Ax ∨ Px) ∨ Gx   2, Impl
     4. (~Ax • ~Px) ∨ Gx   3, DM
     5. Gx ∨ (~Ax • ~Px)   4, Com
     6. (Gx ∨ ~Ax) • (Gx ∨ ~Px)   5, Dist
     7. Gx ∨ ~Ax   6, Simp
     8. ~Ax ∨ Gx   7, Com
     9. Ax ⊃ Gx   8, Impl
     10. (x)(Ax ⊃ Gx)   9, UG

(4)   1. (x)(Cx ⊃ Vx) • (x)(Px ⊃ Fx)
     2. (∃x)(Cx • Gx) • (∃x)(Px • Gx)   / (∃x)(Vx • Gx) • (∃x)(Fx • Gx)
     3. (∃x)(Cx • Gx)   2, Simp
     4. Cm • Gm   3, EI
     5. (∃x)(Px • Gx) • (∃x)(Cx • Gx)   2, Com
     6. (∃x)(Px • Gx)   5, Simp
     7. Pn • Gn   6, EI
     8. (x)(Cx ⊃ Vx)   1, Simp
     9. Cm ⊃ Vm   8, UI
     10. Cm   4, Simp
     11. Vm   9, 10, MP
     12. Gm • Cm   4, Com
     13. Gm   12, Simp
     14. Vm • Gm   11, 13, Conj
     15. (∃x)(Vx • Gx)   14, EG
     16. (x)(Px ⊃ Fx) • (x)(Cx ⊃ Vx)   1, Com
     17. (x)(Px ⊃ Fx)   16, Simp
     18. Pn ⊃ Fn   17, UI
     19. Pn   7, Simp
     20. Fn   18, 19, MP
     21. Gn • Pn   7, Com
     22. Gn   21, Simp
     23. Fn • Gn   20, 22, Conj
     24. (∃x)(Fx • Gx)   23, EG
     25. (∃x)(Vx • Gx) • (∃x)(Fx • Gx)   15, 24, Conj

(5)   1. (x)[(Bx ∨ Px) ⊃ Lx]
     2. (x)(Gx ⊃ ~Lx)   / (x)(Gx ⊃ ~ Bx)
     3. (Bx ∨ Px) ⊃ Lx   1, UI
     4. Gx ⊃ ~Lx   2, UI
     5. ~Lx ⊃ ~(Bx ∨ Px)   3, Trans

179

6. Gx ⊃ ~(Bx ∨ Px)　　　　　　4, 5, HS
7. Gx ⊃ (~Bx • ~Px)　　　　　　6, DM
8. ~Gx ∨ (~Bx • ~Px)　　　　　　7, Impl
9. (~Gx ∨ ~Bx) • (~Gx ∨ ~Px)　　8, Dist
10. ~Gx ∨ ~Bx　　　　　　　　9, Simp
11. Gx ⊃ ~Bx　　　　　　　　　10, Impl
12. (x)(Gx ⊃ ~Bx)　　　　　　　11, UG

(6)　1. (∃x)(Cx • Gx)
　　　2. (∃x)Cx ⊃ (∃x)(Px • Gx)
　　　3. (x)(Px ⊃ Vx)　　　　　/ (∃x)(Vx • Gx)
　　　4. Cm • Gm　　　　　　　1, EI
　　　5. Cm　　　　　　　　　4, Simp
　　　6. (∃x)Cx　　　　　　　　5, EG
　　　7. (∃x)(Px • Gx)　　　　　2, 6, MP
　　　8. Pn • Gn　　　　　　　7, EI
　　　9. Pn　　　　　　　　　8, Simp
　　10. Pn ⊃ Vn　　　　　　　3, UI
　　11. Vn　　　　　　　　　9, 10, MP
　　12. Gn • Pn　　　　　　　8, Com
　　13. Gn　　　　　　　　　12, Simp
　　14. Vn • Gn　　　　　　　11, 13, Conj
　　15. (∃x)(Vx • Gx)　　　　　14, EG

(7)　1. (x)[Gx ⊃ (Ix • Px)]
　　　2. (x)[(Ix • Px) ⊃ Rx]
　　　3. Ga • Gc　　　　　　　/ Ra • Rc
　　　4. Gx ⊃ (Ix • Px)　　　　1, UI
　　　5. (Ix • Px) ⊃ Rx　　　　2, UI
　　　6. Gx ⊃ Rx　　　　　　　4, 5, HS
　　　7. (x)(Gx ⊃ Rx)　　　　　6, UG
　　　8. Ga ⊃ Ra　　　　　　　7, UI
　　　9. Ga　　　　　　　　　3, Simp
　　10. Ra　　　　　　　　　8, 9, MP
　　11. Gc ⊃ Rc　　　　　　　7, UI
　　12. Gc • Ga　　　　　　　3, Com
　　13. Gc　　　　　　　　　12, Simp
　　14. Rc　　　　　　　　　11, 13, MP
　　15. Ra • Rc　　　　　　　10, 14, Conj

(8)　1. (∃x)(Hx • Rx)
　　　2. (∃x)(Bx • Sx)
　　　3. (∃x)Hx ⊃ (x)[Bx ⊃ (Sx ⊃ Ex)]　/ (∃x)(Bx • Ex)
　　　4. Hm • Rm　　　　　　　1, EI
　　　5. Bn • Sn　　　　　　　2, EI
　　　6. Hm　　　　　　　　　4, Simp

7. (∃x)Hx	6, EG
8. (x)[Bx ⊃ (Sx ⊃ Ex)]	3, 7, MP
9. Bn ⊃ (Sn ⊃ En)	8, UI
10. (Bn • Sn) ⊃ En	9, Exp
11. En	5, 10, MP
12. Bn	5, Simp
13. Bn • En	11, 12, Conj
14. (∃x)(Bx • Ex)	13, EG

(9)

1. (∃x)(Rx • Wx) ⊃ (x)(Cx ⊃ Px)	
2. (∃x)(Lx • Wx) ⊃ (x)(Px ⊃ Bx)	
3. (∃x)[(Lx • Rx) • Wx]	/ (x)(Cx ⊃ Bx)
4. (Lm • Rm) • Wm	3, EI
5. Lm • Rm	4, Simp
6. Lm	5, Simp
7. Rm • Lm	5, Com
8. Rm	7, Simp
9. Wm • (Lm • Rm)	4, Com
10. Wm	9, Simp
11. Rm • Wm	8, 10, Conj
12. Lm • Wm	6, 10, Conj
13. (∃x)(Rx • Wx)	11, EG
14. (∃x)(Lx • Wx)	12, EG
15. (x)(Cx ⊃ Px)	1, 13, MP
16. (x)(Px ⊃ Bx)	2, 14, MP
17. Cx ⊃ Px	15, UI
18. Px ⊃ Bx	16, UI
19. Cx ⊃ Bx	17, 18, HS
20. (x)(Cx ⊃ Bx)	19, UG

(10)

1. (x)[(Ax • Kx) ⊃ Rx] ⊃ (x)(Gx ⊃ Sx)	
2. (x)[(Ax • Kx) ⊃ Fx] ⊃ (x)(Gx ⊃ Px)	
3. (x)[(Ax • Kx) ⊃ (Rx • Fx)]	/ (x)[Gx ⊃ (Sx • Px)]
4. (Ax • Kx) ⊃ (Rx • Fx)	3, UI
5. ~(Ax • Kx) ∨ (Rx • Fx)	4, Impl
6. [~(Ax • Kx) ∨ Rx] • [~(Ax • Kx) ∨ Fx]	5, Dist
7. ~(Ax • Kx) ∨ Rx	6, Simp
8. [~(Ax • Kx) ∨ Fx] • [~(Ax • Kx) ∨ Rx]	6, Com
9. ~(Ax • Kx) ∨ Fx	8, Simp
10. (Ax • Kx) ⊃ Rx	7, Impl
11. (Ax • Kx) ⊃ Fx	9, Impl
12. (x)[(Ax • Kx) ⊃ Rx]	10, UG
13. (x)[(Ax • Kx) ⊃ Fx]	11, UG
14. (x)(Gx ⊃ Sx)	1, 12, MP
15. (x)(Gx ⊃ Px)	2, 13, MP
16. Gx ⊃ Sx	14, UI

Exercise 8.3

17. Gx ⊃ Px	15, UI
18. ~Gx ∨ Sx	16, Impl
19. ~Gx ∨ Px	17, Impl
20. (~Gx ∨ Sx) • (~Gx ∨ Px)	18, 19, Conj
21. ~Gx ∨ (Sx • Px)	20, Dist
22. Gx ⊃ (Sx • Px)	21, Impl
23. (x)[Gx ⊃ (Sx • Px)]	22, UG

Exercise 8.3
Part I

(1)
1. (x)Ax ⊃ (∃x)Bx	
2. (x)~Bx	/ (∃x)~Ax
3. ~(∃x)Bx	2, CQ
4. ~(x)Ax	1, 3, MT
5. (∃x)~Ax	4, CQ

(2)
1. (∃x)~Ax ∨ (∃x)~Bx	
2. (x)Bx	/ ~(x)Ax
3. ~(∃x)~Bx	2, CQ
4. (∃x)~Bx ∨ (∃x)~Ax	1, Com
5. (∃x)~Ax	3, 4, DS
6. ~(x)Ax	5, CQ

(3)
1. ~(∃x)Ax	/ (x)(Ax ⊃ Bx)
2. (x)~Ax	1, CQ
3. ~Ax	2, UI
4. ~Ax ∨ Bx	3, Add
5. Ax ⊃ Bx	4, Impl
6. (x)(Ax ⊃ Bx)	5, UG

(4)
1. (∃x)Ax ∨ (∃x)(Bx • Cx)	
2. ~(∃x)Bx	/ (∃x)Ax
3. (x)~Bx	2, CQ
4. ~Bx	3, UI
5. ~Bx ∨ ~Cx	4, Add
6. ~(Bx • Cx)	5, DM
7. (x)~(Bx • Cx)	6, UG
8. ~(∃x)(Bx • Cx)	7, CQ
9. (∃x)(Bx • Cx) ∨ (∃x)Ax	1, Com
10. (∃x)Ax	8, 9, DS

(5) 1. (x)(Ax • Bx) ∨ (x)(Cx • Dx)
    2. ~(x)Dx   / (x)Bx
    3. (∃x)~Dx   2, CQ
    4. ~Dm   3, EI
    5. ~Dm ∨ ~Cm   4, Add
    6. ~Cm ∨ ~Dm   5, Com
    7. ~(Cm • Dm)   6, DM
    8. (∃x)~(Cx • Dx)   7, EG
    9. ~(x)(Cx • Dx)   8, CQ
  10. (x)(Cx • Dx) ∨ (x)(Ax • Bx) 1, Com
  11. (x)(Ax • Bx)   9, 10, DS
  12. Ax • Bx   11, UI
  13. Bx • Ax   12, Com
  14. Bx   13, Simp
  15. (x)Bx   14, UG

(6) 1. (∃x)~Ax ⊃ (x)(Bx ⊃ Cx)
    2. ~(x)(Ax ∨ Cx)   / ~(x)Bx
    3. (∃x)~(Ax ∨ Cx)   2, CQ
    4. ~(Am ∨ Cm)   3, EI
    5. ~Am • ~Cm   4, DM
    6. ~Am   5, Simp
    7. (∃x)~Ax   6, EG
    8. (x)(Bx ⊃ Cx)   1, 7, MP
    9. Bm ⊃ Cm   8, UI
  10. ~Cm • ~Am   5, Com
  11. ~Cm   10, Simp
  12. ~Bm   9, 11, MT
  13. (∃x)~Bx   12, EG
  14. ~(x)Bx   13, CQ

(7) 1. (x)(Ax ⊃ Bx)
    2. ~(x)Cx ∨ (x)Ax
    3. ~(x)Bx   / (∃x)~Cx
    4. (∃x)~Bx   3, CQ
    5. ~Bm   4, EI
    6. Am ⊃ Bm   1, UI
    7. ~Am   5, 6, MT
    8. (∃x)~Ax   7, EG
    9. ~(x)Ax   8, CQ
  10. (x)Ax ∨ ~(x)Cx   2, Com
  11. ~(x)Cx   9, 10, DS
  12. (∃x)~Cx   11, CQ

Exercise 8.3

(8) 1. (x)Ax ⊃ (∃x)~Bx
     2. ~(x)Bx ⊃ (∃x)~Cx   / (x)Cx ⊃ (∃x)~Ax
     3. (x)Ax ⊃ ~(x)Bx   1, CQ
     4. (x)Ax ⊃ (∃x)~Cx   2, 3, HS
     5. ~(∃x)~Cx ⊃ ~(x)Ax   4, Trans
     6. (x)Cx ⊃ (∃x)~Ax   5, CQ

(9) 1. (∃x)(Ax ∨ Bx) ⊃ (x)Cx
     2. (∃x)~Cx   / ~(∃x)Ax
     3. ~(x)Cx   2, CQ
     4. ~(∃x)(Ax ∨ Bx)   1, 3, MT
     5. (x)~(Ax ∨ Bx)   4, CQ
     6. ~(Ax ∨ Bx)   5, UI
     7. ~Ax • ~Bx   6, DM
     8. ~Ax   7, Simp
     9. (x)~Ax   8, UG
     10. ~(∃x)Ax   9, CQ

(10) 1. ~(∃x)(Ax • ~Bx)
     2. ~(∃x)(Bx • ~Cx)   / (x)(Ax ⊃ Cx)
     3. (x)~(Ax • ~Bx)   1, CQ
     4. (x)~(Bx • ~Cx)   2, CQ
     5. ~(Ax • ~Bx)   3, UI
     6. ~(Bx • ~Cx)   4, UI
     7. ~Ax • ~~Bx   5, DM
     8. ~Ax ∨ Bx   7, DN
     9. ~Bx ∨ ~~Cx   6, DM
     10. ~Bx ∨ Cx   9, DN
     11. Ax ⊃ Bx   8, Impl
     12. Bx ⊃ Cx   10, Impl
     13. Ax ⊃ Cx   11, 12, HS
     14. (x)(Ax ⊃ Cx)   13, UG

(11) 1. ~(∃x)(Ax • ~Bx)
     2. ~(∃x)(Ax • ~Cx)   / (x)[Ax ⊃ (Bx • Cx)]
     3. (x)~(Ax • ~Bx)   1, CQ
     4. (x)~(Ax • ~Cx)   2, CQ
     5. ~(Ax • ~Bx)   3, UI
     6. ~(Ax • ~Cx)   4, UI
     7. ~Ax ∨ ~~Bx   5, DM
     8. ~Ax ∨ Bx   7, DN
     9. ~Ax ∨ ~~Cx   6, DM
     10. ~Ax ∨ Cx   9, DN
     11. (~Ax ∨ Bx) • (~Ax ∨ Cx) 8, 10, Conj

184

12. ~Ax ∨ (Bx • Cx)	11, Dist
13. Ax ⊃ (Bx • Cx)	12, Impl
14. (x)[Ax ⊃ (Bx • Cx)]	13, UG

(12)
1. (x)[(Ax • Bx) ⊃ Cx]	
2. ~(x)(Ax ⊃ Cx)	/ ~(x)Bx
3. (∃x)~(Ax ⊃ Cx)	2, CQ
4. ~(Am ⊃ Cm)	3, EI
5. ~(~Am ∨ Cm)	4, Impl
6. ~~Am • ~Cm	5, DM
7. Am • ~Cm	6, DN
8. (Am • Bm) ⊃ Cm	1, UI
9. ~Cm • Am	7, Com
10. ~Cm	9, Simp
11. ~(Am • Bm)	8, 10, MT
12. ~Am ∨ ~Bm	11, DM
13. Am	7, Simp
14. ~~Am	13, DN
15. ~Bm	12, 14, DS
16. (∃x)~Bx	15, EG
17. ~(x)Bx	16, CQ

(13)
1. (x)(Ax • ~Bx) ⊃ (∃x)Cx	
2. ~(∃x)(Cx ∨ Bx)	/ ~(x)Ax
3. (x)~(Cx ∨ Bx)	2, CQ
4. ~(Cx ∨ Bx)	3, UI
5. ~Cx • ~Bx	4, DM,
6. ~Cx	5, Simp
7. (x)~Cx	6, UG
8. ~(∃x)Cx	7, CQ
9. ~(x)(Ax • ~Bx)	1, 8, MT
10. (∃x)~(Ax • ~Bx)	9, CQ
11. ~(Am • ~Bm)	10, EI
12. ~Am ∨ ~~Bm	11, DM
13. ~Am ∨ Bm	12, DN
14. ~Bx • ~Cx	5, Com
15. ~Bx	14, Simp
16. (x)~Bx	15, UG
17. ~Bm	16, UI
18. Bm ∨ ~Am	13, Com
19. ~Am	17, 18, DS
20. (∃x)~Ax	19, EG
21. ~(x)Ax	20, CQ

Exercise 8.3

(14) 1. (∃x)~Ax ⊃ (x)~Bx
      2. (∃x)~Ax ⊃ (∃x)Bx
      3. (x)(Ax ⊃ Cx)   / (x)Cx
      4. ~(x)~Bx ⊃ ~(∃x)~Ax   1, Trans
      5. (∃x)Bx ⊃ ~(∃x)~Ax   4, CQ
      6. (∃x)~Ax ⊃ ~(∃x)~Ax   2, 5, HS
      7. ~(∃x)~Ax ∨ ~(∃x)~Ax   6, Impl
      8. ~(∃x)~Ax   7, Taut
      9. (x)Ax   8, CQ
      10. Ax   9, UI
      11. Ax ⊃ Cx   3, UI
      12. Cx   10, 11, MP
      13. (x)Cx   12, UG

(15) 1. ~(∃x)(Ax ∨ Bx)
      2. (∃x)Cx ⊃ (∃x)Ax
      3. (∃x)Dx ⊃ (∃x)Bx   / ~(∃x)(Cx ∨ Dx)
      4. (x)~(Ax ∨ Bx)   1, CQ
      5. ~(Ax ∨ Bx)   4, UI
      6. ~Ax • ~Bx   5, DM
      7. ~Ax   6, Simp
      8. ~Bx • ~Ax   6, Com
      9. ~Bx   8, Simp
      10. (x)~Ax   7, UG
      11. (x)~Bx   9, UG
      12. ~(∃x)Ax   10, CQ
      13. ~(∃x)Bx   11, CQ
      14. ~(∃x)Cx   2, 12, MT
      15. ~(∃x)Dx   3, 13, MT
      16. (x)~Cx   14, CQ
      17. (x)~Dx   15, CQ
      18. ~Cx   16, UI
      19. ~Dx   17, UI
      20. ~Cx • ~Dx   18, 19, Conj
      21. ~(Cx ∨ Dx)   20, DM
      22. (x)~(Cx ∨ Dx)   21, UG
      23. ~(∃x)(Cx ∨ Dx)   22, CQ

Part II

(1) 1. (x)[Px ⊃ (Hx ∨ Nx)] ⊃ ~(∃x)Cx
     2. Cf   / (∃x)(Px • ~Nx)
     3. (∃x)Cx   2, EG
     4. ~~(∃x)Cx   3, DN

186

5. ~(x)[Px ⊃ (Hx ∨ Nx)]   1, 4, MT
6. (∃x)~[Px ⊃ (Hx ∨ Nx)]   5, CQ
7. ~[Pm ⊃ (Hm ∨ Nm)]   6, EI
8. ~[~Pm ∨ (Hm ∨ Nm)]   7, Impl
9. ~~Pm • ~(Hm ∨ Nm)   8, DM
10. ~~Pm   9, Simp
11. Pm   10, DN
12. ~(Hm ∨ Nm) • ~~Pm   9, Com
13. ~(Hm ∨ Nm)   12, Simp
14. ~Hm • ~Nm   13, DM
15. ~Nm • ~Hm   14, Com
16. ~Nm   15, Simp
17. Pm • ~Nm   11, 16, Conj
18. (∃x)(Px • ~Nx)   17, EG

(2) 1. Ia ∨ (x)(Px ⊃ Ix)
     2. ~(∃x)Ix   / ~Pa
     3. (x)~Ix   2, CQ
     4. ~Ia   3, UI
     5. (x)(Px ⊃ Ix)   1, 4, DS
     6. Pa ⊃ Ia   5, UI
     7. ~Pa   4, 6, MT

(3) 1. (∃x)(Sx • Ax) ⊃ (∃x)(Px • Rx)
     2. (x)(Px ⊃ ~Rx)   / (x)(Sx ⊃ ~Ax)
     3. (x)(~Px ∨ ~Rx)   2, Impl
     4. (x)~(Px • Rx)   3, DM
     5. ~(∃x)(Px • Rx)   4, CQ
     6. ~(∃x)(Sx • Ax)   1, 5, MT
     7. (x)~(Sx • Ax)   6, CQ
     8. (x)(~Sx ∨ ~Ax)   7, DM
     9. (x)(Sx ⊃ ~Ax)   8, Impl

(4) 1. (∃x)(Gx • Px) ∨ (∃x)(Sx • Ex)
     2. ~(∃x)Ex   / (∃x)Px
     3. (x)~Ex   2, CQ
     4. ~Ex   3, UI
     5. ~Ex ∨ ~Sx   4, Add
     6. ~Sx ∨ ~Ex   5, Com
     7. ~(Sx • Ex)   6, DM
     8. (x)~(Sx • Ex)   7, UG
     9. ~(∃x)(Sx • Ex)   8, CQ
     10. (∃x)(Sx • Ex) ∨ (∃x)(Gx • Px)   1, Com
     11. (∃x)(Gx • Px)   9, 10, DS
     12. Gm • Pm   11, EI

13. Pm • Gm   12, Com
14. Pm   13, Simp
15. (∃x) Px   14, EG

(5) 1. (x)[(Px • ~Ax) ⊃ Ix]
     2. ~(∃x)(Px • Ix)   / (x)(Px ⊃ Ax)
     3. (x)~(Px • Ix)   2, CQ
     4. ~(Px • Ix)   3, UI
     5. ~Px ∨ ~Ix   4, DM
     6. ~Ix ∨ ~Px   5, Com
     7. Ix ⊃ ~Px   6, Impl
     8. (Px • ~Ax) ⊃ Ix   1, UI
     9. (Px • ~Ax) ⊃ ~Px   7, 8, HS
    10. (~Ax • Px) ⊃ ~Px   9, Com
    11. ~Ax ⊃ (Px ⊃ ~Px)   10, Exp
    12. ~Ax ⊃ (~Px ∨ ~Px)   11, Impl
    13. ~Ax ⊃ ~Px   12, Taut
    14. Px ⊃ Ax   13, Trans
    15. (x)(Px ⊃ Ax)   14, UG

(6) 1. ~(∃x)(Ix • ~Px)
     2. ~(∃x)(Px • ~Dx)   / (x)(Ix ⊃ Dx)
     3. (x)~(Ix • ~Px)   1, CQ
     4. (x)~(Px • ~Dx)   2, CQ
     5. ~(Ix • ~Px)   3, UI
     6. ~(Px • ~Dx)   4, UI
     7. ~Ix ∨ ~~Px   5, DM
     8. ~Ix ∨ Px   7, DN
     9. ~Px ∨ ~~Dx   6, DM
    10. ~Px ∨ Dx   9, DN
    11. Ix ⊃ Px   8, Impl
    12. Px ⊃ Dx   10, Impl
    13. Ix ⊃ Dx   11, 12, HS
    14. (x)(Ix ⊃ Dx)   13, UG

(7) 1. (x)(Px ⊃ Sx) • (x)(Ix ⊃ Gx)
     2. ~(∃x)(Sx • Gx)   / ~(∃x)(Px • Ix)
     3. (x)~(Sx • Gx)   2, CQ
     4. ~(Sx • Gx)   3, UI
     5. ~Sx ∨ ~Gx   4, DM
     6. (x)(Px ⊃ Sx)   1, Simp
     7. (x)(Ix ⊃ Gx) • (x)(Px ⊃ Sx)   1, Com
     8. (x)(Ix ⊃ Gx)   7, Simp
     9. Px ⊃ Sx   6, UI
    10. Ix ⊃ Gx   8, UI

188

11. ~Sx ⊃ ~Px   9, Trans
12. ~Gx ⊃ ~Ix   10, Trans
13. (~Sx ⊃ ~Px) • (~Gx ⊃ ~Ix)   11, 12, Conj
14. ~Px ∨ ~Ix   5, 13, CD
15. ~(Px • Ix)   14, DM
16. (x)~(Px • Ix)   15, UG
17. ~(∃x)(Px • Ix)   16, CQ

(8)   1. (∃x)(Ox • ~Gx) ⊃ (∃x)(Hx • Rx)
    2. ~(∃x)(Hx ∨ Gx)   / ~(∃x)Ox
    3. (x)~(Hx ∨ Gx)   2, CQ
    4. ~(Hx ∨ Gx)   3, UI
    5. ~Hx • ~Gx   4, DM
    6. ~Hx   5, Simp
    7. ~Hx ∨ ~Rx   6, Add
    8. ~(Hx • Rx)   7, DM
    9. (x)~(Hx • Rx)   8, UG
   10. ~(∃x)(Hx • Rx)   9, CQ
   11. ~(∃x)(Ox • ~Gx)   1, 10, MT
   12. (x)~(Ox • ~Gx)   11, CQ
   13. ~(Ox • ~Gx)   12, UI
   14. ~Ox ∨ ~~Gx   13, DM
   15. ~Ox ∨ Gx   14, DN
   16. ~Gx • ~Hx   5, Com
   17. ~Gx   16, Simp
   18. Gx ∨ ~Ox   15, Com
   19. ~Ox   17, 18, DS
   20. (x)~Ox   19, UI
   21. ~(∃x)Ox   20, CQ

(9)   1. (x){[(Ax ∨ Dx) • Px] ⊃ (Ux • Sx)}
    2. ~(∃x)(Ux • Sx)   / ~(∃x)(Dx • Px)
    3. (x)~(Ux • Sx)   2, CQ
    4. ~(Ux • Sx)   3, UI
    5. [(Ax ∨ Dx) • Px] ⊃ (Ux • Sx)   1, UI
    6. ~[(Ax ∨ Dx) • Px]   4, 5, MT
    7. ~(Ax ∨ Dx) ∨ ~Px   6, DM
    8. (~Ax • ~Dx) ∨ ~Px   7, DM
    9. ~Px ∨ (~Ax • ~Dx)   8, Com
   10. (~Px ∨ ~Ax) • (~Px ∨ ~Dx)   9, Dist
   11. (~Px ∨ ~Dx) • (~Px ∨ ~Ax)   10, Com
   12. ~Px ∨ ~Dx   11, Simp
   13. ~Dx ∨ ~Px   12, Com
   14. ~(Dx • Px)   13, DM

Exercise 8.4

15. (x)~(Dx • Px)	14, UG
16. ~(∃x)(Dx • Px)	15, CQ

(10) 1. ~(∃x)[Px • (Gx ∨ Hx)]
   2. (x)[Nx ⊃ (Px • Hx)]
   3. (∃x)(Px • Cx) ∨ (∃x)(Px • Nx)   / (∃x)(Cx • ~Gx)
   4. (x)~[Px • (Gx ∨ Hx)]   1, CQ
   5. ~[Px • (Gx ∨ Hx)]   4, UI
   6. ~Px ∨ ~(Gx ∨ Hx)   5, DM
   7. ~Px ∨ (~Gx • ~Hx)   6, DM
   8. (~Px ∨ ~Gx) • (~Px ∨ ~Hx)   7, Dist
   9. ~Px ∨ ~Gx   8, Simp
   10. (~Px ∨ ~Hx) • (~Px ∨ ~Gx)   8, Com
   11. ~Px ∨ ~Hx   10, Simp
   12. ~(Px • Hx)   11, DM
   13. Nx ⊃ (Px • Hx)   2, UI
   14. ~Nx   12, 13, MT
   15. ~Nx ∨ ~Px   14, Add
   16. ~Px ∨ ~Nx   15, Com
   17. ~(Px • Nx)   16, DM
   18. (x)~(Px • Nx)   17, UG
   19. ~(∃x)(Px • Nx)   18, CQ
   20. (∃x)(Px • Nx) ∨ (∃x)(Px • Cx) 3, Com
   21. (∃x)(Px • Cx)   19, 20 DS
   22. Pm • Cm   21, EI
   23. (x)(~Px ∨ ~Gx)   9, UG
   24. ~Pm ∨ ~Gm   23, UI
   25. Pm   22, Simp
   26. ~~Pm   25, DN
   27. ~Gm   24, 26, DS
   28. Cm • Pm   22, Com
   29. Cm   28, Simp
   30. Cm • ~Gm   27, 29, Conj
   31. (∃x)(Cx • ~Gx)   30, EG

Exercise 8.4
Part I

(1) 1. (x)(Ax ⊃ Bx)
   2. (x)(Ax ⊃ Cx)   / (x)[(Ax ⊃ (Bx • Cx)]
      3. Ax   ACP
      4. Ax ⊃ Bx   1, UI
      5. Ax ⊃ Cx   2, UI
      6. Bx   3, 4, MP

190

          7. Cx   3, 5, MP
          8. Bx • Cx   6, 7, Conj
       9. Ax ⊃ (Bx • Cx)   3-8, CP
      10. (x)[Ax ⊃ (Bx • Cx)]   9, UG

(2) 1. (∃x)Ax ⊃ (∃x)(Bx • Cx)
     2. (∃x)(Cx ∨ Dx) ⊃ (x)Ex   / (x)(Ax ⊃ Ex)
          3. Ax   ACP
          4. (∃x)Ax   3, EG
          5. (∃x)(Bx • Cx)   1, 4, MP
          6. Bm • Cm   5, EI
          7. Cm • Bm   6, Com
          8. Cm   7, Simp
          9. Cm ∨ Dm   8, Add
         10. (∃x)(Cx ∨ Dx)   9, EG
         11. (x)Ex   2, 10, MP
         12. Ex   11, UI
      13. Ax ⊃ Ex   3-12, CP
      14. (x)(Ax ⊃ Ex)   13, UG

(3) 1. (∃x)Ax ⊃ (∃x)(Bx • Cx)
     2. ~(∃x)Cx   / (x)~Ax
          3. ~(x)~Ax   AIP
          4. (∃x)Ax   3, CQ
          5. (∃x)(Bx • Cx)   1, 4, MP
          6. Bm • Cm   5, EI
          7. Cm • Bm   6, Com
          8. Cm   7, Simp
          9. (x)~Cx   2, CQ
         10. ~Cm   9, UI
         11. Cm • ~Cm   8, 10, Conj
      12. ~~(x)~Ax   3-11, IP
      13. (x)~Ax   12, DN

(4) 1. (x)(Ax ⊃ Cx)
     2. (∃x)Cx ⊃ (∃x)(Bx • Dx)   / (∃x)Ax ⊃ (∃x)Bx
          3. (∃x)Ax   ACP
          4. Am   3, EI
          5. Am ⊃ Cm   1, UI
          6. Cm   4, 5, MP
          7. (∃x)Cx   6, EG
          8. (∃x)(Bx • Dx)   2, 7, MP
          9. Bn • Dn   8, EI
         10. Bn   9, Simp
         11. (∃x)Bx   10, EG
      12. (∃x)Ax ⊃ (∃x)Bx   3-11, CP

                        191

Exercise 8.4

(5) 1. (x)(Ax ⊃ Bx)
     2. (x)[(Ax • Bx) ⊃ Cx]   / (x)(Ax ⊃ Cx)
         3. Ax   ACP
         4. Ax ⊃ Bx   1, UI
         5. (Ax • Bx) ⊃ Cx   2, UI
         6. Bx   3, 4, MP
         7. Ax • Bx   3, 6, Conj
         8. Cx   5, 7, MP
     9. Ax ⊃ Cx   3-8, CP
    10. (x)(Ax ⊃ Cx)   9, UG

(6) 1. (∃x)Ax ⊃ (x)Bx
     2. An ⊃ ~Bn   / ~An
         3. An   AIP
         4. ~Bn   2, 3, MP
         5. (∃x)Ax   3, EG
         6. (x)Bx   1, 5, MP
         7. Bn   6, UI
         8. Bn • ~Bn   4, 7, Conj
     9. ~An   3-8, IP

(7) 1. (x)[(Ax ∨ Bx) ⊃ Cx]
     2. (x)[(Cx ∨ Dx) ⊃ Ex]   / (x)(Ax ⊃ Ex)
         3. Ax   ACP
         4. (Ax ∨ Bx) ⊃ Cx   1, UI
         5. (Cx ∨ Dx) ⊃ Ex   2, UI
         6. Ax ∨ Bx   3, Add
         7. Cx   4, 6, MP
         8. Cx ∨ Dx   7, Add
         9. Ex   5, 8, MP
    10. Ax ⊃ Ex   3-9, CP
    11. (x)(Ax ⊃ Ex)   10, UG

(8) 1. (∃x)(Ax ∨ Bx) ⊃ ~(∃x)Ax   / (x)~Ax
         2. ~(x)~Ax   AIP
         3. (∃x)Ax   2, CQ
         4. Am   3, EI
         5. Am ∨ Bm   4, Add
         6. (∃x)(Ax ∨ Bx)   5, EG
         7. ~(∃x)Ax   1, 6, MP
         8. (x)~Ax   7, CQ
         9. ~Am   8, UI
        10. Am • ~Am   4, 9, Conj
    11. ~~(x)~Ax   2-10, IP
    12. (x)~Ax   11, DN

(9) 1. (x)(Ax ⊃ Bx)
    2. (x)(Cx ⊃ Dx)   / (∃x)(Ax ∨ Cx) ⊃ (∃x)(Bx ∨ Dx)
        3. (∃x)(Ax ∨ Cx)   ACP
        4. Am ∨ Cm   3, EI
        5. Am ⊃ Bm   1, UI
        6. Cm ⊃ Dm   2, UI
        7. (Am ⊃ Bm) • (Cm ⊃ Dm)   5, 6, Conj
        8. Bm ∨ Dm   4, 7, CD
        9. (∃x)(Bx ∨ Dx)   8, EG
    10. (∃x)(Ax ∨ Cx) ⊃ (∃x)(Bx ∨ Dx)   3-9, CP

(10) 1. (x)(Ax ⊃ Bx)
    2. Am ∨ An   / (∃x)Bx
        3. ~(∃x)Bx   AIP
        4. (x)~Bx   3, CQ
        5. Am ⊃ Bm   1, UI
        6. An ⊃ Bn   1, UI
        7. (Am ⊃ Bm) • (An ⊃ Bn)   5, 6, Conj
        8. Bm ∨ Bn   2, 7, CD
        9. ~Bm   4, UI
      10. Bn   8, 9, DS
      11. ~Bn   4, UI
      12. Bn • ~Bn   10, 11, Conj
    13. ~~(∃x)Bx   3-12, IP
    14. (∃x)Bx   13, DN

(11) 1. (x)[(Ax ∨ Bx) ⊃ Cx]
    2. (x)[(Cx ∨ Dx) ⊃ ~Ax]   / (x)~Ax
        3. ~(x)~Ax   AIP
        4. (∃x)Ax   3, CQ
        5. Am   4, EI
        6. (Am ∨ Bm) ⊃ Cm   1, UI
        7. Am ∨ Bm   5, Add
        8. Cm   6, 7, MP
        9. (Cm ∨ Dm) ⊃ ~Am   2, UI
      10. Cm ∨ Dm   8, Add
      11. ~Am   9, 10, MP
      12. Am • ~Am   5, 11, Conj
    13. ~~(x)~Ax   3-12, IP
    14. (x)~Ax   13, DN

(12) 1. (∃x)Ax ⊃ (x)(Bx ⊃ Cx)
    2. (∃x)Dx ⊃ (x)~Cx   / (x)[(Ax • Dx) ⊃ ~Bx]
        3. Ax • Dx   ACP
        4. Ax   3, Simp

193

Exercise 8.4

	5. (∃x)Ax	4, EG
	6. (x)(Bx ⊃ Cx)	1, 5, MP
	7. Bx ⊃ Cx	6, UI
	8. Dx • Ax	3, Com
	9. Dx	8, Simp
	10. (∃x)Dx	9, EG
	11. (x)~Cx	2, 10, MP
	12. ~Cx	11, UI
	13. ~Bx	7, 12, MT
14. (Ax • Dx) ⊃ ~Bx		3-13, CP
15. (x)[(Ax • Dx) ⊃ ~Bx]		14, UG

(13) 1. (∃x)Ax ⊃ (x)(Bx ⊃ Cx)
      2. (∃x)Dx ⊃ (∃x)Bx   / (∃x)(Ax • Dx) ⊃ (∃x)Cx

	3. (∃x)(Ax • Dx)	ACP
	4. Am • Dm	3, EI
	5. Am	4, Simp
	6. (∃x)Ax	5, EG
	7. (x)(Bx ⊃ Cx)	1, 6, MP
	8. Dm • Am	4, Com
	9. Dm	8, Simp
	10. (∃x)Dx	9, EG
	11. (∃x)Bx	2, 10, MP
	12. Bn	11, EI
	13. Bn ⊃ Cn	7, UI
	14. Cn	12, 13, MP
	15. (∃x)Cx	14, EG
16. (∃x)(Ax • Dx) ⊃ (∃x)Cx		3-15, CP

(14) 1. (∃x)Ax ∨ (∃x)(Bx • Cx)
      2. (x)(Ax ⊃ Cx)   / (∃x)Cx

	3. ~(∃x)Cx	AIP
	4. (x)~Cx	3, CQ
	5. ~Cx	4, UI
	6. Ax ⊃ Cx	2, UI
	7. ~Ax	5, 6, MT
	8. (x)~Ax	7, UG
	9. ~(∃x)Ax	8, CQ
	10. (∃x)(Bx • Cx)	1, 9, DS
	11. Bm • Cm	10, EI
	12. Cm • Bm	11, Com
	13. Cm	12, Simp
	14. ~Cm	4, UI
	15. Cm • ~Cm	13, 14, Conj
16. ~~(∃x)Cx		3-15, IP
17. (∃x)Cx		16, DN

194

(15) 1. (∃x)Ax ⊃ (∃x)(Bx • Cx)
    2. (∃x)Cx ⊃ (x)(Dx • Ex)   / (x)(Ax ⊃ Ex)
        3. Ax   ACP
        4. (∃x)Ax   3, EG
        5. (∃x)(Bx • Cx)   1, 4, MP
        6. Bm • Cm   5, EI
        7. Cm • Bm   6, Com
        8. Cm   7, Simp
        9. (∃x)Cx   8, EG
        10. (x)(Dx • ⊃Ex) 2, 9, MP
        11. Dx • Ex   10, UI
        12. Ex • Dx   11, Com
        13. Ex   12, Simp
    14. Ax ⊃ Ex   3-13, CP
    15. (x)(Ax ⊃ Ex)   14, UG

(16) 1. (x)[(Ax ∨ Bx) ⊃ Cx]
    2. (∃x)(~Ax ∨ Dx) ⊃ (x)Ex   / (x)Cx ∨ (x)Ex
        3. ~[(x)Cx ∨ (x)Ex]   AIP
        4. ~(x)Cx • ~(x)Ex   3, DM
        5. ~(x)Cx   4, Simp
        6. (∃x)~Cx   5, CQ
        7. ~Cm   6, EI
        8. (Am ∨ Bm) ⊃ Cm 1, UI
        9. ~(Am ∨ Bm)   7, 8, MT
        10. ~Am • ~Bm   9, DM
        11. ~Am   10, Simp
        12. ~Am ∨ Dm   11, Add
        13. (∃x)(~Ax ∨ Dx) 12, EG
        14. (x)Ex   2, 13, MP
        15. ~(x)Ex • ~(x)Cx 4, Com
        16. ~(x)Ex   15, Simp
        17. (x)Ex • ~(x)Ex 14, 16, Conj
    18. ~~[(x)Cx ∨ (x)Ex] 3-17, IP
    19. (x)Cx ∨ (x)Ex   18, DN

(17) 1. (x)Ax ≡ (∃x)(Bx • Cx)
    2. (x)(Cx ⊃ Bx)   / (x)Ax ≡ (∃x)Cx
    3. [(x)Ax ⊃ (∃x)(Bx • Cx)] • [(∃x)(Bx • Cx) ⊃ (x)Ax]   1, Equiv
        4. (x)Ax   ACP
        5. (x)Ax ⊃ (∃x)(Bx • Cx)   3, Simp
        6. (∃x)(Bx • Cx)   4, 5, MP
        7. Bm • Cm   6, EI
        8. Cm • Bm   7, Com
        9. Cm   8, Simp

10. (∃x)Cx	9, EG
11. (x)Ax ⊃ (∃x)Cx	4-10, CP
12. (∃x)Cx	ACP
13. Cn	12, EI
14. Cn ⊃ Bn	2, UI
15. Bn	13, 14, MP
16. Bn • Cn	13, 15, Conj
17. (∃x)(Bx • Cx)	15, EG
18. [(∃x)(Bx • Cx) ⊃ (x)Ax] • [(x)Ax ⊃ (∃x)(Bx • Cx)]	3, Com
19. (∃x)(Bx • Cx) ⊃ (x)Ax	18, Simp
20. (x)Ax	17, 19, MP
21. (∃x)Cx ⊃ (x)Ax	12-20, CP
22. [(x)Ax ⊃ (∃x)Cx] • [(∃x)Cx ⊃ (x)Ax]	11, 21, Conj
23. (x)Ax ≡ (∃x)Cx	22, Equiv

(18) 1. (x)(Ax ≡ Bx)	
2. (x)[Ax ⊃ (Bx ⊃ Cx)]	
3. (∃x)Ax ∨ (∃x)Bx	/ (∃x)Cx
4. ~(∃x)Cx	AIP
5. (x)~Cx	4, CQ
6. ~Cx	5, UI
7. Ax ⊃ (Bx ⊃ Cx)	2, UI
8. (Ax • Bx) ⊃ Cx	7, Exp
9. ~(Ax • Bx)	6, 8, MT
10. Ax ≡ Bx	1, UI
11. (Ax • Bx) ∨ (~Ax • ~Bx)	10, Equiv
12. ~Ax • ~Bx	9, 11, DS
13. ~Ax	12, Simp
14. (x)~Ax	13, UG
15. ~(∃x)Ax	14, CQ
16. (∃x)Bx	3, 15, DS
17. ~Bx • ~Ax	12, Com
18. ~Bx	17, Simp
19. (x)~Bx	18, UG
20. ~(∃x)Bx	19, CQ
21. (∃x)Bx • ~(∃x)Bx	16, 20, Conj
22. ~~(∃x)Cx	4-21, IP
23. (∃x)Cx	22, DN

(19) 1. (x)[Bx ⊃ (Cx • Dx)]	/ (x)(Ax ⊃ Bx) ⊃ (x)(Ax ⊃ Dx)
2. (x)(Ax ⊃ Bx)	ACP
3. Ax	ACP
4. Ax ⊃ Bx	2, UI
5. Bx	3, 4, MP
6. Bx ⊃ (Cx • Dx)	1, UI

7. Cx • Dx	5, 6, MP
8. Dx • Cx	7, Com
9. Dx	8, Simp
10. Ax ⊃ Dx	3-9, CP
11. (x)(Ax ⊃ Dx)	10, UG
12. (x)(Ax ⊃ Bx) ⊃ (x)(Ax ⊃ Dx)	2-11, CP

(20) 1. (x)[Ax ⊃ (Bx • Cx)]

2. (x)[Dx ⊃ (Ex • Fx)]	/ (x)(Cx ⊃ Dx) ⊃ (x)(Ax ⊃ Fx)
3. (x)(Cx ⊃ Dx)	ACP
4. Ax	ACP
5. Ax ⊃ (Bx • Cx)	1, UI
6. Bx • Cx	4, 5, MP
7. Cx • Bx	6, Com
8. Cx	7, Simp
9. Cx ⊃ Dx	3, UI
10. Dx	8, 9, MP
11. Dx ⊃ (Ex • Fx)	2, UI
12. Ex • Fx	10, 11, MP
13. Fx • Ex	12, Com
14. Fx	13, Simp
15. Ax ⊃ Fx	4-14, CP
16. (x)(Ax ⊃ Fx)	15, UG
17. (x)(Cx ⊃ Dx) ⊃ (x)(Ax ⊃ Fx)	3-16, CP

(21) 1. (∃x)(Ax ∨ Bx)

2. (∃x)Ax ⊃ (x)(Cx ⊃ Bx)	
3. (∃x)Cx	/ (∃x)Bx
4. Am ∨ Bm	1, EI
5. ~(∃x)Bx	AIP
6. (x)~Bx	5, CQ
7. ~Bm	6, UI
8. Bm ∨ Am	4, Com
9. Am	7, 8, DS
10. (∃x)Ax	9, EG
11. (x)(Cx ⊃ Bx)	2, 10, MP
12. Cn	3, EI
13. Cn ⊃ Bn	11, UI
14. Bn	12, 13, MP
15. ~Bn	6, UI
16. Bn • ~Bn	14, 15, Conj
17. ~~(∃x)Bx	5-16, IP
18. (∃x)Bx	17, DN

Exercise 8.4

Part II

(1) 1. (x)(Ax ⊃ Wx)
  2. (x)(Rx ⊃ Cx)   / (x)[(Rx • Ax) ⊃ (Cx • Wx)]
    3. Rx • Ax   ACP
    4. Rx   3, Simp
    5. Ax • Rx   3, Com
    6. Ax   5, Simp
    7. Ax ⊃ Wx   1, UI
    8. Rx ⊃ Cx   2, UI
    9. Cx   4, 8, MP
    10. Wx   6, 7, MP
    11. Cx • Wx   9, 10, Conj
  12. (Rx • Ax) ⊃ (Cx • Wx) 3-11, CP
  13. (x)[(Rx • Ax) ⊃ (Cx • Wx)] 12, UG

(2) 1. (x)(Sx ⊃ Wx)
  2. (∃x)(Wx • Sx) ⊃ Vo   / (∃x)Sx ⊃ Vo
    3. (∃x)Sx   ACP
    4. Sm   3, EI
    5. Sm ⊃ Wm   1, UI
    6. Wm   4, 5, MP
    7. Wm • Sm   4, 6, Conj
    8. (∃x)(Wx • Sx)   7, EG
    9. Vo   2, 8, MP
  10. (∃x)Sx ⊃ Vo   3-9, CP

(3) 1. (x)(Jx ⊃ Wx) ⊃ (∃x)(Ax • Rx)
  2. (∃x)(Jx • ~Wx) ⊃ (∃x)(Ax • Rx) / (∃x)(Ax • Rx)
    3. ~(∃x)(Ax • Rx)   AIP
    4. ~(x)(Jx ⊃ Wx)   1, 3, MT
    5. (∃x)~(Jx ⊃ Wx)   4, CQ
    6. ~(Jm ⊃ Wm)   5, EI
    7. ~(~Jm ∨ Wm)   6, Impl
    8. ~~Jm • ~Wm   7, DM
    9. Jm • ~Wm   8, DN
    10. ~(∃x)(Jx • ~Wx)   2, 3, MT
    11. (x)~(Jx • ~Wx)   10, CQ
    12. ~(Jm • ~Wm)   11, UI
    13. ~Jm ∨ ~~Wm   12, DM
    14. ~Jm ∨ Wm   13, DN
    15. Jm   9, Simp
    16. ~~Jm   15, DN
    17. Wm   14, 16, DS
    18. ~Wm • Jm   9, Com
    19. ~Wm   18, Simp

198

20. Wm • ~Wm	17, 19, Conj	
21. ~~(∃x)(Ax • Rx)	3-20, IP	
22. (∃x)(Ax • Rx)	21, DN	

(4) 1. (x)[(Sx ∨ Ux) ⊃ (Ix • Cx)]
    2. (x)[(Cx ∨ Vx) ⊃ (Rx • Ax)]   / (x)(Sx ⊃ Ax)
       3. Sx   ACP
       4. Sx ∨ Ux   3, Add
       5. (Sx ∨ Ux) ⊃ (Ix • Cx)   1, UI
       6. Ix • Cx   4, 5, MP
       7. Cx • Ix   6, Com
       8. Cx   7, Simp
       9. Cx ∨ Vx   8, Add
      10. (Cx ∨ Vx) ⊃ (Rx • Ax)   2, UI
      11. Rx • Ax   9, 10, MP
      12. Ax • Rx   11, Com
      13. Ax   12, Simp
    14. Sx ⊃ Ax   3-13, CP
    15. (x)(Sx ⊃ Ax)   14, UG

(5) 1. (x)(Ax ⊃ Dx)
    2. (x)[(Ex • Ax) ⊃ Cx] • (x)[(Cx • Dx) ⊃ Fx]   / (x)[(Ex • Ax) ⊃ Fx]
       3. Ex • Ax   ACP
       4. (x)[(Ex • Ax) ⊃ Cx]   2, Simp
       5. (x)[(Cx • Dx) ⊃ Fx] • (x)[(Ex • Ax) ⊃ Cx]   2, Com
       6. (x)[(Cx • Dx) ⊃ Fx]   5, Simp
       7. (Ex • Ax) ⊃ Cx   4, UI
       8. (Cx • Dx) ⊃ Fx   6, UI
       9. Cx   3, 7, MP
      10. Ax • Ex   3, Com
      11. Ax   10, Simp
      12. Ax ⊃ Dx   1, UI
      13. Dx   11, 12, MP
      14. Cx • Dx   9, 13, Conj
      15. Fx   8, 14, MP
    16. (Ex • Ax) ⊃ Fx   3-15, CP
    17. (x)[(Ex • Ax) ⊃ Fx]   16, UG

(6) 1. (∃x)Sx ⊃ (∃x)(Ex • Wx)
    2. (∃x)(Ex ∨ Vx) ⊃ (∃x)Lx
    3. (∃x)Vx ∨ (∃x)Sx   / (∃x)Lx
       4. ~(∃x)Lx   AIP
       5. ~(∃x)(Ex ∨ Vx)   2, 4, MT
       6. (x)~(Ex ∨ Vx)   5, CQ
       7. ~(Ex ∨ Vx)   6, UI
       8. ~Ex • ~Vx   7, DM

9. ~Ex	8, Simp
10. ~Ex ∨ ~Wx	9, Add
11. ~(Ex • Wx)	10, DM
12. (x)~(Ex • Wx)	11, UG
13. ~(∃x)(Ex • Wx)	12, CQ
14. ~(∃x)Sx	1, 13, MT
15. (∃x)Sx ∨ (∃x)Vx	3, Com
16. (∃x)Vx	14, 15, DS
17. ~Vx • ~Ex	8, Com
18. ~Vx	17, Simp
19. (x)~Vx	18, UG
20. ~(∃x)Vx	19, CQ
21. (∃x)Vx • ~(∃x)Vx	16, 20, Conj
22. ~~(∃x)Lx	4-21, IP
23. (∃x)Lx	22, DN

(7) 1. (∃x)Cx ⊃ (x)[Ax ⊃ (Sx • Dx)]
    2. (x)(Cx ⊃ ~Ax) ⊃ (∃x)(Dx • Sx)   / (∃x)(Dx • Sx)
        3. ~(∃x)(Dx • Sx)   AIP
        4. ~(x)(Cx ⊃ ~Ax)   2, 3, MT
        5. (∃x)~(Cx ⊃ ~Ax)   4, CQ
        6. ~(Cm ⊃ ~Am)   5, EI
        7. ~(~Cm ∨ ~Am)   6, Impl
        8. ~~Cm • ~~Am   7, DM
        9. Cm • ~~Am   8, DN
        10. Cm • Am   9, DN
        11. Cm   10, Simp
        12. (∃x)Cx   11, EG
        13. (x)[Ax ⊃ (Sx • Dx)]   1, 12, MP
        14. Am ⊃ (Sm • Dm)   13, UI
        15. Am • Cm   10, Com
        16. Am   15, Simp
        17. Sm • Dm   14, 16, MP
        18. Dm • Sm   17, Com
        19. (∃x)(Dx • Sx)   18, EG
        20. (∃x)(Dx • Sx) • ~(∃x)(Dx • Sx)   3, 19, Conj
    21. ~~(∃x)(Dx • Sx)   3-20, IP
    22. (∃x)(Dx • Sx)   21, DN

(8) 1. (∃x)Vx ⊃ (x)(Px ⊃ Ax)
    2. (∃x)Px ⊃ (x)(Ax ⊃ Cx)   / (∃x)Vx ⊃ (x)(Px ⊃ Cx)
        3. (∃x)Vx   ACP
            4. Px   ACP
            5. (x)(Px ⊃ Ax)   1, 3, MP
            6. (∃x)Px   4, EG

7. (x)(Ax ⊃ Cx)	2, 6, MP
8. Px ⊃ Ax	5, UI
9. Ax	4, 8, MP
10. Ax ⊃ Cx	7, UI
11. Cx	9, 10, MP
12. Px ⊃ Cx	4-11, CP
13. (x)(Px ⊃ Cx)	12, UG
14. (∃x)Vx ⊃ (x)(Px ⊃ Cx)	3-13, CP

(9)	1. (x)(Sx ⊃ ~Px) ∨ (x)(Rx ⊃ ~Px)	
	2. (∃x)(Sx • Px) ∨ (x)(Wx ⊃ ~Px)	/ ~(∃x)[(Rx • Px) • Wx]
	3. (∃x)[(Rx • Px) • Wx]	AIP
	4. (Rm • Pm) • Wm	3, EI
	5. Rm • Pm	4, Simp
	6. ~~Rm • Pm	5, DN
	7. ~~Rm • ~~Pm	6, DN
	8. ~(~Rm ∨ ~Pm)	7, DM
	9. ~(Rm ⊃ ~Pm)	8, Impl
	10. (∃x)~(Rx ⊃ ~Px)	9, EG
	11. ~(x)(Rx ⊃ ~Px)	10, CQ
	12. (x)(Rx ⊃ ~Px) ∨ (x)(Sx ⊃ ~Px)	1, Com
	13. (x)(Sx ⊃ ~Px)	11, 12, DS
	14. Wm • (Rm • Pm)	4, Com
	15. Wm	14, Simp
	16. Pm • Rm	5, Com
	17. Pm	16, Simp
	18. Wm • Pm	15, 17, Conj
	19. ~~Wm • Pm	18, DN
	20. ~~Wm • ~~Pm	19, DN
	21. ~(~Wm ∨ ~Pm)	20, DM
	22. ~(Wm ⊃ ~Pm)	21, Impl
	23. (∃x)~(Wx ⊃ ~Px)	22, EG
	24. ~(x)(Wx ⊃ ~Px)	23, CQ
	25. (x)(Wx ⊃ ~Px) ∨ (∃x)(Sx • Px)	2, Com
	26. (∃x)(Sx • Px)	24, 25, DS
	27. Sn • Pn	26, EI
	28. Sn ⊃ ~Pn	13, UI
	29. Sn	27, Simp
	30. ~Pn	28, 29, MP
	31. Pn • Sn	27, Com
	32. Pn	31, Simp
	33. Pn • ~Pn	30, 32, Conj
	34. ~(∃x)[(Rx • Px) • Wx]	3-33, IP

Exercise 8.5

(10) 1. (∃x)(Gx • Px) ∨ (∃x)(Ax • Px)
      2. (∃x)Px ⊃ (∃x)[Ax • (Cx • Dx)]   / (∃x)(Dx • Cx)
          3. ~(∃x)(Dx • Cx)   AIP
          4. (x)~(Dx • Cx)   3, CQ
          5. ~(Dx • Cx)   4, UI
          6. ~(Cx • Dx)   5, Com
          7. ~(Cx • Dx) ∨ ~Ax   6, Add
          8. ~Ax ∨ ~(Cx • Dx)   7, Com
          9. ~[Ax • (Cx • Dx)]   8, DM
         10. (x)~[Ax • (Cx • Dx)]   9, UG
         11. ~(∃x)[(Ax • (Cx • Dx)]   10, CQ
         12. ~(∃x)Px   2, 11, MT
         13. (x)~Px   12, CQ
         14. ~Px   13, UI
         15. ~Px ∨ ~Gx   14, Add
         16. ~Gx ∨ ~Px   15, Com
         17. ~(Gx • Px)   16, DM
         18. (x)~(Gx • Px)   17, UG
         19. ~(∃x)(Gx • Px)   18, CQ
         20. (∃x)(Ax • Px)   1, 19, DS
         21. Am • Pm   20, EI
         22. Pm • Am   21, Com
         23. Pm   22, Simp
         24. ~Pm   13, UI
         25. Pm • ~Pm   23, 24, Conj
      26. ~~(∃x)(Dx • Cx)   3-25, IP
      27. (∃x)(Dx • Cx)   26, DN

(An alternate method appears in the back of the textbook.)

Exercise 8.5
Part I

1. All cats are animals.
    No cats are dogs.
    Therefore, no dogs are animals.

2. Some animals are fish.
    All cats are animals.
    Therefore, some cats are fish.

3. All women are humans.
    Chuck Norris is a human.
    Therefore, Chuck Norris is a woman.

4. Some mammals are dogs.
   Some mammals write books.
   Therefore, some mammals are dogs that write books.

5. Everything is either an animal, vegetable or mineral.
   Therefore, either everything is an animal, or everything is a vegetable or everything is a mineral

6. All dogs are either animals or sharks.
   All All animals that are sharks are fish.
   Therefore, all dogs are fish.

7. There are flowers.
   There are dogs.
   No flowers are animals.
   Therefore, some dogs are not animals.

8. Anything that is either a dog or a cat is an animal.
   Any animal that has a trunk is an elephant.
   Therefore, all dogs are elephants.

9. All large cats are mammals.
   All large dogs are animals.
   Therefore, all large animals are mammals.

10. Some mammals are felines.
    Some animals are not felines.
    All mammals are animals.
    Therefore, some feline animals are not mammals.

Part II

(1) 1. (x)(Ax ⊃ Bx)
     2. (x)(Ax ⊃ Cx)   / (x)(Bx ⊃ Cx)

For a universe consisting of one member, we have,
Aa ⊃ Ba / Aa ⊃ Ca // Ba ⊃ Ca
 F T T   F T F   T F F

(2) 1. (x)(Ax ∨ Bx)
     2. ~An   / (x)Bx

For a universe consisting of two members, we have,
(An ∨ Bn) • (Aa ∨ Ba) / ~ An // Bn • Ba
 F T T T T T T F   T F   T F F

Exercise 8.5

(3) 1. $(\exists x)Ax \vee (\exists x)Bx$
    2. $(\exists x)Ax$ / $(\exists x)Bx$

For a universe consisting of one member, we have,
Aa ∨ Ba / Aa // Ba
T T F   T   F

(4) 1. $(x)(Ax \supset Bx)$
    2. $(\exists x)Ax$ / $(x)Bx$

For a universe consisting of two members, we have,
(Aa ⊃ Ba) • (Ab ⊃ Bb) / Aa ∨ Ab // Ba • Bb
 T T T   T F T F   T T F   T F F

(5) 1. $(x)[Ax \supset (Bx \vee Cx)]$
    2. $(\exists x)Ax$ /$(\exists x)Bx$

For a universe consisting of one member, we have,
Aa ⊃ (Ba ∨ Ca) / Aa // Ba
T T   F T T   T   F

(6) 1. $(\exists x)Ax$
    2. $(\exists x)Bx$ / $(\exists x)(Ax \cdot Bx)$

For a universe consisting of two members, we have,
Aa ∨ Ab / Ba ∨ Bb // (Aa • Ba) ∨ (Ab • Bb)
T T F   F T T   T F F   F   F F T

(7) 1. $(x)(Ax \supset Bx)$
    2. $(\exists x)Bx \supset (\exists x)Cx$ / $(x)(Ax \supset Cx)$

For a universe consisting of two members, we have,
(Aa ⊃ Ba) • (Ab ⊃ Bb) / (Ba ∨ Bb) ⊃ (Ca ∨ Cb) // (Aa ⊃ Ca) • (Ab ⊃ Cb)
 T T T   T T   T T   T T   T   T   T T F   T T T   F T F F

(8) 1. $(\exists x)(Ax \cdot Bx) \equiv (\exists x)Cx$
    2. $(x)(Ax \supset Bx)$ / $(x)Ax \equiv (\exists x)Cx$

For a universe consisting of two members, we have,
[(Aa • Ba) ∨ (Ab • Bb)] ≡ (Ca ∨ Cb) / (Aa ⊃ Ba) • (Ab ⊃ Bb)
 T T T   T F F F   T T   T   T T T   T F T F

// (Aa • Ab) ≡ (Ca ∨ Cb)
  T F F   F T T

(9) 1. (∃x)(Ax • ~Bx)
    2. (∃x)(Bx • ~Ax)   / (x)(Ax ∨ Bx)

For a universe consisting of three members, we have,
[(Aa • ~ Ba) ∨ (Ab • ~ Bb)] ∨ (Ac • ~ Bc)
 T T T F   T F F F T   T F F T F

/ [(Ba • ~ Aa) ∨ (Bb • ~ Ab)] ∨ (Bc • ~ Ac)
   F F F T   T T T T F   T F F T F

// [(Aa ∨ Ba) • (Ab ∨ Bb)] • (Ac ∨ Bc)
    T T F T F T T   F F F F

(10) 1. (∃x)(Ax • Bx)
     2. (∃x)(~Ax • ~Bx)   / (x)(Ax ≡ Bx)

For a universe consisting of three members, we have,
(Aa • Ba) ∨ [(Ab • Bb) ∨ (Ac • Bc)]
 T T T   T   T F F T F F F

/ (~ Aa • ~ Ba) ∨ [(~ Ab • ~ Bb) ∨ (~ Ac • ~ Bc)]
   F T F F T T   F T F T F T T F T T F

// (Aa ≡ Ba) • [(Ab ≡ Bb) • (Ac ≡ Bc)]
    T T T F T F F F F F T F

Part III

(1) 1. (x)[Vx • Px) ⊃ (Ax • Mx)
    2. (∃x)(Vx • Ox)   / (∃x)(Mx • Ax)

For a universe consisting of one member, we have,
(Va • Pa) ⊃ (Aa • Ma) / Va • Oa // Ma • Aa
 T F F T F F F   T T T   F F F

(2) 1. (x)[(Px ∨ Hx) ⊃ Mx]
    2. Pa   / (x)Mx

For a universe consisting of two members, we have,
[(Pa ∨ Ha) ⊃ Ma] • [(Pc ∨ Hc) ⊃ Mc] / Pa // Ma • Mc
 T T   T T T F F F T F   T   T F F

(3) 1. (∃x)Ox ⊃ (∃x)Bx
    2. (∃x)Cx ⊃ (∃x)Fx
    3. Oa • Ca   / (∃x)(Bx • Fx)

205

Exercise 8.6

For a universe consisting of two members, we have,
(Oa ∨ Ob) ⊃ (Ba ∨ Bb) / (Ca ∨ Cb) ⊃ (Fa ∨ Fb)
 T T   T T T F   T T   T F T T

/ Oa • Ca // (Ba • Fa) ∨ (Bb • Fb)
 T T T   T F F F F F T

 (4) 1. (x)(Tx ⊃ Hx)
      2. (∃x)(Tx • Hx) ⊃ (∃x)(Px • Ox)   / (x)(Tx ⊃ Ox)

For a universe consisting of two members, we have,
(Ta ⊃ Ha) • (Tb ⊃ Hb) / [(Ta • Ha) ∨ (Tb • Hb)] ⊃ [(Pa • Oa) ∨ (Pb • Ob)]
 T T T T T T T   T T T T T T T T F F F T T T

// (Ta ⊃ Oa) • (Tb ⊃ Ob)
  T F F F T T T

 (5) 1. (x)[(Cx ∨ Vx) ⊃ Mx]
      2. (∃x)(Vx • ~Cx)
      3. (∃x)(Cx • ~Vx)   / (x)Mx

For a universe consisting of three members, we have,
{[(Ca ∨ Va) ⊃ Ma] • [(Cb ∨ Vb) ⊃ Mb]} • [(Cc ∨ Vc) ⊃ Mc]
 T T F T T T F T T T T T F F F T F

/ [(Va • ~ Ca) ∨ (Vb • ~ Cb)] ∨ (Vc • ~ Cc)
  F F F T T T T T F T F F T F

/ [(Ca • ~ Va) ∨ (Cb • ~ Vb)] ∨ (Cc • ~ Vc)
  T T T F T F F F T T F F T F

// (Ma • Mb) • Mc
   T T T F F

Exercise 8.6
Part I

 1. Rcp

 2. (x)(Rxp ⊃ Ex)

 3. Fje ∨ Fjc

 4. (∃x)Fxj ⊃ Fmj

 5. (x)(Tjx ⊃ Gx)

206

6. (∃x)(Mx • Tnx)

7. (x)[Px ⊃ (∃y)Sxy]

8. (∃x)[Px • (y)~Sxy]

9. (x)[Px ⊃ (∃y)~Sxy]

10. (∃x)[Px • (y)Sxy]

11. (x)[(Dx • Srx) ⊃ Gx] (assuming the hotel also serves food)
   (x)[Srx ⊃ (Gx • Dx)] (assuming the hotel serves no food)

12. (x)(Pcx ⊃ Acx)

13. (∃x)[(Cx • Lx) • Dpx]

14. (x)[(Cx • Lx) ⊃ Djx]

15. (x)(Isx ⊃ Fxs)

16. (∃x)(Fxc • Icx)

17. (∃x)[Px • (y)(Txy ⊃ Bxy)]

18. (∃x){Px • (y)[(Py • Syx) ⊃ Sxy]}

19. (x){Px ⊃ (∃y)[Py • (Mxy ⊃ Axy)]}

20. (∃x){Px • (y)[(Py • Mxy) ⊃ Axy]}

21. (∃x)[Px • (y)(Axy ⊃ Ty)]

22. (∃x){Px • (y)[(Ty • Sxy) ⊃ Axy]}

23. (∃x)Cx ⊃ (∃x)(Cx • Px)

24. (x){Cx ⊃ [(y)(Ry ⊃ Vy) ⊃ Px]}

25. (x){Lx ⊃ (y)[(Wy • Cy) ⊃ Rxy]}

26. (∃x){Lx • (y)[(Py • ~Ryy) ⊃ Rxy]}

27. (∃x){(Cx • Tx) • (y)[(By • Ly) ⊃ Rxy]}

28. (x){(Cx • Fx) ⊃ (y)[(By • Ly) ⊃ Rxy]}

Exercise 8.6

29. (x){(Sx • Dx) ⊃ [(y)(Ty ⊃ ~By) ⊃ Hx]}

30. (∃x)(Sx • Dx) ⊃ (∃x)[(Sx • Dx) • Hx]

Part II

(1) 1. (x)[Ax ⊃ (y)Bxy]
     2. Am   / (y)Bmy
     3. Am ⊃ (y)Bmy   1, UI
     4. (y)Bmy   2, 3, MP

(2) 1. (x)[Ax ⊃ (y)(By ⊃ Cxy)]
     2. Am • Bn   / Cmn
     3. Am ⊃ (y)(By ⊃ Cmy)   1, UI
     4. Am   2, Simp
     5. (y)(By ⊃ Cmy)   3, 4, MP
     6. Bn ⊃ Cmn   5, UI
     7. Bn • Am   2, Com
     8. Bn   7, Simp
     9. Cmn   6, 8, MP

(3) 1. (∃x)[Ax • (y)(By ⊃ Cxy)]
     2. (∃x)Ax ⊃ Bj   / (∃x)Cxj
     3. Am • (y)(By ⊃ Cmy)   1, EI
     4. Am   3, Simp
     5. (∃x)Ax   4, EG
     6. Bj   2, 5, MP
     7. (y)(By ⊃ Cmy) • Am   3, Com
     8. (y)(By ⊃ Cmy)   7, Simp
     9. Bj ⊃ Cmj   8, UI
     10. Cmj   6, 9, MP
     11. (∃x)Cxj   10, EG

(4) 1. (x)(∃y)(Ax ⊃ By)   / (x)Ax ⊃ (∃y)By
     2. (x)Ax   ACP
     3. Ax   2, UI
     4. (∃y)(Ax ⊃ By)   1, UI
     5. Ax ⊃ Bm   4, EI
     6. Bm   3, 5, MP
     7. (∃y)By   6, EG
     8. (x)Ax ⊃ (∃y)By   2-7, CP

(5) 1. $(\exists x)Ax \supset (\exists y)By$ / $(\exists y)(x)(Ax \supset By)$
       2. Ax   ACP
       3. $(\exists x)Ax$ 2, EG
       4. $(\exists y)By$ 1, 3, MP
       5. Bm   4, EI
   6. $Ax \supset Bm$ 2-5, CP
   7. $(x)(Ax \supset Bm)$ 6, UG
   8. $(\exists y)(x)(Ax \supset By)$ 7, EG

(6) 1. $(x)(y)(Ax \supset By)$
       2. $(x)(\exists y)(Ax \supset Cy)$ / $(x)(\exists y)(Ax \supset (By \cdot Cy)]$
       3. Ax   ACP
       4. $(\exists y)(Ax \supset Cy)$ 2, UI
       5. $Ax \supset Cm$ 4, EI
       6. Cm   3, 5, MP
       7. $(y)(Ax \supset By)$ 1, UI
       8. $Ax \supset Bm$ 7, UI
       9. Bm   3, 8, MP
     10. $Bm \cdot Cm$ 6, 9, Conj
   11. $Ax \supset (Bm \cdot Cm)$ 3-10, CP
   12. $(\exists y)[Ax \supset (By \cdot Cy)]$ 11, EG
   13. $(x)(\exists y)[Ax \supset (By \cdot Cy)]$ 12, UG

(7) 1. $(\exists x)[Ax \cdot (y)(Ay \supset Bxy)]$ / $(\exists x)Bxx$
     2. $Am \cdot (y)(Ay \supset Bmy)$ 1, EI
     3. Am   2, Simp
     4. $(y)(Ay \supset Bmy) \cdot Am$ 2, Com
     5. $(y)(Ay \supset Bmy)$ 4, Simp
     6. $Am \supset Bmm$ 5, UI
     7. Bmm   3, 6, MP
     8. $(\exists x)Bxx$ 7, EG

(8) 1. $(\exists x)[Ax \cdot (y)(By \supset Cxy)]$
     2. $(x)(\exists y)(Ax \supset By)$ / $(\exists x)(\exists y)Cxy$
     3. $Am \cdot (y)(By \supset Cmy)$ 1, EI
     4. Am   3, Simp
     5. $(y)(By \supset Cmy) \cdot Am$ 3, Com
     6. $(y)(By \supset Cmy)$ 5, Simp
     7. $(\exists y)(Am \supset By)$ 2, UI
     8. $Am \supset Bn$ 7, EI
     9. Bn   4, 8, MP
   10. $Bn \supset Cmn$ 6, UI
   11. Cmn   9, 10, MP
   12. $(\exists y)Cmy$ 11, EG
   13. $(\exists x)(\exists y)Cxy$ 12, EG

Exercise 8.6

(9)　1. (∃x)(y)(Axy ⊃ Bxy)
　　　2. (x)(∃y)~Bxy　　　　　　　　/ ~(x)(y)Axy
　　　3. (y)(Amy ⊃ Bmy)　　　　　1, EI
　　　4. (∃y)~Bmy　　　　　　　　2, UI
　　　5. ~Bmn　　　　　　　　　　4, EI
　　　6. Amn ⊃ Bmn　　　　　　　3, UI
　　　7. ~Amn　　　　　　　　　　5, 6, MT
　　　8. (∃y)~Amy　　　　　　　　7, EG
　　　9. (∃x)(∃y)~Axy　　　　　　8, EG
　　　10. (∃x)~(y)Axy　　　　　　9, CQ
　　　11. ~(x)(y)Axy　　　　　　　10, CQ

(10)　1. (x)(∃y)Axy ⊃ (x)(∃y)Bxy
　　　2. (∃x)(y)~Bxy　　　　　　　/ (∃x)(y)~Axy
　　　3. (∃x)~(∃y)Bxy　　　　　　2, CQ
　　　4. ~(x)(∃y)Bxy　　　　　　　3, CQ
　　　5. ~(x)(∃y)Axy　　　　　　　1, 4, MT
　　　6. (∃x)~(∃y)Axy　　　　　　5, CQ
　　　7. (∃x)(y)~Axy　　　　　　　6, CQ

(11)　1. (∃x){Ax • [(∃y)By ⊃ Cx]}
　　　2. (x)(Ax ⊃ Bx)　　　　　　/ (∃x)Cx
　　　3. Am • [(∃y)By ⊃ Cm]　　　1, EI
　　　4. Am　　　　　　　　　　　3, Simp
　　　5. Am ⊃ Bm　　　　　　　　2, UI
　　　6. Bm　　　　　　　　　　　4, 5, MP
　　　7. (∃y)By　　　　　　　　　6, EG
　　　8. [(∃y)By ⊃ Cm] • Am　　　3, Com
　　　9. (∃y)By ⊃ Cm　　　　　　8, Simp
　　　10. Cm　　　　　　　　　　　7, 9, MP
　　　11. (∃x)Cx　　　　　　　　　10, EG

(12)　1. (∃x)(y)[(Ay • By) ⊃ Cxy]
　　　2. (y)(Ay ⊃ By)　　　　　　/ (y)[Ay ⊃ (∃x)Cxy]
　　　　3. Ay　　　　　　　　　　ACP
　　　　4. Ay ⊃ By　　　　　　　2, UI
　　　　5. By　　　　　　　　　　3, 4, MP
　　　　6. Ay • By　　　　　　　　3, 5, Conj
　　　　7. (y)[(Ay • By) ⊃ Cmy]　1, EI
　　　　8. (Ay • By) ⊃ Cmy　　　7, UI
　　　　9. Cmy　　　　　　　　　6, 8, MP
　　　　10. (∃x)Cxy　　　　　　　9, EG
　　　11. Ay ⊃ (∃x)Cxy　　　　　3-10, CP
　　　12. (y)[Ay ⊃ (∃x)Cxy]　　　11, UG

210

(13) 1. (∃x){Ax • (y)[(By ∨ Cy) ⊃ Dxy]}
     2. (∃x)Ax ⊃ (∃y)By   / (∃x)(∃y)Dxy
     3. Am • (y)[(By ∨ Cy) ⊃ Dmy]   1, EI
     4. Am   3, Simp
     5. (∃x)Ax   4, EG
     6. (∃y)By   2, 5, MP
     7. Bn   6, EI
     8. (y)[(By ∨ Cy) ⊃ Dmy] • Am   3, Com
     9. (y)[(By ∨ Cy) ⊃ Dmy]   8, Simp
   10. (Bn ∨ Cn) ⊃ Dmn   9, UI
   11. Bn ∨ Cn   7, Add
   12. Dmn   10, 11, MP
   13. (∃y)Dmy   12, EG
   14. (∃x)(∃y)Dxy   13, EG

(14) 1. (x){Ax ⊃ [(∃y)(By • Cy) ⊃ Dx]}
     2. (x)(Bx ⊃ Cx)   / (x)[Ax ⊃ (Bx ⊃ Dx)]
        3. Ax   ACP
          4. Bx   ACP
          5. Ax ⊃ [(∃y)(By • Cy) ⊃ Dx]   1, UI
          6. (∃y)(By • Cy) ⊃ Dx   3, 5, MP
          7. Bx ⊃ Cx   2, UI
          8. Cx   4, 7, MP
          9. Bx • Cx   4, 8, Conj
         10. (∃y)(By • Cy)   9, EG
         11. Dx   6, 10, MP
      12. Bx ⊃ Dx   4-11, CP
   13. Ax ⊃ (Bx ⊃ Dx)   3-12, CP
   14. (x)[Ax ⊃ (Bx ⊃ Dx)]   13, UG

(15) 1. (∃x)(y)(Ayx ⊃ ~Axy)   / ~(x)Axx
     2. (y)(Aym ⊃ ~Amy)   1, EI
     3. Amm ⊃ ~Amm   2, UI
     4. ~Amm ∨ ~Amm   3, Impl
     5. ~Amm   4, Taut
     6. (∃x)~Axx   5, EG
     7. ~(x)Axx   6, CQ

(16) 1. (x)(∃y)(Ax • By)   / (∃y)(x)(Ax • By)
     2. (∃y)(Ax • By)   1, UI
     3. Ax • Ba   2, EI
     4. Ax   3, Simp
     5. (x)Ax   4, UG
     6. Az   5, UI
     7. Ba • Az   3, Com
     8. Ba   7, Simp

9. Az • Ba	6, 8, Conj
10. (x)(Ax • Ba)	9, UG
11. (∃y)(x)(Ax • By)	10, EG

(17) 1. (x)(∃y)(Ax ∨ By)   / (∃y)(x)(Ax ∨ By)

2. ~(∃y)(x)(Ax ∨ By)	AIP
3. (y)~(x)(Ax ∨ By)	2, CQ
4. (y)(∃x)~(Ax ∨ By)	3, CQ
5. (∃x)~(Ax ∨ By)	4, UI
6. ~(Am ∨ By)	5, EI
7. ~Am • ~By	6, DM
8. (∃y)(Am ∨ By)	1, UI
9. Am ∨ Bn	8, EI
10. ~Am	7, Simp
11. Bn	9, 10, DS
12. ~By • ~Am	7, Com
13. ~By	12, Simp
14. (y)~By	13, UG
15. ~Bn	14, UI
16. Bn • ~Bn	11, 15, Conj
17. ~~(∃y)(x)(Ax ∨ By)	2-16, IP
18. (∃y)(x)(Ax ∨ By)	17, DN

(Note: Attempts to use direct proof on this argument violate the second restriction on UG.)

(18) 1. (x)[Ax ⊃ (∃y)(By • Cxy)]

2. (∃x)[Ax • (y)(By ⊃ Dxy)]   / (∃x)(∃y)(Cxy • Dxy)

3. Am • (y)(By ⊃ Dmy)	2, EI
4. Am ⊃ (∃y)(By • Cmy)	1, UI
5. Am	3, Simp
6. (∃y)(By • Cmy)	4, 5, MP
7. Bn • Cmn	6, EI
8. (y)(By ⊃ Dmy) • Am	3, Com
9. (y)(By ⊃ Dmy)	8, Simp
10. Bn ⊃ Dmn	9, UI
11. Bn	7, Simp
12. Dmn	10, 11, MP
13. Cmn • Bn	7, Com
14. Cmn	13, Simp
15. Cmn • Dmn	12, 14, Conj
16. (∃y)(Cmy • Dmy)	15, EG
17. (∃x)(∃y)(Cxy • Dxy)	16, EG

(19) 1. (x)(∃y)Axy ∨ (x)(y)Bxy
     2. (x)(∃y)(Cx ⊃ ~Bxy)   / (x)(∃y)(Cx ⊃ Axy)
         3. Cx   ACP
         4. (∃y)(Cx ⊃ ~Bxy)   2, UI
         5. Cx ⊃ ~Bxm   4, EI
         6. ~Bxm   3, 5, MP
         7. (∃y)~Bxy   6, EG
         8. (∃x)(∃y)~Bxy   7, EG
         9. (∃x)~(y)Bxy   8, CQ
       10. ~(x)(y)Bxy   9, CQ
       11. (x)(y)Bxy ∨ (x)(∃y)Axy 1, Com
       12. (x)(∃y)Axy   10, 11, DS
       13. (∃y)Axy   12, UI
       14. Axn   13, EI
   15. Cx ⊃ Axn   3-14, CP
   16. (∃y)(Cx ⊃ Axy)   15, EG
   17. (x)(∃y)(Cx ⊃ Axy)   16, UG

(20) 1. (x)(y)[Axy ⊃ (Bx • Cy)]
     2. (x)(y)[(Bx ∨ Dy) ⊃ ~Axy]   / ~(∃x)(∃y)Axy
         3. (∃x)(∃y)Axy   AIP
         4. (∃y)Amy   3, EI
         5. Amn   4, EI
         6. (y)[Amy ⊃ (Bm • Cy)] 1, UI
         7. Amn ⊃ (Bm • Cn)   6, UI
         8. Bm • Cn   5, 7, MP
         9. Bm   8, Simp
       10. (y)[(Bm ∨ Dy) ⊃ ~Amy] 2, UI
       11. (Bm ∨ Dn) ⊃ ~Amn 10, UI
       12. Bm ∨ Dn   9, Add
       13. ~Amn   11, 12, MP
       14. Amn • ~Amn   5, 13, Conj
   15. ~(∃x)(∃y)Axy   3-14, IP

Part III

(1) 1. (x)[Px ⊃ (y)(Ay ⊃ Oxy)]
    2. Pj • ~Ojm   / ~Am
    3. Pj ⊃ (y)(Ay ⊃ Ojy) 1, UI
    4. Pj   2, Simp
    5. (y)(Ay ⊃ Ojy)   3, 4, MP
    6. Am ⊃ Ojm   5, UI
    7. ~Ojm • Pj   2, Com
    8. ~Ojm   7, Simp
    9. ~Am   6, 9, MT

213

Exercise 8.6

(2) 1. (x)[(Fxm ∨ Fxp) ⊃ Rx]
    2. (∃x)Fxm ⊃ Fem   / Fam ⊃ Re
       3. Fam   ACP
       4. (∃x)Fxm   3, EG
       5. Fem   2, 4, MP
       6. (Fem ∨ Fep) ⊃ Re   1, UI
       7. Fem ∨ Fep   5, Add
       8. Re   6, 7, MP
    9. Fam ⊃ Re   3-8, CP

(3) 1. (x)(Hx ⊃ Ax)   / (x)[(∃y)(Hy • Oxy) ⊃ (∃y)(Ay • Oxy)]
       2. (∃y)(Hy • Oxy)   ACP
       3. Hm • Oxm   2, EI
       4. Hm   3, Simp
       5. Hm ⊃ Am   1, UI
       6. Am   4, 5, MP
       7. Oxm • Hm   3, Com
       8. Oxm   7, Simp
       9. Am • Oxm   6, 8, Conj
      10. (∃y)(Ay • Oxy)   9, EG
    11. (∃y)(Hy • Oxy) ⊃ (∃y)(Ay • Oxy)   2-10, CP
    12. (x)[(∃y)(Hy • Oxy) ⊃ (∃y)(Ay • Oxy)]   11, UG

(4) 1. Po
       2. (x)[(Px • Cx) ⊃ Sox]
       3. (x)(Px ⊃ ~Sxx)   / ~Co
         4. Co   AIP
         5. (Po • Co) ⊃ Soo   2, UI
         6. Po • Co   1, 4, Conj
         7. Soo   5, 6, MP
         8. Po ⊃ ~Soo   3, UI
         9. ~Soo   1, 8, MP
       10. Soo • ~Soo   7, 9, Conj
     11. ~Co   4-10, IP

(5) 1. (x){(Hx • Px) ⊃ [(y)(By ⊃ Cy) ⊃ Rx]}
       2. (∃x)[(Hx • Px) • ~Rx]   / (∃x)(Bx • ~Cx)
       3. (Hm • Pm) • ~Rm   2, EI
       4. Hm • Pm   3, Simp
       5. (Hm • Pm) ⊃ [(y)(By ⊃ Cy) ⊃ Rm]   1, UI
       6. (y)(By ⊃ Cy) ⊃ Rm   4, 5, MP
       7. ~Rm • (Hm • Pm)   3, Com
       8. ~Rm   7, Simp
       9. ~(y)(By ⊃ Cy)   6, 8, MT
      10. (∃y)~(By ⊃ Cy)   9, CQ

11. ~(Bn ⊃ Cn)	10, EI
12. ~(~Bn ∨ Cn)	11, Impl
13. ~~Bn • ~Cn	12, DM
14. Bn • ~Cn	13, DN
15. (∃x)(Bx • ~Cx)	14, EG

(6)		
1. (x)[(Px • ~Cxx) ⊃ Crx]		
2. Pr	/ Crr	
3. (Pr • ~Crr) ⊃ Crr	1, UI	
4. Pr ⊃ (~Crr ⊃ Crr)	3, Exp	
5. ~Crr ⊃ Crr	2, 4, MP	
6. ~~Crr ∨ Crr	5, Impl	
7. Crr ∨ Crr	6, DN	
8. Crr	7, Taut	

(7)		
1. (∃x){Px • (y)[(Py • Kxy) ⊃ Fxy]}		
2. (x)[Px ⊃ (∃y)(Py • Kxy)]	/ (∃x)(∃y)[(Px • Py) • Fxy]	
3. Pm • (y)[(Py • Kmy) ⊃ Fmy]	1, EI	
4. Pm ⊃ (∃y)(Py • Kmy)	2, UI	
5. Pm	3, Simp	
6. (∃y)(Py • Kmy)	4, 5, MP	
7. Pn • Kmn	6, EI	
8. (y)[(Py • Kmy) ⊃ Fmy] • Pm	3, Com	
9. (y)[(Py • Kmy) ⊃ Fmy]	8, Simp	
10. (Pn • Kmn) ⊃ Fmn	9, UI	
11. Fmn	7, 10, MP	
12. Pn	7, Simp	
13. Pm • Pn	5, 12, Conj	
14. (Pm • Pn) • Fmn	11, 13, Conj	
15. (∃y)[(Pm • Py) • Fmy]	14, EG	
16. (∃x)(∃y)[(Px • Py) • Fxy]	15, EG	

(8)		
1. (x)[Px ⊃ (y)(Ry ⊃ Axy)]		
2. (x){[Rx • (∃y)(Py • Ayx)] ⊃ Jx}		
3. (∃x)Px • Rm	/ Jm	
4. (∃x)Px	3, Simp	
5. Pc	4, EI	
6. Pc ⊃ (y)(Ry ⊃ Acy)	1, UI	
7. (y)(Ry ⊃ Acy)	5, 6, MP	
8. Rm ⊃ Acm	7, UI	
9. Rm • (∃x)Px	3, Com	
10. Rm	9, Simp	
11. Acm	8, 10, MP	
12. [Rm • (∃y)(Py • Aym)] ⊃ Jm	2, UI	
13. Pc • Acm	5, 11, Conj	
14. (∃y)(Py • Aym)	13, EG	

215

15. Rm • (∃y)(Py • Aym)   10, 14, Conj
16. Jm   12, 15, MP

(9) 1. (x)[Mx ⊃ (∃y)(Py • Syx)]
     2. (x)[Dx ⊃ (∃y)(Py • Byx)]
     3. (∃x)(Mx ∨ Dx)   / (∃x)[Px • (∃y)(Sxy ∨ Bxy)]
     4. Mm ∨ Dm   3, EI
     5. Mm ⊃ (∃y)(Py • Sym)   1, UI
     6. Dm ⊃ (∃y)(Py • Bym)   2, UI
     7. [Mm ⊃ (∃y)(Py • Sym)] • [Dm ⊃ (∃y)(Py • Bym)]   5, 6, Conj
     8. (∃y)(Py • Sym) ∨ (∃y)(Py • Bym)   4, 7, CD
         9. ~(∃y)[(Py • Sym) ∨ (Py • Bym)] AIP
        10. (y)~[(Py • Sym) ∨ (Py • Bym)]   9, CQ
        11. ~[(Py • Sym) ∨ (Py • Bym)]   10, UI
        12. ~(Py • Sym) • ~(Py • Bym)   11, DM
        13. ~(Py • Sym)   12, Simp
        14. (y)~(Py • Sym)   13, UG
        15. ~(∃y)(Py • Sym)   14, CQ
        16. (∃y)(Py • Bym)   8, 15, DS
        17. ~(Py • Bym) • ~(Py • Sym)   12, Com
        18. ~(Py • Bym)   17, Simp
        19. (y)~(Py • Bym)   18, UG
        20. ~(∃y)(Py • Bym)   19, CQ
        21. (∃y)(Py • Bym) • ~(∃y)(Py • Bym) 16, 20, Conj
    22. ~~(∃y)[(Py • Sym) ∨ (Py • Bym)]   9-21, IP
    23. (∃y)[(Py • Sym) ∨ (Py • Bym)]   22, DN
    24. (Pn • Snm) ∨ (Pn • Bnm)   23, EI
    25. Pn • (Snm ∨ Bnm)   24, Dist
    26. (Snm ∨ Bnm) • Pn   25, Com
    27. Snm ∨ Bnm   26, Simp
    28. (∃y)(Sny ∨ Bny)   27, EG
    29. Pn   25, Simp
    30. Pn • (∃y)(Sny ∨ Bny)   28, 29, Conj
    31. (∃x)[Px • (∃y)(Sxy ∨ Bxy)]   30, EG

(10) 1. (x){Ix ⊃ [(∃y)(Cy • Ay) ⊃ Ex]}
     2. [(∃x)Tx ∨ (∃x)Wx] ⊃ [(∃x)Ix • (∃x)Cx]
     3. (x)(Cx ⊃ Ax)   / (∃x)Tx ⊃ (∃x)(Ix • Ex)
         4. (∃x)Tx   ACP
         5. (∃x)Tx ∨ (∃x)Wx   4, Add
         6. (∃x)Ix • (∃x)Cx   2, 5, MP
         7. (∃x)Ix   6, Simp
         8. Im   7, EI
         9. Im ⊃ [(∃y)(Cy • Ay) ⊃ Em]   1, UI
        10. (∃y)(Cy • Ay) ⊃ Em   8, 9, MP
        11. (∃x)Cx • (∃x)Ix   6, Com

12. (∃x)Cx	11, Simp
13. Cn	12, EI
14. Cn ⊃ An	3, UI
15. An	13, 14, MP
16. Cn • An	13, 15, Conj
17. (∃y)(Cy • Ay)	16, EG
18. Em	10, 17, MP
19. Im • Em	8, 18, Conj
20. (∃x)(Ix • Ex)	19, EG
21. (∃x)Tx ⊃ (∃x)(Ix • Ex)	4-20, CP

Exercise 8.7
Part I.

Simple identity statements:
  1. s = g
  2. r ≠ m
  3. m = b
  4. h ≠ g

Statements involving "only," "the only," and "no except":
  5. Wp • (x)(Wx ⊃ x = p)
  6. Pl • (x)(Px ⊃ x = l)
  7. Na • Ma • (x)[(Nx • Mx) ⊃ x = a]
  8. Nc • Mc • (x)[(Nx • Mx) ⊃ x = c]
  9. Uw • Fw • Ua • Fa • (x)[(Ux • Fx) ⊃ (x = w ∨ x = a)]
  10. Sh • Wh • (x)[(Sx • Wx) ⊃ x = h]
  11. Sh • Ph • (x)[(Sx • Px) ⊃ x = h]

Superlative statements:
  12. Eh • (x)[(Ex • x ≠ h) ⊃ Lhx]
  13. Pp • (x)[(Px • x ≠ p) ⊃ Spx]
  14. Ah • Uh • (x)[(Ax • Ux • x ≠ h) ⊃ Ohx]
  15. Rd • Nd • (x)[(Rx • Nx • x ≠ d) ⊃ Ldx]

Statements involving "all except":
  16. Al • ~Sl • (x)[(Ax • x ≠ l) ⊃ Sx]
  17. Uf • ~Wf • (x)[(Ux • x ≠ f) ⊃ Wx]
  18. Mm • ~Sm • (x)[(Mx • x ≠ m) ⊃ Sx]
  19. Pc • ~Wc • (x)[(Px • x ≠ c) ⊃ Wx]

Numerical statements:
  20. (x)(y)[(Cx • Bx • Cy • By) ⊃ x = y]
  21. (x)(y)(z)(Nx • Sx • Ny • Sy • Nz • Sz) ⊃ (x = y ∨ x = z ∨ y = z)]
  22. (x)(y)[(Nx • Jx • Ny • Jy) ⊃ x = y]

Exercise 8.7

23. (x)(y)(z)[(Cx • Mx • Cy • My • Cz • Mz) ⊃ (x = y ∨ x = z ∨ y = z)]
24. (∃x)(Qx • Fx)
25. (∃x)(∃y)(Ax • Wx • Ay • Wy • x ≠ y)
26. (∃x)(∃y)(∃z)(Cx • Cy • Cz • x ≠ y • x ≠ z • y ≠ z)
27. (∃x)[Ux • (y)(Uy ⊃ y = x)]
28. (∃x){Sx • Nx • (y)[(Sy • Ny) ⊃ y = x]}
29. (∃x)(∃y){Sx • Bx • Gx • Sy • By • Gy • x ≠ y • (z)[(Sz • Bz • Gz) ⊃ (z = x ∨ z = y)]}

Statements containing definite descriptions:
30. (∃x)[Wxv • (y)(Wyv ⊃ y = x) • Bx]
31. (∃x)[Wxo • (y)(Wyo ⊃ y = x) • x = d]
32. (∃x){Mx • Cxn • (y)[(My • Cyn) ⊃ y = x] • Rx}
33. (∃x){Ax • Pxa • (y)[(Ay • Pya) ⊃ y = x] • x = b}
34. (∃x)[Cxg • (y)(Cyg ⊃ y = x) • x ≠ s]

Assorted statements:
35. Sr • (x)[(Sx • x ≠ r) ⊃ Srx]
36. (∃x)(Nx • Sx)
37. s = i
38. Ar • Er • (x)[(Ax • Ex) ⊃ x = r]
39. (∃x)(∃y)(Cx • Qx • Cy • Qy • x ≠ y)
40. Pb • (x)(Px ⊃ x = b)
41. (x)(y)[(Sxh • Syh) ⊃ x = y]
42. Mb • Hb • (x)[(Mx • Hx) ⊃ x = b]
43. (x)(y)(z)[(Sx • Nx • Sy • Ny • Sz • Nz) ⊃ (x = y ∨ x = z ∨ y = z)]
44. m ≠ b
45. (∃x){Ex • Dxn • (y)[(Ey • Dyn) ⊃ y = x] • x = a}
46. Rh • (x)[(Rx • x ≠ h) ⊃ Ohx]
47. (∃x)(∃y){Tx • Cx • Ty • Cy • x ≠ y • (z)[(Tz • Cz) ⊃ (z = x ∨ z = y)]}
48. Pj • Rj • ~Ij • (x)[(Px • Rx • x ≠ j) ⊃ Ix]
49. (∃x){Px • Dxr • (y)[(Py • Dyr) ⊃ y = x] • Ex}
50. (∃x)(∃y)(∃z)(Sx • Ox • Sy • Oy • Sz • Oz • x ≠ y • x ≠ z • y ≠ z)

Part II

(1) 1. (x)(x = a)
     2. (∃x)Rx   / Ra
     3. Ri   2, EI
     4. i = a   1, UI
     5. Ra   3, 4, Id

(2) 1. Ke
    2. ~Kn   / e ≠ n
       3. e = n   AIP
        4. Kn   1, 3, Id
        5. Kn • ~Kn   1, 2, Conj
    6. e ≠ n   3-5, IP

(3) 1. (x)(x = c ⊃ Nx)   / Nc
    2. c = c ⊃ Nc   1, UI
    3. c = c   Id
    4. Nc   2, 3, MP

(4) 1. (∃x)(x = g)
    2. (x)(x = i)   / g = i
    3. n = g   1, EI
    4. n = i   2, UI
    5. g = n   3, Id
    6. g = i   4, 5, Id

(5) 1. (x)(Gx ⊃ x = a)
    2. (∃x)(Gx • Hx)   / Ha
    3. Ge • He   2, EI
    4. Ge ⊃ e = a   1, UI
    5. Ge   3, Simp
    6. e = a   4, 5, MP
    7. He • Ge   3, Com
    8. He   7, Simp
    9. Ha   6, 8, Id

(6) 1. (x)(Ax ⊃ Bx)
    2. Ac • ~Bi   / c ≠ i
       3. c = i   AIP
        4. Ac ⊃ Bc   1, UI
        5. Ac   2, Simp
        6. Bc   4, 5, MP
        7. Bi   3, 6, Id
        8. ~Bi • Ac   2, Com
        9. ~Bi   8, Simp
      10. Bi •~Bi   7, 9, Conj
   11. c ≠ i   3-10, IP

(7) 1. (x)(x = a)
    2. Fa   / Fm • Fn
    3. m = a   1, UI
    4. a = m   3, Id
    5. Fm   2, 4, Id
    6. n = a   1, UI

Exercise 8.7

7. a = n	6, Id	
8. Fn	2, 7, Id	
9. Fm • Fn	5, 8, Conj	

(8) 1. (x)(x = r)
2. Hr • Kn   / Hn • Kr
3. n = r   1, UI
4. Hr   2, Simp
5. r = n   3, Id
6. Hn   4, 5, Id
7. Kn • Hr   2, Com
8. Kn   7, Simp
9. Kr   3, 8, Id
10. Hn • Kr   6, 9, Conj

(9) 1. (x)(Lx ⊃ x = e)
2. (x)(Sx ⊃ x = i)
3. (∃x)(Lx • Sx)   / i = e
4. Ln • Sn   3, EI
5. Ln ⊃ n = e   1, UI
6. Ln   4, Simp
7. n = e   5, 6, MP
8. Sn ⊃ n = i   2, UI
9. Sn • Ln   4, Com
10. Sn   9, Simp
11. n = i   8, 10, MP
12. i = n   11, Id
13. i = e   7, 12, Id

(10) 1. (x)(Px ⊃ x = a)
2. (x)(x = c ⊃ Qx
3. a = c   / (x)(Px ⊃ Qx)
     4. Px   ACP
     5. Px ⊃ x = a   1, UI
     6. x = a   4, 5, MP
     7. x = c   3, 6, Id
     8. x = c ⊃ Qx   2, UI
     9. Qx   7, 8, MP
10. Px ⊃ Qx   4-9, CP
11. (x)(Px ⊃ Qx)   10, UG

(11) 1. (x)(y)(Txy ⊃ x = e)
2. (∃x)Txi   / Tei
3. Tni   2, EI
4. (y)(Tny ⊃ n = e)   1, UI
5. Tni ⊃ n = e   4, UI

6. n = e   3, 5, MP
7. Tei   3, 6, Id

(12) 1. (x)[Rx ⊃ (Hx • x = m)]   / Rc ⊃ Hm
      2. Rc   ACP
      3. Rc ⊃ (Hc • c = m)   1, UI
      4. Hc • c = m   2, 3, MP
      5. Hc   4, Simp
      6. c = m • Hc   4, Com
      7. c = m   6, Simp
      8. Hm   5, 7, Id
      9. Rc ⊃ Hm   2-8, CP

(13) 1. (x)(Ba ⊃ x ≠ a)
      2. Bc   / a ≠ c
      3. a = c   AIP
      4. c = a   3, Id
      5. Ba   2, 4, Id
      6. Ba ⊃ c ≠ a   1, UI
      7. c ≠ a   5, 6, MP
      8. c = a • c ≠ a   4, 7, Conj
      9. a ≠ c   3-8, IP

(14) 1. (∃x)Gx ⊃ (∃x)(Kx • x = i)   / Gn ⊃ Ki
      2. Gn   ACP
      3. (∃x)Gx   2, EG
      4. (∃x)(Kx • x = i)   1, 3, MP
      5. Ks • s = i   4, EI
      6. Ks   5, Simp
      7. s = i • Ks   5, Com
      8. s = i   7, Simp
      9. Ki   6, 8, Id
     10. Gn ⊃ Ki   2-9, CP

(15) 1. (x)(Rax ⊃ ~Rxc)
      2. (x)Rxx   / c ≠ a
      3. c = a   AIP
      4. Rac ⊃ ~Rcc   1, IU
      5. Rcc   2, UI
      6. Rac   3, 5, Id
      7. ~Rcc   4, 6, MP
      8. Rcc • ~Rcc   5, 7, Conj
      9. c ≠ a   3-8, IP

221

Exercise 8.7

(16) 1. (x)[Nx ⊃ (Px • x = m)]
    2. ~Pm   / ~Ne
        3. Ne   AIP
        4. Ne ⊃ (Pe • e = m)   1, UI
        5. Pe • e = m   3, 4, MP
        6. Pe   5, Simp
        7. e = m • Pe   5, Com
        8. e = m   7, Simp
        9. Pm   6, 8, Id
        10. Pm • ~Pm   2, 9, Conj
    11. ~Ne   3-10, IP

(17) 1. (x)(Fx ⊃ x = e)
    2. (∃x)(Fx • x = a)   / a = e
    3. Fn • n = a   2, EI
    4. Fn ⊃ n = e   1, UI
    5. Fn   3, Simp
    6. n = e   4, 5, MP
    7. n = a • Fn   3, Com
    8. n = a   7, Simp
    9. a = e   6, 8, Id

(18) 1. (x)[Ex ⊃ (Hp • x = e)]
    2. (∃x)(Ex • x = p)   / He
    3. Es • s = p   2, EI
    4. Es ⊃ (Hp • s = e)   1, UI
    5. Es   3, Simp
    6. Hp • s = e   4, 5, MP
    7. Hp   6, Simp
    8. s = p • Es   3, Com
    9. s = p   8, Simp
    10. p = s   9, Id
    11. Hs   7, 10, Id
    12. s = e • Hp   6, Com
    13. s = e   12, Simp
    14. He   11, 13, Id

(19) 1. (x)(∃y)(Cxy ⊃ x = y)
    2. (∃x)(y)(Cxy • x = a)   / Caa
    3. (y)(Cny • n = a)   2, EI
    4. (∃y)(Cay ⊃ a = y)   1, UI
    5. Cam ⊃ a = m   4, EI
    6. Cnm • n = a   3, UI
    7. Cnm   6, Simp
    8. n = a • Cnm   6, Com
    9. n = a   8, Simp
    10. Cam   7, 9, Id

11. a = m	5, 10, MP
12. m = a	11, Id
13. Caa	10, 12, Id

(20) 1. (x)[Fx ⊃ (Gx • x = n)]
     2. Gn ⊃ (∃x)(Hx • x = e)   / Fm ⊃ He
       3. Fm   ACP
       4. Fm ⊃ (Gm • m = n)   1, UI
       5. Gm • m = n   3, 4, MP
       6. Gm   5, Simp
       7. m = n • Gm   5, Com
       8. m = n   7, Simp
       9. Gn   6, 8, Id
     10. (∃x)(Hx • x = e)   2, 9, MP
     11. Ha • a = e   10, EI
     12. Ha   11, Simp
     13. a = e • Ha   11, Com
     14. a = e   13, Simp
     15. He   12, 14, Id
    16. Fm ⊃ He   3-15, CP

Part III.

(1) 1. (∃x)(Nx • Wjx • Ix)
     2. Nc • Wjc • (x)[(Nx • Wjx) ⊃ x = c]   / Ic
     3. Na • Wja • Ia   1, EI
     4. (x)[(Nx • Wjx) ⊃ x = c] • Nc • Wjc   2, Com
     5. (x)[(Nx • Wjx) ⊃ x = c]   4, Simp
     6. (Na • Wja) ⊃ a = c   5, UI
     7. Na • Wja   3, Simp
     8. a = c   6, 7, MP
     9. Ia • Na • Wja   3, Com
    10. Ia   9, Simp
    11. Ic   8, 10, Id

(2) 1. Ur • (x)[(Ux • x ≠ r) ⊃ Orx]
     2. Uw
     3. w ≠ r   / Orw
     4. (x)[(Ux • x ≠ r) ⊃ Orx] • Ur   1, Com
     5. (x)[(Ux • x ≠ r) ⊃ Orx]   4, Simp
     6. (Uw • w ≠ r) ⊃ Orw   5, UI
     7. Uw • w ≠ r   2, 3, Conj
     8. Orw   6, 7, MP

Exercise 8.7

(3) 1. (∃x){Ax • Pxm • (y)[(Ay • Pym) ⊃ y = x] • Fx}
    2. (∃x){Ax • Pxm • (y)[(Ay • Pym) ⊃ y = x] • x = 1}   / Fl
    3. Aa • Pam • (y)[(Ay • Pym) ⊃ y = a] • Fa   1, EI
    4. Ac • Pcm • (y)[(Ay • Pym) ⊃ y = c] • c = 1   2, EI
    5. c = 1 • Ac • Pcm • (y)[(Ay • Pym) ⊃ y = c]   4, Com
    6. (y)[(Ay • Pym) ⊃ y = c] • c = 1 • Ac • Pcm   5, Com
    7. (y)[(Ay • Pym) ⊃ y = c]   6, Simp
    8. (Aa • Pam) ⊃ a = c   7, UI
    9. Aa • Pam   3, Simp
   10. a = c   8, 9, MP
   11. c = 1   5, Simp
   12. a = 1   10, 11, Id
   13. Fa • Aa • Pam • (y)[(Ay • Pym) ⊃ y = a]   3, Com
   14. Fa   13, Simp
   15. Fl   12, 14, Id

(4) 1. (∃x){Nx • Tx • (y)[(Ny • Ty) ⊃ y = x] • Wmx}
    2. Ng • Wmg • (x)[(Nx • Wmx) ⊃ x = g]
             / (∃x){Nx • Tx • (y)[(Ny • Ty) ⊃ y = x] • x = g}
    3. Na • Ta • (y)[(Ny • Ty) ⊃ y = a] • Wma   1, EI
    4. (x)[(Nx • Wmx) ⊃ x = g] • Ng • Wmg   2, Com
    5. (x)[(Nx • Wmx) ⊃ x = g]   4, Simp
    6. (Na • Wma) ⊃ a = g   5, UI
    7. Na   3, Simp
    8. Wma • Na • Ta • (y)[(Ny • Ty) ⊃ y = a]   3, Com
    9. Wma   8, Simp
   10. Na • Wma   7, 9, Conj
   11. a = g   6, 10, MP
   12. Na • Ta • (y)[(Ny • Ty) ⊃ y = a]   3, Simp
   13. Na • Ta • (y)[(Ny • Ty) ⊃ y = a] • a = g   11, 12, Conj
   14. (∃x){Nx • Tx • (y)[(Ny • Ty) ⊃ y = x] • x = g}   13, EG

(5) 1. (∃x)[Wxk • (y)(Wyk ⊃ y = x) • Ex • Ax]
    2. Em • ~Am   / ~Wmk
    3. Wak • (y)(Wyk ⊃ y = a) • Ea • Aa   1, EI
    4. (y)(Wyk ⊃ y = a) • Ea • Aa • Wak   3, Com
    5. (y)(Wyk ⊃ y = a)   4, Simp
    6. Wmk ⊃ m = a   5, UI
       7. Wmk   5, AIP
       8. m = a   6, 7, MP
        9. Aa • Wak • (y)(Wyk ⊃ y = a) • Ea   3, Com
   10. Aa   10, Simp
   11. a = m   8, Id
   12. Am   10, 11, Id
   13. ~Am • Em   2, Com
   14. ~Am   13, Simp

| 15. Am • ~Am | 12, 14, Conj |
| 16. ~Wmk | 7-15, IP |

(6) 1. (∃x){(Dx • Bx) • (y)[(Dy • By) ⊃ y = x] • Lx • Tx}
    2. ~La • Da   / ~Ba
    3. Dc • Bc • (y)[(Dy • By) ⊃ y = c] • Lc • Tc   1, EI
    4. Lc • Tc • Dc • Bc • (y)[(Dy • By) ⊃ y = c]   3, Com
    5. (y)[(Dy • By) ⊃ y = c] • Lc • Tc • Dc • Bc   4, Com
    6. (y)[(Dy • By) ⊃ y = c]   5, Simp
    7. (Da • Ba) ⊃ a = c   6, UI
       8. a = c   AIP
       9. Lc   4, Simp
      10. c = a   8, Id
      11. La   9, 10, Id
      12. ~La   2, Simp
      13. La • ~La   11, 12, Conj
    14. a ≠ c   6-10, IP
    15. ~(Da • Ba)   7, 14, MT
    16. ~Da ∨ ~Ba   15, DM
    17. Da • ~La   2, Com
    18. Da   17, Simp
    19. ~~Da   18, DN
    20. ~Ba   16, 19, DS

(7) 1. Me • ~Se • (x)[(Mx • x ≠ e) ⊃ Sx]
    2. Mn • ~Gn • (x)[(Mx • x ≠ n) ⊃ Gx]
    3. e ≠ n   / Ge • Sn
    4. (x)[(Mx • x ≠ e) ⊃ Sx] • Me • ~Se   1, Com
    5. (x)[(Mx • x ≠ e) ⊃ Sx]   4, Simp
    6. (Mn • n ≠ e) ⊃ Sn   5, UI
    7. Mn   2, Simp
    8. n ≠ e   3, Id
    9. Mn • n ≠ e   7, 8, Conj
    10. Sn   6, 9, MP
    11. (x)[(Mx • x ≠ n) ⊃ Gx] • Mn • ~Gn   2, Com
    12. (x)[(Mx • x ≠ n) ⊃ Gx]   11, Simp
    13. (Me • e ≠ n) ⊃ Ge   12, UI
    14. Me   1, Simp
    15. Me • e ≠ n   3, 14, Conj
    16. Ge   13, 15, MP
    17. Ge • Sn   10, 16, Conj

(8) 1. Pa • Oa • (y)[(Py • Oy) ⊃ y = a]
    2. Pw • Sw • (y)[(Py • Sy) ⊃ y = w]
    3. (∃x)(Px • Ox • Sx)   / a = w
    4. Pc • Oc • Sc   3, EI

5. (y)[(Py • Oy) ⊃ y = a] • Pa • Oa   1, Com
6. (y)[(Py • Oy) ⊃ y = a]   5, Simp
7. (Pc • Oc) ⊃ c = a   6, UI
8. Pc • Oc   4, Simp
9. c = a   7, 8, MP
10. (y)[(Py • Sy) ⊃ y = w] • Pw • Sw   2, Com
11. (y)[(Py • Sy) ⊃ y = w]   10, Simp
12. (Pc • Sc) ⊃ c = w   11, UI
13. Sc • Pc • Oc   4, Com
14. Sc • Pc   13, Simp
15. Pc • Sc   14, Com
16. c = w   12, 15, MP
17. a = c   8, Id
18. a = w   16, 17, Id

(9) 1. (∃x){Mx • Tx • (y)[(My • y ≠ x) ⊃ Hxy]}
                    / (∃x){Mx • Tx • (y)[(My • ~Ty) ⊃ Hxy]}
2. Ma • Ta • (y)[(My • y ≠ a) ⊃ Hay]   1, EI
3. Ma • Ta   2, Simp
  4. ~(y)[(My • ~Ty) ⊃ Hay]   AIP
  5. (∃x)~[(My • ~Ty) ⊃ Hay]   4, CQ
  6. ~[(Mc • ~Tc) ⊃ Hac]   5, EI
  7. ~[~(Mc • ~Tc) ∨ Hac]   6, Impl
  8. ~~(Mc • ~Tc) • ~Hac   7, DM
  9. Mc • ~Tc • ~Hac   8, DN
  10. (y)[(My • y ≠ a) ⊃ Hay] • Ma • Ta   2, Com
  11. (y)[(My • y ≠ a) ⊃ Tay]   10, Simp
  12. (Mc • c ≠ a) ⊃ Hac   11, UI
  13. Mc ⊃ (c ≠ a ⊃ Hac)   12, Exp
  14. Mc   9, Simp
  15. c ≠ a ⊃ Hac   13, 14, MP
  16. ~Hac • Mc • ~Tc   9, Com
  17. ~Hac   16, Simp
  18. ~(c ≠ a)   15, 17, MT
  19. c = a   18, DN
  20. Ta • Ma   3, Com
  21. Ta   20, Simp
  22. ~Tc • ~Hac • Mc   16, Com
  23. ~Tc   22, Simp
  24. ~Ta   19, 23, Id
  25. Ta • ~Ta   21, 24, Conj
26. ~~(y)[(My • ~Ty) ⊃ Hay]   4-25, IP
27. (y)[(My • ~Ty) ⊃ Hay]   26, DN
28. Ma • Ta • (y)[(My • ~Ty) ⊃ Hay]   3, 20, Conj
29. (∃x){Mx • Tx • (y)[(My • ~Ty) ⊃ Hxy]}   28, EG

(10) 1. Bs • (x)[(Bx • x ≠ s) ⊃ Tsx]
    2. (∃x){Bx • (y)[(By • y ≠ x) ⊃ Txy] • Cx}
    3. (x)(y)(Txy ⊃ ~Tyx)   / Cs
    4. Ba • (y)[(By • y ≠ a) ⊃ Tay] • Ca   2, EI
    5. (x)[(Bx • x ≠ s) ⊃ Tsx] • Bs   1, Com
    6. (x)[(Bx • x ≠ s) ⊃ Tsx]   5, Simp
    7. (Ba • a ≠ s) ⊃ Tsa   6, UI
        8. a ≠ s   AIP
        9. Ba   4, Simp
      10. Ba • a ≠ s   8, 9, Conj
      11. Tsa   7, 10, MP
      12. (y)[(By • y ≠ a) ⊃ Tay] • Ca • Ba 4, Com
      13. (y)[(By • y ≠ a) ⊃ Tay]   12, Simp
      14. (Bs • s ≠ a) ⊃ Tas   13, UI
      15. Bs   1, Simp
      16. s ≠ a   8, Id
      17. Bs • s ≠ a   15, 16, Conj
      18. Tas   14, 17, MP
      19. (y)(Tay ⊃ ~Tya)   3, UI
      20. Tas ⊃ ~Tsa   19, UI
      21. ~Tsa   18, 20, MP
      22. Tsa • ~Tsa   11, 21, Conj
   23. ~(a ≠ s)   8-22, IP
   24. a = s   23, DN
   25. Ca • Ba • (y)[(By • y ≠ a) ⊃ Tay] 4, Com
   26. Ca   25, Simp
   27. Cs   24, 26, Id

(11) 1. (∃x)(∃y)(Px • Lx • Py • Ly • x ≠ y)
    2. Pr • Fr • Lr • (y)[(Py • Fy • Ly) ⊃ y = r] / (∃x)(Px • Lx • ~Fx)
        3. ~(∃x)(Px • Lx • ~Fx)   AIP
        4. (∃y)(Pa • La • Py • Ly • a ≠ y)   1, EI
        5. Pa • La • Pc • Lc • a ≠ c   4, EI
        6. (y)[(Py • Fy • Ly) ⊃ y = r] • Pr • Fr • Lr 2, Com
        7. (y)[(Py • Fy • Ly) ⊃ y = r]   6, Simp
        8. (Pa • Fa • La) ⊃ a = r   7, UI
        9. (Pc • Fc • Lc) ⊃ c = r   7, UI
      10. (x)~(Px • Lx • ~Fx)   3, CQ
      11. ~(Pa • La • ~Fa)   10, UI
      12. ~Pa ∨ ~La ∨ ~~Fa   11, DM
      13. ~(Pa • La) ∨ ~~Fa   12, DM
      14. Pa • La   5, Simp
      15. ~~(Pa • La)   14, DN
      16. ~~Fa   13, 15, DS
      17. Fa   16, DN
      18. Pa • La • Fa   14, 17, Conj

19. Pa • Fa • La	18, Com
20. a = r	8, 19, MP
21. ~(Pc • Lc • ~Fc)	10, UI
22. ~Pc ∨ ~Lc ∨ ~~Fc	21, DM
23. ~(Pc • Lc) ∨ ~~Fc	22, DM
24. a ≠ c • Pa • La • Pc • Lc	5, Com
25. Pc • Lc • a ≠ c • Pa • La	24, Com
26. Pc • Lc	25, Simp
27. ~~(Pc • Lc)	26, DN
28. ~~Fc	23, 27, DS
29. Fc	28, DN
30. Pc • Lc • Fc	26, 29, Conj
31. Pc • Fc • Lc	30, Com
32. c = r	9, 31, MP
33. r = c	32, Id
34. a = c	20, 33, Id
35. a ≠ c	24, Simp
36. a = c • a ≠ c	34, 35, Conj
37. ~~(∃x)(Px • Lx • ~Fx)	3-36, IP
38. (∃x)(Px • Lx • ~Fx)	37, DN

(12) 1. Df • Bf • Dp • Bp • (x)[(Dx • Bx) ⊃ (x = f ∨ x = p)]
    2. f ≠ p
    3. Df • ~Rf • (x)[(Dx • x ≠ f) ⊃ Rx]
                      / (∃x){Dx • Bx • Rx • (y)[(Dy • By • Ry) ⊃ y = x]}

4. (x)[(Dx • x ≠ f) ⊃ Rx] • Df • ~Rf	3, Com
5. (x)[(Dx • x ≠ f) ⊃ Rx]	4, Simp
6. (Dp • p ≠ f) ⊃ Rp	5, UI
7. Dp • Bp • (x)[(Dx • Bx) ⊃ (x = f ∨ x = p)] • Df • Bf	1, Com
8. Dp	7, Simp
9. p ≠ f	2, Id
10. Dp • p ≠ f	8, 9, Conj
11. Rp	6, 10, MP
12. Bp • (x)[(Dx • Bx) ⊃ (x = f ∨ x = p)] • Df • Bf • Dp	7, Com
13. Bp	12, Simp
14. Dp • Bp	8, 13, Conj
15. Dp • Bp • Rp	11, 14, Conj
16. ~(y)[(Dy • By • Ry) ⊃ y = p]	AIP
17. (∃y)~[(Dy • By • Ry) ⊃ y = p]	16, CQ
18. ~[(Da • Ba • Ra] ⊃ a = p]	17, EI
19. ~[~(Da • Ba • Ra) ∨ a = p]	18, Impl
20. ~~(Da • Ba • Ra) • a ≠ p	19, DM
21. Da • Ba • Ra • a ≠ p	20, DN
22. (x)[(Dx • Bx) ⊃ (x = f ∨ x = p)] • Df • Bf • Dp • Bp	1, Com
23. (x)[(Dx • Bx) ⊃ (x = f ∨ x = p)]	22, Simp
24. (Da • Ba) ⊃ (a = f ∨ a = p)	23, UI

25. Da • Ba	24, Simp
26. a = f ∨ a = p	24, 25, MP
27. a ≠ p • Da • Ba • Ra	21, Com
28. a ≠ p	27, Simp
29. a = p ∨ a = f	26, Com
30. a = f	28, 29, DS
31. Ra • a ≠ p • Da • Ba	27, Com
32. Ra	31, Simp
33. Rf	30, 32, Id
34. ~Rf • (x)[(Dx • x ≠ f) ⊃ Rx] • Df	3, Com
35. ~Rf	34, Simp
36. Rf • ~Rf	33, 35, Conj
37. ~~(y)[(Dy • By • Ry) ⊃ y = p]	16, 36, IP
38. (y)[(Dy • By • Ry) ⊃ y = p]	37, DN
39. Dp • Bp • Rp • (y)[(Dy • By • Ry) ⊃ y = p]	15, 38, Conj
40. (∃x){Dx • Bx • Rx • (y)[(Dy • By • Ry) ⊃ y = x]}	39, EG

(13) 1. (∃x)(∃y)(Ax • Ox • Ay • Oy • x ≠ y)

2. (x)(Ax ⊃ Px)

3. (x)(y)(z)[(Px • Ox • Py • Oy • Pz • Oz) ⊃ (x = y ∨ x = z ∨ y = z)]
     / (∃x)(∃y){Px • Ox • Py • Oy • x ≠ y • (z)[(Pz • Oz) ⊃ (z = x ∨ z = y)]}

4. (∃y)(Aa • Oa • Ay • Oy • a ≠ y)	1, EI
5. Aa • Oa • Ab • Ob • a ≠ b	4, EI
6. Aa ⊃ Pa	2, UI
7. Aa	5, Simp
8. Pa	6, 7, MP
9. Ab ⊃ Pb	2, UI
10. Ab • Ob • a ≠ b • Aa • Oa	5, Com
11. Ab	10, Simp
12. Pb	9, 11, MP
13. Oa • Ab • Ob • a ≠ b • Aa	10, Com
14. Oa	13, Simp
15. Ob • a ≠ b • Aa • Oa • Ab	5, Com
16. Ob	15, Simp
17. a ≠ b • Aa • Oa • Ab • Ob	5, Com
18. a ≠ b	17, Simp
19. Pa • Oa • Pb • Ob • a ≠ b	8, 14, 12, 16, 18, Conj
20. ~(z)[(Pz • Oz) ⊃ (z = a ∨ z = b)]	AIP
21. (∃z)~[(Pz • Oz) ⊃ (z = a ∨ z = b)]	20, CQ
22. ~[(Pc • Oc) ⊃ (c = a ∨ c = b)]	21, EI
23. ~[~(Pc • Oc) ∨ (c = a ∨ c = b)]	22, Impl
24. ~~(Pc • Oc) • ~(c = a ∨ c = b)	23, DM
25. Pc • Oc • ~(c = a ∨ c = b)	24, DN
26. (y)(z)[(Pa • Oa • Py • Oy • Pz • Oz) ⊃ (a = y ∨ a = z ∨ y = z)]	3, UI

229

27. (z)[(Pa • Oa • Pb • Ob • Pz • Oz) ⊃

        (a = b ∨ a = z ∨ b = z)]   26, UI

28. (Pa • Oa • Pb • Ob • Pc • Oc) ⊃

        (a = b ∨ a = c ∨ b = c)   27, UI

29. Pc • Oc   25, Simp

30. Pa • Oa • Pb • Ob   19, Simp

31. Pa • Oa • Pb • Ob • Pc • Oc   29, 30, Conj

32. a = b ∨ a = c ∨ b = c   28, 31, MP

33. a = c ∨ b = c   18, 32, DS

34. ~(c = a ∨ c = b) • Pc • Oc   25, Com

35. ~(c = a ∨ c = b)   34, Simp

36. ~(a = c ∨ c = b)   35, Id

37. ~(a = c ∨ b = c)   36, Id

38. (a = c ∨ b = c) • ~(a = c ∨ b = c)   33, 37, Conj

39. ~~(z)[(Pz • Oz) ⊃ z = a ∨ z = b)]   20-38, IP

40. (z)[(Pz • Oz) ⊃ z = a ∨ z = b)]   39, DN

41. Pa • Oa • Pb • Ob • a ≠ b •

        (z)[(Pz • Oz) ⊃ (z = a ∨ z = b)]   19, 40, Conj

42. (∃y){Pa • Oa • Py • Oy • a ≠ y •

        (z)[(Pz • Oz) ⊃ (z = a ∨ z = y)]}   41, EG

43. (∃x)(∃y){Px • Ox • Py • Oy • x ≠ y •

        (z)[(Pz • Oz) ⊃ (z = x ∨ z = y)]}   42, EG

(14) 1. (x)(y)(z)[(Sx • Lx • Sy • Ly • Sz • Lz) ⊃ (x = y ∨ x = z ∨ y = z)]

    2. (∃x)(∃y)(Sx • Lx • Rx • Sy • Ly • Ry • x ≠ y)

    3. (x)(Rx ⊃ ~Cx)   / (Sn • Cn) ⊃ ~Ln

    4. (∃y)(Sa • La • Ra • Sy • Ly • Ry • a ≠ y)   2, EI

    5. Sa • La • Ra • Sc • Lc • Rc • a ≠ c   4, EI

    6. (y)(z)[(Sa • La • Sy • Ly • Sz • Lz) ⊃

        (a = y ∨ a = z ∨ y = z)]   1, UI

    7. (z)[(Sa • La • Sc • Lc • Sz • Lz) ⊃

        (a = c ∨ a = z ∨ c = z)]   6, UI

    8. (Sa • La • Sc • Lc • Sn • Ln) ⊃

        (a = c ∨ a = n ∨ c = n)   7, UI

    9. Sn • Cn • Ln   AIP

   10. Sn • Ln • Cn   9, Com

   11. Sn • Ln   10, Simp

   12. Sa • La   5, Simp

   13. Sc • Lc • Rc • a ≠ c • Sa • La • Ra   5, Com

   14. Sc • Lc   13, Simp

   15. Sa • La • Sc • Lc • Sn • Ln   11, 12, 14, Conj

   16. a = c ∨ a = n ∨ c = n   8, 15, MP

   17. a ≠ c • Sa • La • Ra • Sc • Lc • Rc   5, Com

   18. a ≠ c   17, Simp

   19. a = n ∨ c = n   16, 18, DS

   20. Ra ⊃ ~Ca   3, UI

21. Ra • Sc • Lc • Rc • a ≠ c • Sa • La	5, Com
22. Ra	21, Simp
23. ~Ca	20, 22, MP
24. a = n	AIP
25. ~Cn	23, 24, Id
26. Cn • Ln • Sn	9, Com
27. Cn	26, Simp
28. Cn • ~Cn	25, 27, Conj
29. a ≠ n	20-23, IP
30. c = n	19, 29, DS
31. Rc ⊃ ~Cc	3, UI
32. Rc • a ≠ c • Sa • La • Ra • Sc • Lc	17, Com
33. Rc	32, Simp
34. ~Cc	31, 33, MP
35. ~Cn	30, 34, Id
36. Cn • Sn • Ln	10, Com
37. Cn	36, Simp
38. Cn • ~Cn	35, 37, Conj
39. ~(Sn • Cn • Ln)	9-38, IP
40. ~Sn ∨ ~Cn ∨ ~Ln	39, DM
41. ~(Sn • Cn) ∨ ~Ln	40, DM
42. (Sn • Cn) ⊃ ~Ln	33, Impl

(15) 1. Cm • ~Em • (x)[(Cx • x ≠ m) ⊃ Ex]
    2. Cr • Er • (x)[(Cx • Ex) ⊃ x = r]
    3. m ≠ r

                / (∃x)(∃y){Cx • Cy • x ≠ y • (z)[Cz ⊃ (z = x ∨ z = y)]}

4. Cm	1, Simp
5. Cr	2, Simp
6. ~(z)[Cz ⊃ (z = m ∨ z = r)]	AIP
7. (∃z)~[Cx ⊃ (z = m ∨ z = r)]	6, CQ
8. ~[Ca ⊃ (a = m ∨ a = r)]	7, EI
9. ~(~Ca ∨ a = m ∨ a = r)	8, Impl
10. ~~Ca • a ≠ m • a ≠ r	9, DM
11. Ca • a ≠ m • a ≠ r	10, DN
12. (x)[(Cx • x ≠ m) ⊃ Ex] • Cm • ~Em	1, Com
13. (x)[(Cx • x ≠ m) ⊃ Ex]	13, Simp
14. (Ca • a ≠ m) ⊃ Ea	13, UI
15. Ca • a ≠ m	11, Simp
16. Ea	14, 15, MP
17. (x)[(Cx • Ex) ⊃ x = r] • Cr • Er	2, Com
18. (x)[(Cx • Ex) ⊃ x = r]	17, Simp
19. (Ca • Ea) ⊃ a = r	18, UI
20. Ca	11, Simp
21. Ca • Ea	16, 20, Conj
22. a = r	19, 21, MP

23. a ≠ r • Ca • a ≠ m   11, Com
24. a ≠ r   23, Simp
25. a = r • a ≠ r   22, 24, Conj
26. ~~(z)[Cz ⊃ (z = m ∨ z = r)]   6-25, IP
27. (z)[Cz ⊃ (z = m ∨ z = r)]   26, DN
28. Cm • Cr • m ≠ r • (z)[Cz ⊃ (z = m ∨ z = r)]   3-5, 27, Conj
29. (∃y){Cm • Cy • m ≠ y • (z)[Cz ⊃ (z = m ∨ z = y)]}   28, EG
30. (∃x)(∃y){Cx • Cy • x ≠ y • (z)[Cz ⊃ (z = x ∨ z = y)]}   29, EG

(16) 1. Sc • ~Pc • Sn • ~Pn • (x)[(Sx • x ≠ c • x ≠ n) ⊃ Px]
     2. Sn • Dn • (x)[(Sx • Dx) ⊃ x = n]
     3. (x){Sx ⊃ [Rx ≡ (~Dx • ~Px)]}
     4. c ≠ n   / (∃x){(Sx • Rx) • (y)[(Sy • Ry) ⊃ y = x]}
     5. Sc   1, Simp
     6. Sc ⊃ [Rc ≡ (~Dc • ~Pc)]   3, UI
     7. Rc ≡ (~Dc • ~Pc)   5, 6, MP
     8. [Rc ⊃ (~Dc • ~Pc)] • [(~Dc • ~Pc) ⊃ Rc]   7, Equiv
     9. [(~Dc • ~Pc) ⊃ Rc] • [Rc ⊃ (~Dc • ~Pc)]   8, Com
    10. (~Dc • ~Pc) ⊃ Rc   9, Simp
    11. (x)[(Sx • Dx) ⊃ x = n] • Sn • Dn   2, Com
    12. (x)[(Sx • Dx) ⊃ x = n]   11, Simp
    13. (Sc • Dc) ⊃ c = n   12, UI
    14. ~(Sc • Dc)   4, 13, MT
    15. ~Sc ∨ ~Dc   14, DM
    16. ~~Sc   5, DN
    17. ~Dc   15, 16, DS
    18. ~Pc • Sn • ~Pn • (x)[(Sx • x ≠ c • x ≠ n) ⊃ Px] • Sc   1, Com
    19. ~Pc   18, Simp
    20. ~Dc • ~Pc   17, 19, Conj
    21. Rc   10, 20, MP
    22. Sc • Rc   5, 21, Conj
         23. ~(y)[(Sy • Ry) ⊃ y = c]   AIP
         24. (∃y)~[(Sy • Ry) ⊃ y = c]   23, CQ
         25. ~[(Sa • Ra) ⊃ a = c]   24, EI
         26. ~[~(Sa • Ra) ∨ a = c]   25, Impl
         27. ~~(Sa • Ra) • a ≠ c   26, DM
         28. Sa • Ra • a ≠ c   27, DN
         29. Sa ⊃ [Ra ≡ (~Da • ~Pa)]   3, UI
         30. Sa   28, Simp
         31. Ra ≡ (~Da • ~Pa)   29, 30, MP
         32. [Ra ⊃ (~Da • ~Pa)] • [(~Da • ~Pa) ⊃ Ra]   31, Equiv
         33. Ra ⊃ (~Da • ~Pa)   32, Simp
         34. Ra • a ≠ c • Sa   28, Com
         35. Ra   34, Simp
         36. ~Da • ~Pa   33, 35, MP
         37. (x)[(Sx • x ≠ c • x ≠ n) ⊃ Px] • Sc • ~Pc • Sn • ~Pn   1, Com

232

38. $(x)[(Sx \cdot x \neq c \cdot x \neq n) \supset Px]$	37, Simp
39. $(Sa \cdot a \neq c \cdot a \neq n) \supset Pa$	38, UI
40. $(Sa \cdot a \neq c) \supset (a \neq n \supset Pa)$	39, Exp
41. $a \neq c \cdot Sa \cdot Ra$	28, Com
42. $a \neq c$	41, Simp
43. $Sa \cdot a \neq c$	30, 42, Conj
44. $a \neq n \supset Pa$	40, 43, MP
45. $\sim Pa \cdot \sim Da$	36, Com
46. $\sim Pa$	45, Simp
47. $\sim(a \neq n)$	44, 46, MT
48. $a = n$	47, DN
49. $n = a$	48, Id
50. $Dn \cdot (x)[(Sx \cdot Dx) \supset x = n] \cdot Sn$	2, Com
51. Dn	50, Simp
52. Da	49, 51, Id
53. $\sim Da$	36, Simp
54. $Da \cdot \sim Da$	52, 53, Conj
55. $\sim\sim(y)[(Sy \cdot Ry) \supset y = c]$	23-54, IP
56. $(y)[(Sy \cdot Ry) \supset y = c]$	55, DN
57. $Sc \cdot Rc \cdot (y)[(Sy \cdot Ry) \supset y = c]$	22, 56, Conj
58. $(\exists x)\{Sx \cdot Rx \cdot (y)[(Sy \cdot Ry) \supset y = x]\}$	57, EG

Exercise 9.1
Part II

1. a. Has no affect.   f. Strengthens.
   b. Strengthens.   g. Weakens.
   c. Weakens.   h. Strengthens.
   d. Weakens.   i. Strengthens.
   e. Strengthens.   j. Weakens.

2. a. Strengthens.   f. Strengthens.
   b. Weakens.   g. Has no affect.
   c. Weakens.   h. Weakens.
   d. Weakens.   i. Weakens.
   e. Strengthens.   j. Strengthens.

3. a. Strengthens.   f. Weakens.
   b. Has no affect.   g. Strengthens.
   c. Strengthens.   h. Weakens.
   d. Weakens.   i. Weakens.
   e. Strengthens.   j. Strengthens.

4. a. Has no effect.
   b. Weakens.
   c. Strengthens.
   d. Weakens.
   e. Strengthens.
   f. Has no effect.
   g. Strengthens
   h. Weakens.
   i. Weakens
   j. Strengthens.

5. a. Strengthens
   b. Weakens.
   c. Has no effect.
   d. Weakens.
   e. Weakens.
   f. Strengthens.
   g. Weakens.
   h. Strengthens.
   i. Strengthens.
   j. Strengthens.

6. a. Weakens.
   b. Strengthens.
   c. Weakens.
   d. Weakens.
   e. Weakens.
   f. Has no effect.
   g. Strengthens.
   h. Weakens.
   i. Strengthens.
   j. Strengthens.

7. a. Weakens.
   b. Strengthens.
   c. Has no effect.
   d. Strengthens.
   e. Strengthens.
   f. Weakens.
   g. Weakens.
   h. Strengthens.
   i. Strengthens.
   j. Weakens.

8. a. Weakens.
   b. Strengthens.
   c. Strengthens.
   d. Strengthens.
   e. Weakens.
   f. Weakens.
   g. Weakens.
   h. Has no effect.
   i. Weakens.
   j. Weakens.

9. The central issue is whether Dr. Wacko's occupancy of Mica Peak was open, notorious, and hostile. For Dr. Wacko's argument, note the fact that every evening for 20 years he could be seen climbing the road to Mica Peak, and every night he had his equipment set up on the peak and his vehicle parked there, in open view of anyone in the vicinity. Whether anyone actually saw him there is irrelevant. Such occupation is more notorious than merely parking one's car in front of a house, as Crick had done. The car could have been owned by someone other than Crick. Also, evidence of Dr. Wacko's nightly occupation for twenty years must have been apparent during the day: weeds trampled down, footprints, tire marks, etc. After rainy nights, these indications must have been even more apparent. Such indications of occupancy are similar to Crick's mowing the lawn. Furthermore, Crick probably worked during the day and actually occupied the house only at night, just as Dr. Wacko occupied Mica Peak only at night. Lastly, unlike Raymond, who was gone 3 months of the year, Dr. Wacko occupied Mica Peak day in and day out.

   For Tom Bell's argument note the fact that Crick occupied urban property in open view of thousands of people. Neighbors would have seen Crick come and go, and some of them probably would have notified Hoskins. Because Mica Peak is relatively remote and because Dr. Wacko was there only at night, no neighbors would have been able to report Dr. Wacko's presence to Tom Bell. Also, the owner of a house would be expected to enter it periodically and check for evidence of occupancy. Such evidence would be obvious (clothes in the closet, dishes in the sink, etc.). Since Hoskins apparently did not do this, he/she apparently did not care if the house was occupied. On the other hand, Mica Peak almost certainly stretches over a much larger area than a house, and evidence of Dr. Wacko's occupancy would be harder to detect. Even if Bell saw the tire marks, etc., why should he think they were anything other than evidence of people enjoying a weekend picnic? Finally, even though Raymond set up a large tent on rural property and presumably left it there during the day time, Raymond was refused title to the land. By leaving no structures at all on Mica Peak during the day, Dr. Wacko's occupancy was even less notorious than Raymond's. The fact that Raymond was gone for three months is irrelevant because given the inaccessible condition of the land at this time, no one would have seen Raymond occupying it even if he had chosen to stay.

10. For Maxie's argument, concentrate on the similarities between a home and a car (a car is an extended living space with heating, air conditioning, stereo, telephone, etc.), the dissimilarities between a plane and a car (greater difficulty in controlling, ease of crossing international borders, greater danger in operating, etc.). Also, people outside U.S. borders are not accorded the same constitutional protections as people inside, and a phone message normally suggests greater privacy than a radio message. In addition, the teenagers parked in the lot were acting in plain view, and a telescope only enhances ordinary sense perception (so there was no search). Maxie, on the other hand, was talking while speeding down the freeway, and was thus not acting in plain view (in the same sense), and a radio receiver (used by the agents) does not enhance ordinary sense perception.

For the agents' argument, concentrate on the similarities between a car and a plane (both are means of transportation, both can cross state lines, both are relatively hard to keep track of, etc.), and the dissimilarities between a car or plane and a house (houses do not move, so a search warrant can be obtained without the risk of a house moving away in the mean time). Also, cell phones use radio transmitters just like planes, the cell phone message was received inside U.S. borders just as was the radio message from the plane, and the cell phone message was received inadvertently, just as was the radio message from the plane and the image through the telescope (thus making it impossible to plan ahead for a search warrant). Also, in a sense, Maxie *was* acting in plain view: A lip reader traveling in an adjacent car might interpret his message. Lastly, controlling illicit drugs is a high priority for the government.

11. In support of the group, note the fact that the Gay Freedom Day parade involves sexual expression just as Lester's paintings did, and Lester's First Amendment rights were upheld. Indeed, the parade probably would have been less offensive than the paintings because it presumably involved no nudity. Similar parades were "calm and orderly." If Lester's rights were upheld, then surely the group's rights should be upheld too. Also, analogously to the Nazi group, the gay group's expression was in the form of a parade. If the Nazi's rights were upheld, then surely the gay's should be too. After all, Nazi activities led to the death of millions of innocent people during World War II. If any deaths have resulted from gay activities, they were unintended and they were only accidentally connected with the activity itself. Furthermore, the

gay parade is directly tied to the remediation of a severe social injustice, and therefore First Amendment protections should surely be extended to it. Finally, unlike the film, the parade would not be erotic and would not motivate viewers to engage in sexual activity they would not otherwise be disposed to engage in. By holding a parade, the gays are not seeking converts but only the recognition of their rights as human beings. In support of the police chief, note that the gay parade could be said to promote the spread of AIDS just as the erotic film would. The parade would promote homosexual awareness and openness in homosexual expression, and it would thus lead some people who are not openly homosexual to become so. Since AIDS is spread by homosexual activity, the parade would spread AIDS. In contrast to the Nazi parade, which involved political expression, the gay parade involves sexual expression. The First Amendment is intended chiefly to protect political expression, not sexual expression. Also unlike Lester's art, which involved a relatively limited area of park space, the parade will be large and will be seen by hundreds or thousands of people, and will thus have a great influence. Also, Lester's art involved heterosexual nudity and therefore could not be said to promote homosexuality and the spread of AIDS.

12. In favor of Isabel, note that constant noise is at least as disruptive as cold temperatures. Without sleep, Isabel's efficiency at work would undoubtedly be impaired, and thus her livelihood would be adversely affected. Linder could at least get some sleep by purchasing an electric blanket that would keep out the cold, but it is doubtful that earplugs would be equally effective for Isabel. Also, Carolyn's decision not to enforce the noise clause in the lease was a free act on her part, just as was Garvin's decision not to provide heat. If Garvin was not permitted to collect rent, then neither should Carolyn. In contrast, Quincy's decision to shut down the elevator was probably mandated by necessary repairs. Furthermore, Fulton's arthritis was a condition peculiar to her, whereas hearing is something everybody has. Also, when Isabel moved in, she had good reason to expect that the noise clause in the lease would be enforced. Otherwise, why would the lease contain such a clause? But when Fulton moved into the tenth floor apartment she had no reason to expect that the elevator would be operating every single day, and if she could not climb the stairs, she should not have taken the apartment. Finally, there was reason to believe that the elevator problem was temporary, whereas the noise problem might have lasted for years.

For Caroline, note that the lack of heat can have a direct impact on one's physical health. Without heat, Linder could have caught pneumonia. However, a little noise has no such impact. Also, did Isabel ever talk to the owner of the stereo about turning down the volume? Apartment living can be expected to involve the inconvenience of noisy neighbors, and if Isabel did nothing to remedy the problem, she arguably consented to it. Also, Isabel's problem with the noise was similar to Fulton's problem with climbing flights of stairs: they both resulted from the location of their apartment within the building, and not with the building as a whole. Fulton could have asked Quincy for a new apartment closer to the ground, and if she had asked, she might have gotten one. Instead, Fulton simply moved out. Similarly, Isabel could have asked Caroline for a new apartment some distance from the loud stereo, but instead she just moved out.

13. For Liz's argument note that there were several events that intervened between the car accident and the amputation: Mary's being taken to the hospital, Mary's being treated by doctors for bumps and bruises, Mary's apparent mix-up with some other patient scheduled for leg amputation, the doctors' failure to check Mary's proper identity before operating, etc. Liz did not directly control any of these events, and therefore she could not have foreseen them. Liz could not have foreseen what hospital Mary would be taken to, the fact that Mary would be mixed up with another patient, etc. Because Liz should not be held liable for an event utterly unforeseen to her, she should not be liable for Mary's amputated leg. The facts are similar to those in *Gomez v. Hunt*, where Gomez could not foresee the exact route that Hunt would take when walking home, the fact that a worker would drop a brick, the fact that the brick would strike Hunt, etc. The facts are dissimilar to those in *Sacco v. Lane*, where Lane was in direct control over the flames in the barbecue, and it was those very same flames that spread to the houses.

For Mary's argument note that Liz initiated a chain of events that flowed naturally from the car accident to the amputation. Once the car accident occurred, it was foreseeable that Mary would be taken to the hospital, once Mary was in the hospital it was foreseeable that mix-ups would occur (after all, mix-ups occur in hospitals every day), and given the nature of these mix-ups, it was foreseeable that Mary's leg would be amputated. Granted, Liz might not have been able to foresee each event in the chain, but once an event occurred, someone familiar with it could have foreseen the next event. Therefore, given that each event was foreseeable by *someone*--at least some hypothetical person--Liz should be held liable. The events are similar to those in *Sacco v. Lane*. When the flames were leaping from the barbecue, it was foreseeable that they would ignite the trees, once the trees were aflame, it was foreseeable that a house would be ignited, then another house, etc. Lane would not have been able to foresee the whole chain of events at the time he was tending the barbecue, but once one event occurred, the next was foreseeable. Also, even though the wind constituted an intervening event, Lane was still held liable. Finally, the facts are dissimilar to those in *Gomez v. Hunt*. When Hunt was walking home, he was in complete control over his own actions. He freely chose to walk past the building under construction, and he should have been on the lookout for falling objects. The fact that he was struck by a falling brick was partly the result of his own failure to observe. On the contrary, from the time of the accident until the amputation, Mary was in the hands of others: the person who took her to the hospital, nurses in the hospital, etc. In no sense was the amputation the result of Mary's free choices.

Exercise 9.2
Part I

1. Sufficient condition. The window can also be broken by throwing a stone or baseball through it.

2. Sufficient and necessary condition.

3. Sufficient condition. The tire will also go flat if it is punctured with a bullet or if the valve is removed.

4. Necessary condition. For an image to appear on the film the camera must also be loaded and focused, and there must be sufficient light.

5. Necessary condition--the gun must also be loaded.

6. Sufficient and necessary condition.

7. Sufficient condition. The fire will also go out if it is smothered.

8. Sufficient condition. Catching the flu will also cause one to become ill.

9. Sufficient and necessary condition.

10. Necessary condition--electricity must also be supplied from the main lines.

Part II

1. A = a certain make, B = a certain year, C = a certain model, D = driven 30,000 miles, E = a certain gasoline, F = a certain oil, G = a certain driver, H = certain road conditions, I = the additive.

Occurrence	Possible Conditions									Phenomenon (Less Wear)
	A	B	C	D	E	F	G	H	I	
1	*	*	*	*	*	*	*	*	*	*
2	*	*	*	*	*	*	*	*	-	-

By the method of difference, I is the cause in the sense of a sufficient condition.

2. A = large family, B = wealthy parents, C = professional parents, D = phonics training, E = reads novels, F = lives close to library, G = watches educational TV.

Occurrence	Possible Conditions							Phenomenon (Read Well)
	A	B	C	D	E	F	G	
Tom	*	-	*	*	*	*	*	*
Andy	-	*	*	*	-	-	*	*
Cindy	*	*	*	*	-	*	-	*
April	*	*	-	*	*	*	*	*
Joe	*	-	*	*	*	-	*	*

By the method of agreement, B (phonics training) is the cause of the phenomenon in the sense of a necessary condition.

3. The method of residues.

4. A = type X circuitry, B = shipped to a coastal region, C = sold to a business customer, D = manufactured in the Kansas City plant, E = used to play computer games, F = shipped to a large city.

Occurrence	Possible Conditions						Phenomenon (Returned)
	A	B	C	D	E	F	
1	*	*	-	*	*	-	*
2	-	*	*	*	-	*	*
3	*	*	*	-	*	*	*
4	-	*	-	*	*	*	*
5	*	*	-	*	*	-	*
6	*	*	*	-	-	*	*
7	*	*	*	*	-	*	*

By the method of agreement, B (salty air) is the cause of the phenomenon in the sense of a necessary condition.

5. A = Dynamite lure, B = Hot Spot lure, C = Sure Catch lure, D = Trusty rod, E = Best Bet rod, F = Spiffy reel, G = Husky reel, H = monofiliment line.

Occurrence	Possible Conditions								Phenomenon (Caught fish)
	A	B	C	D	E	F	G	H	
Jake	-	-	*	-	*	*	-	*	*
Bill	-	-	*	*	-	-	*	*	*
Kat	-	-	*	-	*	*	-	*	*
Amy	-	-	*	*	-	-	*	-	*
Dan	*	-	-	*	-	-	*	*	-
Ed	-	*	-	-	*	*	-	-	-
Flo	-	*	-	*	-	-	*	-	-
Tim	*	-	-	-	*	-	*	-	-

By the joint method of agreement and difference, C (Sure Catch lure) is the cause of the phenomenon in the sense of a sufficient and necessary condition.

6. A = a certain baking time, B = certain ingredients, C = a certain temperature, D = 2:00 PM, E = a certain relative humidity, F = a dish of a certain size and configuration, G = electric oven.

Occurrence	Possible Conditions							Phenomenon (Moist)
	A	B	C	D	E	F	G	
1	*	*	*	*	*	*	*	*
2	*	*	*	*	*	*	-	-

Exercise 9.2

By the method of difference, G (Baking in an electric oven) is the cause of the phenomenon in the sense of a sufficient condition.

7. A = camomile tea, B = late dinner, C = hot bath, D = read book, E = walk, F = wine, G = massage.

Occurrence	Possible Conditions							Phenomenon (Slept Well)
	A	B	C	D	E	F	G	
Mon	*	*	*	*	*	-	-	*
Tu	-	*	-	*	-	-	-	-
Wed	-	-	-	-	*	*	*	-
Th	-	*	*	*	-	*	*	*
Fri	*	*	-	*	*	-	*	*
Sat	*	-	*	-	*	*	*	*
Sun	*	-	*	*	-	-	-	-

By the joint method of agreement and difference, none of the possible conditions is a cause of the phenomenon.

8. The method of concomitant variation.

9. A = coconut, B = chocolate, C = nuts, D = milk products, E = shellfish, F = peppers, G = eggs, H = wheat products.

Occurrence	Possible Conditions								Phenomenon (Reaction)
	A	B	C	D	E	F	G	H	
1	*	*	*	*	*	*	*	*	*
2	-	-	-	-	-	-	-	-	-
3	*	-	-	-	-	-	-	-	-
4	-	*	-	-	-	-	-	-	-
5	-	-	*	-	-	-	-	-	-
6	-	-	-	*	-	-	-	-	*
7	-	-	-	-	*	-	-	-	-
8	-	-	-	-	-	*	-	-	-
9	-	-	-	-	-	-	*	-	-
10	-	-	-	-	-	-	-	*	-

By the joint method of agreement and difference, D (milk products) is the cause of the phenomenon in the sense of a necessary and sufficient condition.

10. A = corporal punishment, B = siblings, C = adopted, D = male figure, E = sexual abuse, F = domineering mother, G = uprooted often, H = day care facility.

Occurrence	Possible Conditions								Phenomenon (Blurred Bound.)
	A	B	C	D	E	F	G	H	
Meg	*	*	*	_	*	*	_	_	*
Sue	*	*	_	*	*	_	_	*	*
Dot	*	_	*	*	*	*	*	*	*
Jane	*	*	*	*	*	*	*	_	*
Lynn	_	*	*	*	*	_	_	*	*
Flo	*	*	_	*	*	*	*	_	*

By the method of agreement, E (sexual abuse) is the cause of the phenomenon in the sense of a necessary condition.

11. A = zinc, B = tin, C = sodium, D = silver, E = copper, F = silicon, G = nickel, H =iron.

Occurrence	Possible Conditions								Phenomenon (Resistance.)
	A	B	C	D	E	F	G	H	
1	*	*	_	_	*	*	*	_	*
2	_	*	*	_	*	*	_	*	*
3	_	*	_	_	*	_	*	_	_
4	*	_	*	_	_	_	_	_	_
5	_	_	*	_	*	*	_	_	*
6	_	_	_	*	_	_	_	*	_
7	*	_	_	*	_	*	*	*	*

By the joint method of agreement and difference, C (sodium) is the cause of the phenomenon in the sense of a sufficient and necessary condition.

12. A = smoggy area, B = high tension power lines, C = smoke cigarettes, D = defoliant chemicals, E = nuclear power plant, F = red meat.

Occurrence	Possible Conditions						Phenomenon (Cancer)
	A	B	C	D	E	F	
Davis	*	*	_	*	*	*	*
Jones	*	*	*	*	_	_	*
Ellis	*	*	_	*	*	*	*
Smith	*	_	*	*	*	*	*
Frank	_	_	*	*	*	_	*

By the method of agreement, D (defoliant chemicals) is the cause of the phenomenon in the sense of a necessary condition.

Exercise 9.3

13. A = malathion, B = American Beauty, C = five years old, D = a certain location, E = a certain amount of water, F = a certain amount of sun, G = a certain kind of soil, H = a certain amount of cultivation, I = a certain amount of Bandini rose food.

Occurrence	Possible Conditions									Phenomenon (No Aphids)
	A	B	C	D	E	F	G	H	I	
1	*	*	*	*	*	*	*	*	*	*
2	-	*	*	*	*	*	*	*	*	-

By the method of difference, A (malathion) is the cause of the phenomenon in the sense of a sufficient condition.

14. This study is similar to Mill's method of concomitant variation. A correlation coefficient of +0.2 indicates a weak positive correlation between GPA and income. This is a retrospective study because the subjects fulfilled the requirements prior to the time the study was conducted.

15. The experiment is equivalent to forty simultaneous applications of Mill's method of difference. The experiment is followed by a generalization that extends the results to other rabbits. The experiment indicates a cause in the sense of a sufficient condition.

Part III

1. By the method of agreement, D is the cause in the sense of a necessary condition.

2. By the method of difference, B is the cause in the sense of a sufficient condition.

3. By the joint method of agreement and difference, C is the cause in the sense of a sufficient and necessary condition.

4. By the joint method of agreement and difference, D is the cause in the sense of a sufficient (but not a necessary) condition.

5. By the joint method of agreement and difference, B is the cause in the sense of a necessary (but not a sufficient) condition.

Exercise 9.3
Part I

1.	1/6	6.	6:11
2.	.028	7.	3/12 or ¼
3.	8/13 or .615	8.	$8
4.	.853	9.	4:8 or 1:2
5.	2/52 or 1/26	10.	Approximately $17

Part II

1. P(6 or 1) = P(6) + P(1) = 1/6 + 1/6 = 2/6 = 1/3

2. $P(H_1$ and H_2 and $H_3) = P(H_1) \times P(H_2) \times P(H_3)$
   = 1/2 × 1/2 × 1/2
   = 1/8

3. P(K or Q) = P(K) + P(Q)
   = 4/52 + 4/52
   = 2/13

4a. $P(A_1$ and $A_2) = P(A_1) \times P(A_2)$
    = 4/52 × 4/52
    = 1/169 = .0059

4b. $P(A_1$ and $A_2) = P(A_1) \times P(A_2$ given $A_1)$
    = 4/52 × 3/51
    = 1/221 = .0045

5. $P(A_1$ or $A_2) = P(A_1) + P(A_2) - P(A_1$ and $A_2)$
   = 4/52 + 4/52 − (4/52 × 4/52)
   = 25/169
   = .148

6. First compute the probability of getting no heads:

   $P(no heads) = P(T_1$ and T_2 and $T3)$
   $= P(T_1) \times P(T_2) \times P(T3)$
   = 1/2 × 1/2 × 1/2
   = 1/8

   Then use the negation rule:

   P(at least one head) = 1 − P(no heads)
   = 1 − 1/8
   = 7/8

7. First compute the probability of getting no sixes:
   P(no sixes) = 5/6 × 5/6 × 5/6
   = 125/216

   Then use the negation rule:

   P(at least one six) = 1 − P(no sixes)
   = 1 − 125/216
   = 91/216 = .4213

Exercise 9.3

8a. $P(5) = P(1 \text{ and } 4) + P(2 \text{ and } 3) + P(3 \text{ and } 2) + P(4 \text{ and } 1)$
$\quad = (1/6 \times 1/6) + (1/6 \times 1/6) + (1/6 \times 1/6) + (1/6 \times 1/6)$
$\quad = 1/9 = .1111$

8b. $P(6) = P(1 \text{ and } 5) + P(2 \text{ and } 4) + P(3 \text{ and } 3) + P(4 \text{ and } 2) + P(5 \text{ and } 1)$
$\quad = (1/6 \times 1/6) + (1/6 \times 1/6) + (1/6 \times 1/6) + (1/6 \times 1/6) + (1/6 \times 1/6)$
$\quad = 5/36 = .1389$

8c. $P(7) = P(1 \text{ and } 6) + P(2 \text{ and } 5) + P(3 \text{ and } 4) + P(4 \text{ and } 3) + P(5 \text{ and } 2) +$
$\quad P(6 \text{ and } 1)$
$\quad = (1/6 \times 1/6) + (1/6 \times 1/6) + (1/6 \times 1/6) + (1/6 \times 1/6) + (1/6 \times 1/6) +$
$\quad (1/6 \times 1/6)$
$\quad = 1/6 = .1667$

9a. $P(R_1 \text{ and } R_2) = P(R_1) \times P(R_2)$
$\quad = 2/9 \times 4/9$
$\quad = 8/81 = .0988$

9b. $P(G_1 \text{ or } G_2) = P(G_1) + P(G_2) - P(G_1 \text{ and } G_2)$
$\quad = (3/9 + 2/9) - (3/9 \times 2/9)$
$\quad = 13/27 = .4815$

9c. $P(\text{one R, one Y}) = P(R_1 \text{ and } Y_2) + P(Y_1 \text{ and } R_2)$
$\quad = (2/9 \times 3/9) + P(4/9 \times 4/9)$
$\quad = 22/81 = .2716$

9d. First compute the probability that neither is red or yellow:
$P(G_1 \text{ and } G_2) = 3/9 \times 2/9$
$\quad = 2/27$
Then use the negation rule:

$P(R \text{ or } Y) = 1 - P(G_1 \text{ and } G_2)$
$\quad = 1 - 2/27$
$\quad = 25/27 = .9259$

9e. $P(\text{same color}) = P(R_1 \text{ and } R_2) + P(G_1 \text{ and } G_2) + P(Y_1 \text{ and } Y_2)$
$\quad = (2/9 \times 4/9) + (3/9 \times 2/9) + (4/9 \times 3/9)$
$\quad = 26/81 = .3210$

10a. $P(R_1 \text{ and } R_2) = P(R_1) \times P(R_2 \text{ given } R_1)$
$\quad = 3/12 \times 2/11$
$\quad = 6/132 = .045$

b. $P(Y \text{ and } G) = P(Y_1 \text{ and } G_2) + P(G_1 \text{ and } Y_2)$
$\quad = (5/12 \times 4/11) + (4/12 \times 5/11)$
$\quad = 20/132 + 20/132$
$\quad = 10/33 = .303$

c. $P(R \text{ or } G) = 1 - P(Y_1 \text{ and } Y_2)$
$= 1 - (5/12 \times 4/11)$
$= 1 - 20/132$
$= 28/33 = .848$

d. $P(G_1 \text{ or } G_2) = 1 - P(\text{not-}G)$
$= 1 - [P(R_1 \text{ and } R_2) + P(R_1 \text{ and } Y_2) + P(Y_1 \text{ and } R_2) + P(Y_1 \text{ and } Y_2)$
$= 1 - [(3/12 \times 2/11) + (3/12 \times 5/11) + (5/12 \times 3/11) + (5/12 \times 4/11)]$
$= 1 - [6/132 + 15/132 + 15/132 + 20/132]$
$= 1 - 56/132$
$= 19/33 = .57$

e. $P(\text{same color}) = P(R_1 \text{ and } R_2) + P(G_1 \text{ and } G_2) + P(Y_1 \text{ and } Y_2)$
$= (3/12 \times 2/11) + (4/12 \times 3/11) + (5/12 \times 4/11)$
$= 6/132 + 12/132 + 20/132$
$= 19/66 = .288$

11. First compute the probability of drawing neither an ace nor a king:
$P(\text{not-}A \text{ and not-}K) = P(\text{not-}A \text{ and not-}K)_1 \times P(\text{not-}A \text{ and not-}K)_2 \times$
$P(\text{not-}A \text{ and not-}K)_3$
$= 44/52 \times 43/51 \times 42/50$
$= 79464/132600$

Then use the negation rule:
$P(A \text{ or } K) = 1 - P(\text{not-}A \text{ and not-}K)$
$= 1 - 79464/132600$
$= 53136/132600 = .4007$

12. First compute the probability of the event not happening; i.e., the probability of drawing either not an ace or not a king:
$P(\text{not-}A \text{ or not-}K)$
$= P(\text{not-}A) + P(\text{not-}K) - P(\text{not-}A \text{ and not-}K)$
$= (48/52 \times 47/51 \times 46/50) + (48/52 \times 47/51 \times 46/50) -$
$(44/52 \times 43/51 \times 42/50)$
$= 128088/132600$

Then use the negation rule:
$P(A \text{ and } K) = 1 - P(\text{not-}A \text{ or not-}K)$
$= 1 - 128088/132600$
$= 4512/132600 = .0340$

13a. $P(M \text{ or } W) = P(M) + P(W) - P(M \text{ and } W)$
$= .74 + .82 - (.74 \times .82)$
$= .95$

13b. P(M and W and S) = P(M) × P(W) × P(S)

    = .74 × .82 × 8/9

    = .54

14. P(WS) = P(I) × P(C)

    = 5/8 × 7/12

    = 35/96 = .36

15. P(two on same day) = 1 − P(separate days)

    = 1 − (7/7 × 6/7 × 5/7 × 4/7)

    = 1 − 840/2401 = .65

16. $P(N \text{ given } R) = \dfrac{P(N) \times P(R \text{ given } N)}{[P(N \times P(R \text{ given } N)] + [P(O) \times P(R \text{ given } O)]}$

$= \dfrac{3/5 \times 7/15}{[3/5 \times 7/15] + [2/5 \times 5/15]} = \dfrac{21/75}{21/75 + 10/75} = \dfrac{21/75}{31/75}$

= 21/31 = .68

Answer: New urn

17. $P(S \text{ given } P) = \dfrac{P(S) \times P(P \text{ given } S)}{[P(S) \times P(P \text{ given } S)] + [P(\text{not-}S) \times P(P \text{ given not-}S)]}$

$= \dfrac{.4 \times .9}{[.4 \times .9] + [.6 \times .3]} = \dfrac{.36}{.36 + .18} = .36/.54 = 2/3$

18. $P(L \text{ given } T) = \dfrac{P(L) \times P(T \text{ given } L)}{[P(L) \times P(T \text{ given } L)] + [P(H) \times P(T \text{ given } H)]}$

$= \dfrac{1/3 \times .9}{[1/3 \times .9] + [2/3 \times 1/6]} = \dfrac{.3}{.3 + 1/9} = .73$

19. $P(R \text{ given } N) = \dfrac{P(R) \times P(N \text{ given } R)}{[P(R) \times P(N \text{ given } R)] + [P(T) \times P(N \text{ given } T)]}$

$= \dfrac{.2 \times .7}{[.2 \times .7] + [.8 \times .2]} = \dfrac{.14}{.14 + .16} = \dfrac{.14}{.30} = .47$

20. $P(N \text{ given } C) = \dfrac{P(N) \times P(C \text{ given } N)}{[P(N) \times P(C \text{ given } N)] + [P(S) \times P(C \text{ given } S)]}$

$= \dfrac{.6 \times .3}{[.6 \times .3] + [.4 \times .65]} = \dfrac{.18}{.18 + .26} = \dfrac{.18}{.44} = .407$

Exercise 9.4
Part I

1. Since the water in the lake might not be circulating, the algae content of the water at one end might not be representative of the whole lake. Thus, the sample might be biased.

2. The sample is probably biased. Homeowners in fashionable neighborhoods would be expected to support the convention center because, once constructed, it would bring increased business to the city.

3. The sample might be biased. Suppose that each box contains 24 cans of fruit and that a defect in the machine that filled the cans resulted in only one in 24 being filled to capacity. If the can filled to capacity turned up at regular intervals and was always packed in the left-front corner of each box, the sample would be clearly biased. Similarly, if only the first 24 of every 240 cans was filled to capacity, the engineer would have taken his sample only from boxes that contained filled cans.

4. According to Table 7, the margin of error for a random sample of 600 is) five percent. Since the sample taken indicates a difference of only two percent, the results of the sample are inconclusive.

5. Since the calls were placed at a time when most people are working, and since most of the people with 9-to-5 jobs are not avid soap opera viewers, the sample is probably biased.

6. According to Table 7, the margin of error for a random sample of 750 is) four percent, and the margin of error for a random sample of 1500 is) three percent. Thus, the second sample is only 25 percent (i.e., one percentage point) more accurate than the first.

7. Since no mention is made of the size of the sample or of the expected sampling error, the sample might be biased. The manufacturer might have taken 25 separate samples consisting of ten dentists per sample and reported the results of only the most favorable one.

8. The sample is probably biased as a result of psychological factors. Few self-respecting Americans would admit to having never read the Constitution.

9. The sample is probably biased as a result of psychological factors. Few patients would admit to their doctor that they failed to follow his/her advice.

10. The problem concerns the meaning of "average." If the average is a mean, most of the toys could be over $15, and a few very cheap toys could bring the average down to $15. If the average is a mode, there might be a few toys priced at $15, and all the other toys might have varying prices exceeding $15. Only if the average is a median can one be assured that half the toys are $15 or less.

11. The conclusion follows only if the average is a mean. If the average is a median, then it might be the case that 50 salmon weigh eleven pounds each and the other 50 weigh two pounds each, for a total weight of only 650 pounds and a total value of only $1300. Similarly, if the average is a mode, then it might be the case that five or six salmon weigh ten pounds each and that the rest have varying weights less than ten pounds.

12. The conclusion follows only if the average is a mode, in which case there are more shoes of size eight than any other size. If the average is a mean or median, there might be no size eight shoes at all.

13. Since no mention is made of the dispersion, the argument is weak. The rock pile might consist of several pieces weighing 500 pounds and enough weighing only four or five pounds to bring the average down to 50 pounds. If the range were only ten pounds or so, the conclusion would follow.

14. Since no mention is made of the dispersion, the argument is weak. The class might consist of ten students having IQs of 50, 60, 70, 80, 120, 120, 160, 170, 180, and 190, respectively, for an average (in the sense of mean, median, and mode) of 120 (and a range of 140). If the range were 20 points or less, the conclusion would follow.

15. Since the axes are not scaled, there is no way of knowing how many bugs are killed with one application or how long the spray remains potent. Furthermore, no information is given on the conditions under which these results are supposed to be obtained.

16. If the scale on the vertical axis does not begin at "0," the conclusion does not follow.

17. In fact the total costs have been reduced by less than five percent.

18. For high volume businesses, such as grocery stores, expressing profits as a percentage of sales is not an accurate reflection of how well the business is doing. If profits were expressed as a percentage of investment, the figure would probably be much higher.

19. Since there were many more cars on the road in 1980 than there were in 1950, the comparison is faulty.

20. The goal was to increase the productivity 500 units per week. The actual increase was 200 units per week. Thus, the effort of the efficiency expert was only 40 percent successful.

Part II

1. mean = 180
   median = 170
   mode = 160

2. mean = $40,000
   median = $30,000
   mode = $15,000

3. mean = 3
   variance = 5.2
   standard deviation = 2.28

4. mean = 3   5. mean = 8
   variance = 3   variance = 1.5
   standard deviation = 1.73   standard deviation = 1.22

Part III

1. False	6. True	11. False	16. False
2. True	7. True	12. True	17. True
3. True	8. False	13. True	18. False
4. False	9. True	14. True	19. False
5. False	10. False	15. True	20. False

Exercise 9.5
Part II

1. Radium:
   Problem: Why were the rays emitted by pitchblende stronger than the rays emitted by pure uranium?

   I.   Hypothesis: The intensified rays were triggered by impurities.

        Implication: Mixing pure uranium with impurities would intensify the emission of rays.

        Test: Mixing pure uranium with impurities failed to intensify the emission of rays.

   II. Hypothesis: The intensified rays came directly from some impurity.

        Implications: 1. The intensified rays were caused by an unknown element.
                       2. This element could be separated through a process of refinement.
                       3. The unknown element could be identified through spectrographic analysis.

        Tests: 1. The only other radioactive element known to exist was thorium, and the pitchblende was found to contain no thorium.
                       2. Prolonged processing and refinement produced a visible quantity of pure radium.
                       3. Spectrographic analysis of the white powder revealed a characteristic spectrum line.

Exercise 9.5

2. Neptune:

Problem: Why did the astronomical tables predict accurate results for Jupiter and Saturn but not for Uranus?

Hypothesis: The deviations in the orbit of Uranus were caused by gravitational interactions with an eighth planet.

Implications: If an eighth planet exists, its motion will be depicted by Adams's and Leverrier's tables.

Tests: 1. A preliminary search was made, but the eighth planet was not discovered.
2. A second search was made using star charts. The eighth planet was discovered.

3. Atmospheric Pressure:

Problem: If nature abhors a vacuum, why did pumps and siphons fail to work through heights of 30 feet or more, why was a vacuum created in Berti's glass vessel, and why did the water level always descend to the same level in the pipe?

Hypothesis: The water is supported in Berti's pipe (and in other vacuum devices) by the pressure of the atmosphere.

Implications: 1. The pressure of the atmosphere would support a column of mercury 29 inches high.

2. A tube filled with mercury could be used to measure fluctuations in atmospheric pressure.
3. If a tube filled with mercury were carried to the top of a mountain, the mercury level would descend.

Tests: 1. Viviani poured mercury into a tube closed at one end. He found that when the tube was inverted the mercury was supported about 29 inches from the level of the mercury in the dish.
2. Later experimenters proved that such a device could be used to measure fluctuations in atmospheric pressure.
3. Perier carried a disassembled barometer to a mountaintop and found that the mercury level descended.

4. Spontaneous Generation:

A. Re: Redi

Problem: How can life arise from nonliving matter?

Hypothesis: Worms are deposited in rotting meat by flies.

Implications: If flies are kept away from rotting meat, worms will not develop.

Test: Pieces of meat sealed in a glass container developed no worms.

B. Re: Pasteur

	Problem:	How can life arise from nonliving matter in view of the fact that the occurrence of fermentation requires the introduction of living yeast?
I.	Hypothesis:	Life comes only from life.
	Implication:	No life will develop in a sterilized nutrient solution exposed only to sterilized air.
	Test:	A flask containing a nutrient solution was boiled, and the surrounding atmosphere was replaced by sterilized air. No life developed.
II.	Hypothesis:	Life forms are carried by dust particles.
	Implication:	The microbes carried by dust particles can be discovered through microscopic inspection.
	Test:	A wad of cotton in which dust particles had been trapped was washed in an alcohol mixture. Microbes were discovered when the fluid was examined under a microscope.
III.	Hypothesis:	Life forms that developed in sterile nutrient solutions were deposited in the solutions by dust particles.
	Implication:	Sterile nutrient solutions in which no life forms developed after a prolonged wait would exhibit microbial life forms when exposed to dust particles.
	Tests:	1. A sealed flask containing a sterile nutrient solution was reopened, and dust particles were introduced. Later, life forms developed.
		2. A goose-necked flask containing a sterile nutrient solution was shaken vigorously, dislodging the dust particles trapped in the neck. Later, life forms developed.

Part III

Problem: Why is the patient in a coma when there is no obvious injury?

1.	Hypothesis:	(By Dr. Rosenthal) The patient is faking it.
	Implication:	Shaking him and lifting his torso should bring him out it.
	Test:	The patient was shaken and his torso lifted and dropped back on the bed. This had no effect.

2. Hypothesis: The patient is suffering from a heroin overdose.
    Implication: The patient's pupils would have shrunk.
    Test: The patients pupils were observed. No shrinking was noticed.

3. Hypothesis: The patient is suffering from a valium overdose.
    Implication: The patient's heart rate would have dipped.
    Test: The patient's heart rate was checked and found to be normal.

4. Hypothesis: The patient is suffering from an antidepressant overdose.
    Implication: The patient's heart would be racing.
    Test: The patient's heart was checked, and it was not found to be racing.

5. Hypothesis: The patient took an overdose of pills.
    Implication: A residue of the pills would still be in his stomach.
    Test: The patient's stomach was pumped, but nothing was found.

6. Hypothesis: The patient is suffering from poison and/or drugs.
    Implication: Poison and/or drugs would register in the patient's blood.
    Test: A blood sample was taken, but nothing turned up.

7. Hypothesis: The patient is suffering from a brain hemorrhage or stroke.
    Implicaiont: A hemorrhage or stroke would be visible on a CT scan.
    Test: A CT scan was done, but nothing unusual was seen.

8. Hypothesis: (By Dr. Green) The patient is faking or in some kind of trance.
    Implication: Pain would bring the patient out of it.
    Test: A reflex hammer was pressed hard against the patient's toenail and he
                  was given a sternal rub. This had no effect.

9. Hypothesis: The patient is suffering from a brainstem malfunction.
    Implication: If the brainstem is normal, then squirting ice water into the patient's
                  ear would cause his eyes to jiggle. Also, if the patient is conscious, it
                  would cause him to become dizzy and sick to his stomach.
    Test: Ice water was squirted into the patient's ear. This caused his eyes to
                  jiggle, and there was a slight indication of nausea.

10. Hypothesis: The patient is capable of voluntary movement:
    Implication: Sprinkling ice water on the patient's face would elicit a response.
    Test: Ice water was sprinkled on the patient's face. The patient exhibited a
                  slight wince.

11. Hypothesis: The patient is conscious.
    Implication: If the patient's arm is raised a foot above his face and dropped, it
                  would veer away and not strike his face directly.
    Test: The patient's arm was raised a foot above his face and dropped. On
                  descending, it veered away from his face.

12. Hypothesis: The patient's problem is psychiatric.
    Implication: The patient's relatives would have noticed the patient behaving strangely in the recent past.
    Test: The patient's relatives were contacted and asked about the patient's behavior. They reported strange forms of behavior.

13. Hypothesis: The patient is having a seizure.
    Implication: Indications of a seizure would register on an EEG.
    Test: The patient was given an EEG. There were no indications of a seizure.

14. Hypothesis: The patient is suffering from a brain tumor.
    Implication: A tumor would show up on a dye-enhanced CT scan.
    Test: The patient was given a die-enhanced CT scan. No tumor showed up.

15. Hypothesis: The patient is suffering from a bladder or kidney problem.
    Implication: Evidence of a bladder or kidney problem would appear in the patient's urine.
    Test: Catheterize the patient and check his urine. This test was interrupted, so no results were obtained.

Note: The shots of narcon and dextrose given to the patient by the paramedics were standard emergency measures, so they were probably unrelated to any consciously formed hypotheses. Also, taking the patient's temperature, giving him a chest X-ray, and taking a blood count were probably not related to any hypotheses.

Part VI

1. True
2. False
3. True
4. False
5. True
6. False
7. True
8. False
9. True
10. True
11. True
12. True
13. True
14. False
15. False
16. False
17. True
18. True
19. False
20. True

Truth Tree Supplement
Exercise T-1

1. Self-consistent, K false, M true.
2. Self-contradictory.
3. Self-consistent, N false, B true.
4. Self-consistent, E true, G true.
5. Self-contradictory.
6. Self-contradictory.
7. Self-consistent, R false, N false.
8. Self-contradictory.
9. Self-consistent, S false, R false.
10. Self-contradictory.

Exercise T 1-4

Exercise T-2

1. Consistent, M true, D false, K true.
2. Inconsistent.
3. Consistent, C false, N false, H true.
4. Consistent, P false, B false, Q false, D false.
5. Inconsistent.
6. Inconsistent.
7. Inconsistent.
8. Consistent, S false, C true, H true.
9. Consistent, D true, N true, T true, Q true.
10. Inconsistent.

Exercise T-3

1. Valid.
2. Invalid, B true, H true, T true, E false.
3. Valid.
4. Invalid, R true, T false, K true, P false.
5. Invalid, S false, F true.
6. Valid.
7. Valid.
8. Invalid, E true, A true, T false, M false.
9. Valid.
10. Invalid, P true, B false, Q false, D false.
11. Invalid, N true, J false, G false, K true.
12. Valid.
13. Valid.
14. Invalid, L false, N true, C false.
15. Valid.

Exercise T-4

1. For a universe of one (a): Fa true, Ga true, Ha false.
2. For a universe of two (c, e): Fc false, Fe false, Ge true.
3. For a universe of one (a): Fa false, Ga true, Ha true.
4. For a universe of two (a, c): Fa false, Fc true, Ga false, Gc true.
5. For a universe of one (a): Fa false, Ga true.
6. For a universe of two (a, b): Fa true, Fb false, Ga false, Gb false.
7. For a universe of two (a, b): Fa false, Fb true, Ga false, Gb true.
8. For a universe of two (a, b): Fa false, Fb true, Ga false, Gb true.
9. For a universe of two (a, b): Fa true, Fb false, Ga false, Gb false.
10. For a universe of two (a, b): Fa false, Fb false, Ja false.
11. For a universe of two (a, b): Fa false, Fb true, Ga true, Gb true, Ha true, Hb false.
12. For a universe of two (a, b): Fa true, Fb true, Ga true, Gb false, Da false, Db true.
13. For a universe of two (a, b): Fa true, Fb false Ga false, Gb false.
14. For a universe of two (a, b): Fa false, Fb true, Ga false, Gb true, Hb false.
15. For a universe of two (a, b): Fa false, Fb true, Ga false, Gb true, Ha false, Hb true.